Esports and the Law

A Game Plan for Business and Legal Trends

Marc Edelman
Thomas A. Baker
John Holden
Rebecca Rosenthal

ABA
AMERICAN BAR ASSOCIATION
Business Law Section

Cover design by Catherine Zaccarine.

Excerpts from this book previously appeared in John T. Holden, Marc Edelman & Thomas Baker III, *A Short Treatise on Esports and the Law*, 2020 U. Ill. L. Rev. 509 (2020).

Printed in the United States of America.

25 24 23 22 21   5 4 3 2 1

ISBN: 978-1- 63905-017-8

CONTENTS

Introduction

The Emergence of Esports

In May of 2018, more than 127 million fans across the globe tuned in to watch the Mid-season Invitational of *League of Legends* online. In the Mid-season Invitational finals, team Royal Never Give Up from China defeated Korea's Kingzone Dragon X, three games to one, to earn the Midseason Invitational $527,650 first-place prize. Team Liquid, which was the highest-ranking team to include American players, finished fifth, earning a total of $68,526 in prize money. As of March 2020, Team Liquid is the highest-earning esports team, making an annual profit of $32 million.[1] The second-best team in esports, OG, features three of the best esports players in the world,[2] all of whom are between the ages of 20 and 28.[3] In 2020, these three players had annual salaries of $6.6 million, $6 million, and $5.9 million, respectively.[4]

To many Americans, the emerging popularity of electronic sports (or, as they are colloquially known, "esports") may seem like little more than a passing fad. Indeed, older American sports fans who have already lived through the fleeting, mainstream popularity of indoor soccer in the 1980s, and the X-Games in the 1990s, may be especially skeptical of the rise of any new forms of sports entertainment. If fan interest in each of these other games quickly faded away, why should longstanding American sports fans perceive the current appeal of esports to be anything more than a current trend?

However, a number of factors differentiate esports from those other activities that only enjoyed short-lived success. Most notably, the trend toward growing interest in esports is global rather than local. Not only does esports enjoy a large and loyal fan base in the United States, but it has also garnered a substantial following in China, Korea, Japan, Vietnam,

---

1. Tarvin Gill, *3 esports teams made a whopping US $93 million in 2020 just by playing video games*, Mashable, https://sea.mashable.com/entertainment/9960/3-esports-teams-made-a-whopping-us93-million-in-2020-just-by-playing-video-games (last visited Aug. 14, 2020).

2. *Id.*

3. *Top 100 Highest Overall Earnings*, eSports Earnings, https://www.esportsearnings.com/players (last visited Aug. 15, 2020).

4. Gill, *supra* note 1.

Brazil, and Russia, among many other countries. While the potential of esports emerging as the "next national pastime" in America still seems several years away, in Asia, it is already on the horizon. Further, esports does not necessarily compete with any of the traditional sports for fans, as the esports fan base includes large numbers of individuals who are neither traditional athletes nor spectators of traditional sports. Thus, there is less risk of a substitution effect for esports and this allows for ample opportunity for marketers who advertise on traditional sports broadcasts to reach entirely different audiences by advertising on esports broadcasts. Finally, both real-life and online communities evolve around esports in a way that helps to strengthen the fan bases of professional esports players and fosters more of a personal connection between fans and particular games. Indeed, esports are distinct from traditional, major professional sports because esports fans are able to play the same games at home in nearly the exact same manner as the professionals. As such, the accessibility of esports games to anyone interested in playing them is a model that professional sports have never had and likely can never provide.

At present, many valuation experts project continued growth of esports fans and revenues well into the future. According to market research firm Newzoo, by the end of 2021, esports will have approximately 250 million enthusiasts and produce upwards of $1.1 billion in revenue around the world. By 2023, Newzoo predicts that esports will have a total global audience of 646 million annually, with 295 million of these viewers being esports enthusiasts.[5] When viewed in this light, the future economic potential of esports is colossal.

Esports and the Law

Of course, the rapid growth of the esports industry also presents a range of new questions about underlying legal issues. First, there are questions about whether esports actually constitute sports. Whereas, until recently, sports fandom pertained exclusively to competitions in physical activities, the emergence of esports is changing that conception and forcing society to revisit who is perceived as a competitive athlete. Questions of this nature not only matter from the standpoint of the discipline of linguistics and sociology, but they also matter when determining whether a wide

---

5. 2020 Global Esports Market Report, NEWZOO, https://newzoo.com/key-numbers/ (last visited Mar. 30, 2021).

variety of laws and other codes that pertain to "sports" also apply to esports.

Second, there are questions about which laws govern esports, and how the bodies of law that apply in the context of traditional sports are both similar to, and distinct from, those governing esports. Of course, there are a number of similarities between how the law governs traditional sports and how it governs esports. For example, both traditional sports and esports entail important contractual relationships between contest hosts and their players, as well as between contest hosts and their television broadcast and other business partners. However, at present, the "athletes" who compete in esports are not unionized, whereas players in the four premier U.S. professional sports leagues—Major League Baseball (MLB), the National Basketball Association (NBA), the National Football League (NFL), and the National Hockey League (NHL)—are *all* union members. Additionally, the publishers of esports video games enjoy copyright over their games and thus can prevent rival leagues from easily forming and using their game. In traditional team sports, on the other hand, the underlying contests are clearly in the public domain. Finally, antitrust law plays an important role in regulating commercial team sports based on the complex relationships between teams in a sports league that simultaneously must compete and cooperate in the creation of their product. It is less clear what role, if any, antitrust law will play in governing the behavior of esports owners.

Third, there are questions about who will emerge as the lawyers who play an important role in developing the structure of commercial esports, and what credentials will make them most qualified. Despite the esports industry's rapid growth, the industry remains in its infancy. As such, there are many young attorneys who are interested in video games but lack meaningful experience in the doctrinal bodies of sports and entertainment who promote themselves as experts in the field. At the same time, there are a number of established sports and entertainment attorneys who represent esports entities, but they often lack a nuanced understanding of how esports operate and the unique challenges underlying the burgeoning industry. Unfortunately, there are few attorneys with both a substantial understanding of esports and sophisticated legal practice experience. However, this will likely change with time.

This book, which is the first of its kind to address these issues, is broken into twelve separate chapters plus a conclusion. The first two chapters outline the history and business environment of electronic gaming. Chapters 3 through 6 then explore the primary legal issues related to the esports industry: the ownership of intellectual property rights within the esports industry; issues pertaining to gamers' rights of publicity; esports labor and employment matters; and issues pertaining to contest broadcasts. Subsequently, Chapters 8 through 12 explore more nuanced legal and public policy issues pertaining to esports, including the treatment of violent content in video games, the emergence of collegiate esports competitions, issues pertaining to the fair treatment of women, esports gambling, doping, and immigration matters. The book ends with a conclusion projecting the long-term viability of esports and predicting future business and legal trends in the industry.

Chapter 1

A Brief History of Esports

The Early Days

Many commentators describe esports as a new and emerging segment of the commercial sports industry—one as young as Generation Z itself. In some ways, this description is accurate. Only in the past ten years has real money been involved in electronic gaming. Nevertheless, the origins of the esports industry date back nearly a century, to the period between World War I and World War II.

In this era, long before there was modern gaming, there was pinball. The popularity of pinball exploded in 1932 with the launch of Raymond Maloney's *Ballyhoo* machine.[1] First manufactured by the Bally Manufacturing Company of Chicago, Illinois, the *Ballyhoo* machine had no flippers or bumpers like more modern pinball machines.[2] Instead, the machine relied on a set of pins and holes with point totals ranging from 100 to 500 points.[3] Yet, despite these limitations, when compared to modern gaming consoles (e.g., Microsoft Xbox), the *Ballyhoo* machine was a remarkable innovation for its time and quickly gained popularity.

---

1. Ashley Sanders Lipson & Robert D. Brain, Videogame Law: Cases, Statutes, Forms, Problems & Materials 6 (2d ed. 2015).

2. *Pinball Machine: Ballyhoo Pinball Game,* Google Arts & Culture (last accessed May 12, 2020), https://artsandculture.google.com/asset/pinball-machine-ballyhoo-pinball-game-bally-manufacturing-company/HAHCac1v537Z1w?hl=en.

3. *Id.*

Pinball machines would continue to grow in popularity throughout the United States in the post-World War II period until March 6, 1948, when a non-uniformed New York City patrolman placed a penny into a *Marvel Pop Up* pinball machine, competed successfully, and won a free play based on his performance.[4] Rather than proceed to enjoy his free play, the patrolman turned around and arrested the shop owner for the illegal possession of a gambling machine—contending that the early version of pinball was nothing more than a guise for an illegal lottery that violated state gambling laws.[5] At this time, under most state laws, any activity that included consideration (an entry fee) and a prize was illegal if it were deemed to be a "game of chance."[6] The earliest versions of pinball machines, without flippers and bumpers, were quite likely games of chance.

Although the war on pinball could have conceivably died down with that one New York City incident, by the end of the 1940s, cities across the country were actively banning pinball machines that required users to insert a penny and compete to win free plays.[7] It was not until 1974—long after pinball machines evolved to include flippers and other devices to add a bona fide element of skill to the game—that the California Supreme Court, in assessing pinball's legality, ruled that these games were indeed skill-based and thus legal under state law.[8] The court's notable decision in *Cossack v. Los Angeles*[9] explained the following:

> Whether a game is a game of skill or a game of chance depends upon which factor predominates, and this is a fact question for the trial court. In the present case, the trial court found, supported by substantial evidence, that the games in question are games predominantly of skill. In addition, the Attorney General has indicated that although pinball machines which are predominantly games of chance are prohibited by section 330b of the Penal Code, pinball machines equipped with flippers, permitting manipulation of the ball by the player, are predominantly games of skill.[10]

---

4. Christopher Klein, *That Time America Outlawed Pinball*, History (Aug. 22, 2018), https://www.history.com/news/that-time-america-outlawed-pinball.

5. *Id.*

6. *Id.*

7. *See id.*

8. *Id.*

9. Cossack v. Los Angeles, 523 P.2d 260 (Cal. 1974).

10. *Id.* at 264.

As pinball games once again began to capture the attention of the American entertainment industry in the 1970s, other companies began to garner a foothold into a similar market segment with early video game machines. One such company was the Japanese corporation Nintendo, which started manufacturing playing cards called "hafanuda," or "flower cards," in 1889.[11] By the 1960s, Nintendo took advantage of changing technology and began exploring the possibility of producing simple electronic video games.[12] At around the same time, the Connecticut Leather Company ("Coleco"), which until then served primarily as a manufacturer of leather goods, also invested in what eventually became the video game market.[13] Additionally, David Rosen, a businessman and Korean War veteran, launched Service Games—a company that shipped coin-operated machines to U.S. military bases.[14] Years later, Service Games reemerged as the video game company SEGA.

Further, during the 1960s, students at the Massachusetts Institute of Technology (MIT) began to use their electrical engineering experience to work toward developing and fine-tuning the underlying technology needed to produce video games.[15] Using Cathode Ray Tube monitors and a PDP-1 computer, MIT students ultimately won the race to build the world's first true video game, *Spacewar*.[16] *Spacewar* was a *Missile Command*-type game where players would fire missiles at each other's spaceships with the objective of destroying their opponent's spacecraft first. *Spacewar* would form the basis for early coin-operated games like *Asteroids*. These early video gaming computers built by MIT students in the post-World War II era laid the foundation for the modern gaming computers that fuel the esports industry today.

Arcade Gaming in the 1970s

With both the business structures and early technologies now in place to allow for electronic gaming, the 1970s and 1980s ushered in the second era

11. *History of Nintendo: Where Did Nintendo Come From?*, BBC (Jun. 12, 2019), https://www.bbc.co.uk/newsround/48606526.

12. Gamester81, *History of Consoles: ColecoVision (1982)*, GAMESTER 81 (Aug. 29, 2012), http://gamester81.com/history-of-consoles-colecovision/.

13. *Id.*

14. John T. Holden, Marc Edelman & Thomas A. Baker III, *A Short Treatise on Esports and the Law: How America Regulates Its Next National Pastime*, 2020 U. ILL. L. REV. 509, 513 (2020).

15. *Id.* at 514 (citing LIPSON & BRAIN, *supra* note 1, at 8).

16. Holden, Edelman & Baker, *supra* note 14, at 514.

that would lead to the contemporary emergence of esports—the era of arcade gaming. The arcade gaming era would see not only the emergence of Nintendo, Coleco, and SEGA but also the company Atari, which, for a time, was the most well known of all arcade gaming companies.

After playing *Spacewar* as a student at the University of Utah, Nolan Bushnell would begin a journey that monumentally shaped the course of the history of video gaming—the launching of Atari. Bushnell believed that while the MIT students' development of *Spacewar* marked important technological progress, *Spacewar* was missing a coin slot that would allow the game to be played in the same way as pinball machines.[17] Thus, Bushnell set out to change this. By pairing the underlying technology developed by the MIT students with a coin slot, he built his own video game, *Computer Space*, which allowed for pay-to-enter gaming, just like in pinball.

Bushnell would debut *Computer Space* at a Palo Alto restaurant, the Dutch Goose, in the summer of 1971.[18] While *Computer Space* was not a huge commercial success, it was the first arcade game of its kind, and it provided the technological groundwork for a future Bushnell project that launched video gaming into the mainstream: *Pong*. *Pong* was created for Atari and released in 1972—the business venture that Bushnell ultimately started with his colleague, Ted Dabney—by an engineer named Al Alcorn.[19] Alcorn's *Pong* was a technological wonder. Not only could the game be played in its arcade form, but there was also a console version that could be played at home on a television. The game marked an important introduction to the idea of home computing, and thereby home gaming, for Americans. Rather than enjoy the profits generated from *Pong* for personal gain, Bushnell and Dabney instead invested the proceeds from *Pong* into Atari to further game development, which allowed them to continue launching technologically sophisticated games.

By the late 1970s, the new arcade games that emerged were far more nuanced and complex than those designed in previous years. Although these new arcade games were technologically sophisticated, many of the games faced backlash from critics who were concerned about the games'

---

17. Benj Edwards, *Computer Space and the Dawn of the Arcade Videogame*, TECHNOLOGIZER (Dec. 11, 2011), https://www.technologizer.com/2011/12/11/computer-space-and-the-dawn-of-the-arcade-video-game/.

18. *Id.*

19. Matt Barton & Bill Loguidice, *The History of Pong: Avoid Missing Game to Start Industry*, GAMASUTRA (Jan. 9, 2009), https://www.gamasutra.com/view/feature/132293/the_history_of_pong_avoid_missing_.php.

violence or encouragement of antisocial tendencies. Perhaps most notably, in 1976, a game called *Death Race,* developed by the company Exidy, attracted significant negative attention because it encouraged players to drive a car and strike pedestrians. The game even drew the ire of the National Safety Council, which criticized it as making a mockery of the 9,000 pedestrians killed each year.[20] At least momentarily, this negative backlash raised doubts about the future potential of arcade and in-home games. However, the backlash did not have any broad, negative effects on the emerging video game industry, as by the late 1970s, there were approximately 13,000 arcades around the country, and by 1982, popular video game machines could generate up to $400 a week.[21]

Even with the great popularity of certain arcade games, such as *Pac-Man,* that generated revenues in the billions of dollars, the costs associated with maintaining arcade machines, the constant demand for new games, and the ubiquity of competition made it difficult for game operators to make a profit.[22] As a result, ultra-popular games like *Space Invaders* had a limited shelf life in arcades.[23] Despite the launch of the U.S. National Videogame Team in 1983, arcades were experiencing the beginning of the end, which was set in motion by the launch of the Atari 2600 in 1980 and the increased proliferation of the in-home gaming console.[24]

Home Gaming Emerges with Atari

Until 1980, most people who played video games did so in arcades. However, the arrival of the Atari 2600 meant that Americans who wanted to play video games no longer had to leave their homes. Instead, they could purchase cartridges and play games through a console, which they purchased, plugged into their televisions. In addition to being able to play video games in the privacy of their own homes, the Atari 2600 allowed heavy gamers to save money because they could now pay a one-time fee to purchase a console instead of placing a quarter into an arcade machine each time they wanted to play a particular game.

---

20. Holden, Edelman & Baker, *supra* note 14, at 514.

21. Laura June, *For Amusement Only: The Life and Death of the American Arcade,* THE VERGE (Jan. 16, 2013), https://www.theverge.com/2013/1/16/3740422/the-life-and-death-of-the-american-arcade-for-amusement-only.

22. *Id.*

23. *Id.*

24. Holden, Edelman & Baker, *supra* note 14, at 515.

Atari 2600 video game consoles gained immediate popularity among many gamers, and the pinnacle for Atari was in 1982. But a year later, in 1983, the video game market crashed as video game makers flooded the market with many new games, and customers only allocated discretionary income to a select few. The video game market crash of 1983 saw revenues fall nearly 97 percent in two years, leaving the industry with only a few surviving companies.[25] With video game supply far exceeding demand, most gaming companies had to sell games at discounted prices and hope to recoup some of their losses through the sale of consoles.[26]

The video game market crash would lead to a personnel shakeup at Atari that marked the end of Atari's brief market dominance and resulted in a number of key personnel leaving Atari to start Activision.[27] Then, in 1985, Nintendo entered the video game console market with the Nintendo Entertainment System (NES). From a business perspective, the NES was superior to the Atari 2600 in one very specific way—it would only allow games to operate if they included a Nintendo-manufactured computer chip. The NES-chip system allowed Nintendo to restrict non-licensed third-party game makers from producing games for their console system. Nintendo also was able to use its market power over the video game console market to negotiate exclusivity with certain third parties so that they would not manufacture games for competitors. Although Atari would challenge Nintendo's practice under antitrust law, Nintendo and the NES were ultimately successful.[28] While Atari was unsuccessful in its challenge to Nintendo's success in the United States, the Federal Trade Commission (FTC) criticized Nintendo's business practices and Nintendo ultimately agreed to settle their dispute with the FTC by issuing $25 million in rebates, without an admission of guilt.[29]

As the early console companies like Atari and Coleco faded from the scene toward the end of the 1980s, a new competitive battle emerged in

---

25. Ryan Lambie, *The 1983 Videogame Crash: Could It Happen Again?*, Den of Geek (Feb. 20, 2013), https://www.denofgeek.com/games/the-1983-videogame-crash-what-went-wrong-and-could-it-happen-again/.

26. Matt Barton & Bill Loguidice, *A History of Gaming Platforms: Atari 2600 Video Computer Systems / VCS*, Gamasutra (last accessed May 12, 2020), https://www.gamasutra.com/view/feature/131956/a_history_of_gaming_platforms_.php?print=1.

27. Holden, Edelman & Baker, *supra* note 14, at 515.

28. Jonathan Weber, *Jury Sides with Nintendo in Suit Brought by Atari: * Verdict: Panel Exonerates the Videogame Giant of Trying to Monopolize the Market and Rules It Had Not Damaged Its Rival*, L.A. Times (May 2, 1992), https://www.latimes.com/archives/la-xpm-1992-05-02-fi-1361-story.html.

29. Robert E. Tomasson, *Nintendo to Pay $25 Million In Rebates on Price Fixing*, N.Y. Times (Apr. 11, 1991), https://www.nytimes.com/1991/04/11/business/nintendo-to-pay-25-million-in-rebates-on-price-fixing.html.

1989 between Nintendo and SEGA, when SEGA launched its Genesis console. The rivalry between these two companies featured a battle between two iconic game franchises: *Mario* for Nintendo and *Sonic the Hedgehog* for SEGA. While Nintendo performed especially well among children and young teenagers, SEGA's Genesis succeeded in pushing the video game console market towards older users, with games like *Mortal Kombat*, which featured significantly more blood and gore than many of the Nintendo titles of the time.[30] In a period of just a few short years, SEGA captured nearly half the United States video gaming market share. But much as Atari found itself facing economic trouble by 1983 due to the emergence of many competitive video game makers for their own consoles, the later trouble for the console makers such as Nintendo and SEGA came in the form of the rapidly dropping cost of personal computers (PCs). As the price for computers came down, making them accessible for middle-income families, PCs became bona fide competitors to the video game consoles. In some ways, PCs were actually more desirable options for many consumers, especially families, as unlike game consoles, PCs offered word processing software in addition to gaming options.

Electronic Arts Inc. and the Sports Gaming Segment

The 1980s also saw the advent of the sports-based video game, which, for the first time, would emerge as an important sub-segment of gaming—especially on in-home consoles. While early sports video games such as *One on One: Dr. J vs. Larry Bird* were limited in their ability to replicate team sporting events, in 1984, the company Electronic Arts (EA) began to develop more realistic video games in which users could navigate any of the players of a team in a team-based traditional sport. To intensify the realism in its football video game, EA's founder reached out to then-head coach of the NFL's Oakland Raiders (now the Las Vegas Raiders), John Madden. In 1988, Madden agreed to be the face and name for one of the most successful and long-running American video game franchises with the launch of *John Madden Football*.[31] In 1994, EA would reach licensing

30. Leo Kelion, *Sega v. Nintendo: Sonic, Mario and the 1990's Console War*, BBC (May 13, 2014), https://www.bbc.com/news/technology-27373587.

31. Holden, Edelman & Baker, *supra* note 14, at 516.

deals with the National Football League (NFL) and the National Football League Players Association (NFLPA) that would enable the game makers to use actual NFL team names, logos, and rosters in their game.[32]

As EA was cornering the market for video games based on America's most popular sports, it was also increasing its global footprint by expanding its line of products to games involving international sports. Working with Fédération Internationale de Football Association (FIFA), EA launched an electronic version of the world's most popular sport (soccer) with the establishment of the FIFA video game franchise. EA's FIFA game now has licensing agreements with more than 400 different sports clubs and other entities ranging from international federations to individual players.[33] It is this relationship, as well as the relationship between EA and domestic professional sports leagues, that later helped yield the emergence of esports competitions based on real-world sports video games and the ongoing joint ventures in this arena between video game makers and some of the world's largest professional sports leagues.

More Games, More Variety, and More Regulation

The 1990s, meanwhile, saw video games move beyond entertainment products such as sports and shooting games, as game makers began to capitalize on the educational market with the creation of games for both PCs and traditional gaming consoles (e.g. the original Nintendo NES system). Games like *Oregon Trail*, *Where in the World Is Carmen Sandiego?* and *Math Blaster* marked the beginning of this new generation of products.[34] Furthermore, the era saw the establishment of games like *SimCity*, which incorporated educational aspects, but was marketed for mass appeal because it taught users the basics of managing a city.[35] By expanding games beyond just pure entertainment, the video game industry was able to gain mass societal appeal—moving far beyond the period of

32. *Id.*

33. Arjun Reddy, *FIFA's Videogame Is Leaving Its Competition In The Dust Because of 2 Key Advantages (EA)*, Bus. Insider (Mar. 7, 2019), https://markets.businessinsider.com/news/stocks/fifa-video-game-leaving-competition-in-the-dust-2019-3-1028013682.

34. Stephen Baer, *The Rise of Educational Games*, eLearning Industry (Feb. 3, 2018), https://elearningindustry.com/rise-of-educational-games.

35. Holden, Edelman & Baker, *supra* note 14, at 516.

time back in the 1970s when the National Safety Council cautioned society about the industry's proliferation. The value of video games was even recognized by the California Bar Association, which approved the game *Objection!* as a potential means of earning continuing legal education credits for bar members.[36]

Nevertheless, certain video games still attracted concern. For example, in the 1990s, video games became increasingly graphic, with games like *Doom, Mortal Combat, and Wolfenstein 3D* focusing on shooting and blood. These games would eventually draw both the attention and ire of Congress.[37] With the support of children's advocates, Joe Lieberman, a Senator from Connecticut, sponsored legislation to require the video game industry to establish a warning label system like that used by the Motion Picture Association of America to warn parents about graphic content.[38] The hearings scared some game makers, and SEGA elected to pull its controversial game *Night Trap* from shelves, and to revise the version of the game for its Genesis platform to remove some of its more controversial elements.[39] The game industry would move to voluntarily enact some content advisory labels, heading off the immediate threat posed by Congress in the mid-1990s.

During the same era that Congress became focused on violent video games, consoles were becoming more technologically advanced. In turn, these advancements allowed video games to appear more realistic. Within a year of each other, SEGA released the 32-bit Saturn, and Nintendo released the 64-bit Nintendo 64.[40] Before the Christmas shopping season of 1995, Sony would also enter the video game industry. The Sony PlayStation made its American debut in September 1995[41] and would go on to sell more than 100 million units. The emergence of Sony as a powerful entity in the console market would have unfortunate timing for Nintendo. While Nintendo survived antitrust challenges regarding some of their practices in the United States, the company would not be so lucky

---

36. Lipson & Brain, *supra* note 1, at 17.

37. *Id.*

38. *Senator Calls for Warnings on Videogames*, Wash. Post (Dec. 2, 1993), https://www.washingtonpost.com/archive/lifestyle/1993/12/02/senator-calls-for-warnings-on-video-games/74450503-ed9a-4084-9910-b8e65ac6f0cb/.

39. John Burgess, *SEGA to Withdraw, Revise 'Night Trap,'* Wash. Post (Jan. 11, 1994), https://www.washingtonpost.com/archive/business/1994/01/11/sega-to-withdraw-revise-night-trap/d221ba3c-c19d-4d40-b88e-cc1905878cf4/.

40. Holden, Edelman & Baker, *supra* note 14, at 516.

41. D.S. Cohen, *The History of the Sony PlayStation*, Lifewire (Nov. 23, 2019), https://www.lifewire.com/history-of-sony-playstation-729672.

with the European Economic Commission, which ruled that Nintendo could not continue to exclude third-party game makers from making Nintendo cartridges.[42]

As the content of video games became more realistic in the late 1990s and the first decade of the twenty-first century, courts began to look at video games differently, extending First Amendment protections to the content of games. In *American Amusement Machine Association v. Kendrick*,[43] the Seventh Circuit Court of Appeals ruled that an Indianapolis ordinance that restricted the access of minors to violent video games was unconstitutional.[44] The Supreme Court would also wrestle with a similar question a decade later, in *Brown v. Entertainment Merchants Association*,[45] holding that California's restrictions on the sale of violent video games to minors failed to satisfy strict scrutiny.[46] The landmark *Brown* decision provided a firm constitutional basis for the sale of video games, even violent ones, to minors. The decision was critical for video game producers because children and adolescents were, and remain, one of the most important demographics for the industry. Even today, the younger market is the driving force behind the growth of both the electronic gaming and esports industries. Without the *Brown* decision, it is unclear whether esports could have attained the success that it enjoys in the United States today.

Gaming Competitions

Not only have recent decades seen profound growth in video games, but they have also experienced the emergence of gaming competitions—events that have ultimately morphed into the modern activity known as esports. It is believed that the earliest video game competition took place at Stanford University in 1982.[47] The event, in the form of the "Intergalactic *Spacewar* Olympics," permitted eligible entrants the chance to compete for

42. Commission Decision No. 2003/675/EC of 30 October 2002. *See also* Lipson & Brain, *supra* note 11, at 18.

43. Am. Amusement Machine Ass'n v. Kendrick, 244 F.3d 572 (7th Cir. 2001).

44. *Id.* at 580.

45. Brown v. Ent. Merch. Ass'n, 564 U.S. 786 (2011).

46. *Id.* at 804–05 (2011).

47. Megan Farokmanesh, *First Game Tournament, 'Intergalactic Spacewar Olympics," held 50 years ago*, Polygon (Oct. 20, 2012), https://www.polygon.com/2012/10/20/3529662/first-game-tournament-intergalactic-spacewar-olympics-held-40-years.

the prize of a one-year subscription to *Rolling Stone* magazine.[48] Additionally, at this time, game makers themselves saw the opportunity to capitalize on video gaming competitions, with Atari hosting its first-ever competition—a *Space Invaders* tournament—which reportedly attracted 10,000 entrants.[49]

The 1980s also saw the emergence of video gaming record keeping, with the *Guinness Book of World Records* keeping track of the high scores associated with certain game titles.[50] Perhaps no video gaming figure was more renowned in the early 1980s than Billy Mitchell, a talented gamer who possessed high scores in both *Donkey Kong* and *Pac-Man*.[51] Mitchell would become one-fifth of the U.S. National Videogame Team. The team was the concept of event promoter Jim Riley and Twin Galaxies co-founder Walter Day. Riley and Day thought of the idea to select America's best video game players and take them on a roadshow, *The Electric Circus Tour*, around the country.[52] While the tour was not a commercial success, it set the stage for what has become the highly commercialized esports environment of today.

Meanwhile, the 1990s brought something more akin to the video game competitions we today call "esports." In 1994, Nintendo would host *Powerfest*, bringing together the best video game players from around the country to compete in three different specially modified games of *Super Mario All-Stars*, *Super Mario Kart*, and *Ken Griffey Jr. Presents Major League Baseball* .[53] Nintendo created only thirty-three cartridges of the specially modified versions of the games, thirty-one of which were collected at the conclusion of the finals that were held at Sea World in San Diego, California. The two remaining cartridges remain sought after collector's items, with one listing for $300,000.[54] Then, in 1997, Id Software hosted its Red Annihilation *Quake* tournament, in which the winner,

48. *Id.*

49. Holden, Edelman & Baker, *supra* note 14, at 517.

50. *Id.*

51. Owen S. Good, *Billy Mitchell Threatens Legal Action Over Vacated Donkey Kong Scores*, Polygon (Sep. 14, 2019), https://www.polygon.com/2019/9/14/20865828/billy-mitchell-the-king-of-kong-records-thrown-out-twin-galaxies-guinness-lawsuit.

52. Patrick S. Patterson, *History*, US Nat'l Videogame Team (last accessed May 13, 2020), https://www.usnationalvideogameteam.com/history.

53. *Id.*

54. *Nintendo Powerfest*, Nintendo Wiki (last accessed May 13, 2020), https://nintendo.fandom.com/wiki/Nintendo_PowerFest_%2794.

Dennis Fong, was rewarded with $5,000 in cash and the company cofounder's Ferrari.[55]

In 2000, the World Cyber Games held its first competition.[56] The World Cyber Games were one of the premier international esports events, drawing competitors from more than seventy-five countries throughout the first decade of the twenty-first century.[57] Likewise, the Electronic Sports World Cup (now Electronic Sports World Convention) also gained popularity at this time, eventually awarding more than $3 million in prize money.[58] However, in America, no esports league had the same presence as Major League Gaming (MLG). MLG was an esports league featured on the USA Network, which used a logo that looked similar to those of other American sports leagues, but instead of a professional athlete swinging a baseball bat or dribbling a basketball, it featured the image of a game controller with a connector cable. MLG would spend the early years of its existence focused on first-person shooter games, such as *Halo*. As the twenty-first century continued, the organization would branch out across different genres of games.[59] MLG's live events grew to attract more than 15,000 spectators and generated more than $50 million in advertising deals, making it perhaps the first American esports league to attain some level of sustained success.[60] In late 2015, Activision Blizzard acquired MLG for a reported $46 million in the hopes of launching a dedicated esports network.[61]

The Present Day

Today, esports attract more money than ever before, with investors ranging from professional sports teams or celebrities to hedge funds and

---

55. Chris Baker, *Meet Dennis 'Thresh' Fong, the Original Pro Gamer*, Rolling Stone (Aug. 30, 2016), https://www.rollingstone.com/culture/culture-news/meet-dennis-thresh-fong-the-original-pro-gamer-103208/.

56. Holden, Edelman & Baker, *supra* note 14, at 518.

57. *Id.*

58. *About ESWC*, ESWC (last accessed May 13, 2020), https://www.eswc.com/page/about-eswc.

59. Holden, Edelman & Baker, *supra* note 14, at 518.

60. Alex Wilhelm, *The Rise of Major League Gaming and the Future of Esports*, The Next Web (Jun. 26, 2011), https://thenextweb.com/insider/2011/06/26/the-rise-of-major-league-gaming-and-the-future-of-esports/.

61. Dean Takahashi, *Activision Blizzard Buys MLG for Estimated $46M to Build 'ESPN of Esports,'* Venture Beat (Jan. 4, 2016), https://venturebeat.com/2016/01/04/activision-blizzard-buys-mlg-for-estimated-46m-to-build-espn-of-esports/.

venture capital firms. While some leagues have attempted to navigate the traditional delivery of a sports model to consumers via television broadcasting contracts, the majority of esports competitions are streamed on platforms like Twitch and YouTube.[62] Despite the departure from the traditional vehicle for sport delivery that has characterized much of the last seventy-five years, esports are attracting significant crowds to live events, selling out arenas like New York's Barclays' Center and the Staples Center in Los Angeles, in under an hour.[63] Even though most consumers view esports content for free over the internet, the numbers of viewers exceed even some of the most-watched traditional sporting events. In 2018, the *League of Legends* World Championship had more than 205 million concurrent viewers at its peak.[64] In 2019, more viewers watched the *League of Legends* World Championship than the NBA Finals.[65] This, of course, represents a very far cry from the humbling beginnings of video games in the form of pinball machines and other simple gaming consoles (e.g., the Atari 2600) that were seen just a couple of generations earlier.

---

62. C.J. Hughes, *As E-Sports Grow, So Do Their Homes*, N.Y. Times https://www.nytimes.com/2019/05/28/business/esports-arenas-developers.html (May 28, 2019); AJ Willingham, *What is eSports? A look at an explosive billion-dollar industry*, CNN (Aug. 27, 2018, 2:18 PM), https://www.cnn.com/2018/08/27/us/esports-what-is-video-game-professional-league-madden-trnd/index.html; Steven Asarch, *What Is Twitch? Understanding the Explosive Live-Streaming Service*, Newsweek, (May 3, 2018, 11:00 AM), https://www.newsweek.com/2018/05/11/twitch-909594.html.

63. *See* Angelos Anastasopoulos, *AEG Part 1: Why a Mainstream Entertainment Company Invested in Esports*, The eSports Observer (Jan. 22, 2018), https://esportsobserver.com/aeg-esports-part-one/.

64. Thomas Baker, *League of Legends: Chinese Viewership Drives Worlds To Highest Peak In Esports History*, Game Haus (Nov. 12, 2018), https://thegamehaus.com/columns/league-worlds-viewership-esports-2018/2018/11/12/.

65. *Compare* Kevin Webb, *More than 100 million people watched the 'League of Legends' World Championship, cementing its place as the most popular esport*, Bus. Insider (Dec. 18, 2019, 12:09 PM), https://www.businessinsider.com/league-of-legends-world-championship-100-million-viewers-2019-12 (explaining that the *League of Legends* World Championship had 44 million viewers), *with* Rick Porter, *TV Ratings: Strong Numbers for Toronto Raptors' NBA Title Clincher*, The Hollywood Reporter (Jun. 14, 2019, 8:03 AM), https://www.hollywoodreporter.com/live-feed/nba-finals-close-strong-tv-ratings-thursday-june-13-2019-1218363 (sharing that Game 6 of the NBA Finals had 18.34 million viewers).

Chapter 2

The Esports Industry Today

Industry Growth

Measuring the economic growth of the esports industry is a difficult task because the overarching video game industry far surpasses the size of the competitive esports scene. By the end of 2019, the video game industry was worth $120 billion.[1] Despite COVID-related setbacks, the industry still grew by 12 percent in 2020 to be worth $139.9 billion.[2] By the end of 2021, the global esports market will likely amass revenue of over $1.08 billion.[3] This translates to year-over-year growth of 14 percent, as the esports industry generated roughly $974 million in revenue in 2020.[4]

The esports industry's revenue growth is impressive. Notably, more than 40 percent of esports enthusiasts boast annual household incomes in excess of $75,000,[5] and more than 30 percent of esports enthusiasts have

1. Dean Takahashi, *SuperData: Games grew 12% to $139.9 billion in 2020 amid pandemic*, VentureBeat (Jan. 6, 2021, 6:00 AM), https://venturebeat.com/2021/01/06/superdata-games-grew-12-to-139-9-billion-in-2020-amid-pandemic/.

2. *Id.*

3. Christina Gough, *eSports market revenue worldwide from 2019 to 2024*, Statista (Mar. 18, 2021), https://www.statista.com/statistics/490522/global-esports-market-revenue/.

4. *Newzoo: Esports industry revenue expected to surpass $1B in 2021*, Reuters (Mar. 9, 2021, 7:49 PM), https://www.reuters.com/article/esports-business-esports-growth/newzoo-esports-industry-revenue-expected-to-surpass-1b-in-2021-idUSFLM4K2cJ7.

5. Joss Wood, *New Research: Esports Fans May Not Be Exactly Who You Think They Are*, The Lines (last updated Jan. 22, 2018), https://www.thelines.com/esports-fan-demographic-research/.

annual household incomes exceeding $90,000 annually.[6] In addition to having more disposable income than the typical consumer, esports fans are also much younger than fans of traditional sports, with 65 percent of them being between the ages of 18 and 34.[7] By contrast, in 2016, the average age of a viewer of Major League Baseball was 57 years old.[8]

Esports are not only attracting younger and wealthier fans than traditional sports, but esports enthusiasts also consume more esports than traditional sports fans.[9] According to one study in America, young gamers between the ages of 18 and 25 "spend an average of 3 hours and 25 minutes each week watching others play video games online."[10] This consumption pattern appears to hold for esports enthusiasts around the globe, as researchers studied a group that included more than 3,000 consumers from different countries and found similar results.[11] Further, it is likely that esports fandom and consumption will only continue to grow. For example, research group *Newzoo* expects esports to have more than 300 million casual viewers by 2021.[12]

Investing in Esports

As esports continues to expand in popularity, there has been a steady stream of outside investment seeking to capitalize on the ascent of one of the fastest-growing entertainment segments in recent memory. Investors are interested in the esports space for a number of reasons. Most notably, investor interest in esports has intensified due to the fact that the industry transcends virtually all demographics.[13] Additionally, those who work in both traditional sports and esports see continued growth potential for esports. For example, Steve Borenstein of Activision Blizzard and former

---

6. *Id.*

7. *Id.*

8. Jason Notte, *The Sports With The Oldest—and Youngest—TV Audiences*, MarketWatch (Jun. 30, 2017), https://www.marketwatch.com/story/the-sports-with-the-oldest-and-youngest-tv-audiences-2017-06-30.

9. Darren Heitner, *Watching Video Games Is Now Bigger Than Traditional Spectator Sporting Events*, Inc. (Apr. 2, 2018), https://www.inc.com/darren-heitner/watching-video-games-is-now-bigger-traditional-spectator-sporting-events.html.

10. *Id.*

11. *Id.*

12. John T. Holden, Marc Edelman & Thomas A. Baker III, *A Short Treatise on Esports and the Law: How America Regulates Its Next National Pastime*, 2020 U. Ill. L. Rev. 509, 522 (2020).

13. *Id.*

CEO of ESPN and the NFL Network stated that he believes esports will rival the most prominent traditional sports leagues in the future because due to advertising and ticket sales opportunities the industry has tremendous opportunity for growth.[14] Likewise, Johanna Faries, the current Commissioner of the *Call of Duty* League and former Vice President at the NFL, has shared that esports allow for "innovation and in-game opportunities that . . . go farther than traditional sports can stretch," because esports allows fans to engage with players through virtual experiences spearheaded by technological advancements.[15]

While institutional investors, high-net-worth individuals, and venture capital firms are attracted to direct investment in esports, there are numerous avenues through which casual investors also can indirectly invest in the industry. For example, investors can purchase stock shares for ownership in video game makers like Activision Blizzard or make investments in companies that support an underlying aspect of competitive video gaming, such as virtual reality. This is distinguishable from traditional sports, where other than investing in World Wrestling Entertainment Inc. (NYSE: WWE), there are few opportunities for fans to hold shares of a professional sports team or league.

Not only has esports gained investments from a traditional investing crowd, but it also has attracted its share of celebrities ranging from NBA superstar Michael Jordan to the musician, Drake.[16] Much of the investment into esports is being placed back into the product itself to further enhance the appearance and reputation of esports contests. In 2018, Las Vegas opened the Esports Arena Las Vegas—a state-of-the-art space dedicated to esports inside the Luxor hotel—on the strip.[17] While the Esports Arena Las Vegas was the first dedicated esports arena, plans for a $10 million esports facility in the city of Arlington, Texas, quickly followed suit.[18] The Arlington

---

14. Josh Chapman, *Esports: A Guide to Competitive Video Gaming*, TOPTAL (last visited Jun. 9, 2020), https://www.toptal.com/finance/market-research-analysts/esports.

15. Noah Smith, *As curtain rises on Call of Duty League, big questions loom. How will they be answered?*, SPORTS ILLUSTRATED (Jan. 24, 2020, 9:08 AM), https://www.washingtonpost.com/video-games/esports/2020/01/24/curtain-rises-call-duty-league-big-questions-loom-how-will-they-be-answered/.

16. Tom Huddleston, Jr., *From Michael Jordan to Drake: The Athletes and Celebs Who Invested Millions in Esports in 2018*, CNBC (Dec. 27, 2018), https://www.cnbc.com/2018/12/19/from-michael-jordan-to-drake-athletes-celebrities-invested-millions-esports.html.

17. *Id.*

18. David Malone, *The Largest eSports Stadium in North America Opens in Arlington, Texas*, BLDG., DESIGN AND CONSTR. (Nov. 27, 2018), https://www.bdcnetwork.com/largest-esports-stadium-north-america-opens-arlington-texas.

facility converted 100,000 square feet of the former convention center into a state-of-the-art esports facility.[19]

Las Vegas and Arlington were merely the tip of the iceberg. Today, cities across the country are planning for the construction of dedicated esports facilities, including a $50 million investment in Philadelphia by Comcast subgroup, Spectator.[20] Schools have also begun to explore the value of esports as a means of not only offering activities that students are interested in but also as a means of attracting students. The process began with Robert Morris University offering scholarships to competitive video gamers[21] and has now trickled down to educational institutions of nearly all levels, including major universities like Ohio State.[22] In 2019, there were approximately 125 varsity esports teams in the United States, and several schools now offer majors that center around esports.[23] Nevertheless, despite the collegiate-level presence of esports, the National Collegiate Athletic Association (NCAA) does not recognize it as a sanctioned activity and thus participants on college esports teams are not restricted in their economic opportunities by the NCAA's growingly controversial Principle of Amateurism.[24]

The Game Genres of Esports

Esports is a term that covers a lot of ground. The term represents competitive video gaming across a wide variety of games and game genres. Some games reward a player's fast reflexes, whereas others value a competitor's more cerebral and strategic moves. While new video games are released for public consumption every week, only those that produce esports competitions qualify as "esports." Although there is no standard definition for what

---

19. *Id.*

20. David Bloom, *Esports Stadiums Are Popping Up Everywhere*, Forbes (May 31, 2019), https://www.forbes.com/sites/dbloom/2019/05/31/esports-stadiums-are-popping-up-everywhere/#176398252105.

21. John T. Holden, Anastasios Kaburakis, & Ryan M. Rodenberg, *The Future Is Now: Esports Policy Considerations and Potential Litigation*, 27 J. Legal Aspects of Sport 46, 54 (2017).

22. *See* Calvin Hendrick, *Esports Programs Start to Pop Up in K-12 Schools*, EdTech (Jan. 11, 2019), https://edtechmagazine.com/k12/article/2019/01/esports-programs-start-pop-k-12-schools.

23. Eric Stoller, *An Epic Update on Collegiate Esports*, Inside Higher Ed (May 16, 2019), https://www.insidehighered.com/blogs/student-affairs-and-technology/epic-update-collegiate-esports.

24. *See* Joe Lemire, *NCAA President Criticizes Esports for Misogyny, Violence, Gamer Health*, Sport Techie (Jan. 28, 2019), https://www.sporttechie.com/ncaa-president-criticizes-esports-for-misogyny-violence-gamer-health/.

constitutes an "esport," there are three primary characteristics that lend themselves to accepting an activity as an esport. First, games with a strong competitive element,[25] such as games involving suspense and action as opposed to a slow meandering storyline, are likely esports. Second, games that have a strong following with recreational players tend to project better as esports than games that are more niche. The reason for this is primarily profit-driven, but as esports rely on outside investment, investors expect there to be a product that consumers desire. Third, esports typically involve games that are easy for a newcomer to watch and understand—like fighting games.

Fighting Games

As an outsider trying to understand an esports genre, the fighting game is perhaps the most straightforward game type to understand. Fighting games revolve around the idea that one player must defeat the other player, usually in one-on-one combat. The player who inflicts the most damage on the other player is declared the winner. These games have occasionally featured graphic death scenes that, although controversial, leave little doubt as to which player is victorious.[26] Fighting games have a long history, dating to the arcades of the early 1980s. Indeed, games like *Street Fighter* are now prominent esports. Other fighting games like *Tekken* and *Super Smash Bros.* are also notable titles in the realm of fighting games.[27]

Unlike team-based esports games, fighting games appeal to individual amateurs and fans. As such, fighting games are unique in esports, as they provide an opportunity for amateur players and fans to attempt to play their way into a number of prominent esports events through an "open bracket."[28] The top event for fighting games is the Evolution Championship Series, known as Evo,[29] which is the longest continually running esports event for the fighting game genre.[30] The Evo typically takes place over a series of weekends and features up to eight championships for fighting game titles such as *Street Fighter V, Granblue Fantasy: Versus;*

25. Holden, Edelman & Baker, *supra* note 12, at 524.

26. *See e.g.*, Rob Crossley, *Mortal Kombat: Violent Game That Changed Video Games Industry*, BBC News (Jun. 2, 2014), https://www.bbc.com/news/technology-27620071 (describing the controversy surrounding the launch of *Mortal Kombat,* which prominently encouraged players to "Finish him!" when an opponent was close to defeat).

27. Holden, Edelman & Baker, *supra* note 12, at 524.

28. *Id.*

29. *Id.*

30. *See* Evo Championship Series, EVO, http://evo.shoryuken.com/ (last accessed Jun. 10, 2020).

Samurai Shodown; DragonBall FighterZ; Super Smash Bros. Ultimate; Under Night In Birth: EXE [CL-R]; Tekken 7; and *Soul Caliber 6.*[31] The similarities between some fighting games and real-world combat sports, like boxing and mixed martial arts, also lend to their approachability for novice esports fans, and at some events, competitors even have pre-fight handshakes and staredowns like those that traditionally occur in combat sports during weigh-ins.[32]

First- and Third-Person Shooter Games (and Battle Royale)

First-person shooter games (or FPS games), place the human player in the viewpoint of the on-screen person (avatar) they are controlling.[33] This commonly results in a human player being able to see the avatar's arms, weapons, and sometimes its legs and torso, much like someone would if they were looking at their own body. The games also typically include sounds and actions that mimic real life, such as panting after extreme exertion or grunting if an avatar is asked to move a heavy object.[34] Additionally, FPS games involve a player shooting opponents in an effort to achieve an objective on a map. Objectives can range from eliminating all members of an opposing team to disarming a virtual bomb.[35]

The first FPS game, *Maze War,* was actually played on computers at the NASA Ames Research Center.[36] The FPS game genre would also transition to the console system in 1980, with Atari's tank-based game, *Battlezone.*[37] In the early 1990s, FPS games would assert themselves as mainstays in the gaming world with the launch of games like *Wolfenstein 3D* and *Doom,* which sold hundreds of thousands of copies.[38] Those games eventually gave way to enduring game franchises such as *Counter-Strike: Global Offensive* and *Call of Duty,* as well as emergent games like *Overwatch.*

There are a number of prominent championship events for FPS esports competitors, including the *Call of Duty World Championships* and

31. Evo Championship Series, *EVO 21 Frequently Asked Questions,* EVO, https://www.evo.gg/faq/ (last accessed Aug. 19, 2021).

32. Holden, Edelman & Baker, *supra* note 12, at 525.

33. *Id.*

34. *Id.*

35. *Id.*

36. K. Thor Jenson, *The Complete History of First-Person Shooters,* Pc Mag. (Oct. 11, 2017, 9:00 AM), https://www.pcmag.com/news/the-complete-history-of-first-person-shooters.

37. *Id.*

38. *Id.*

Electronic Sports League (ESL) competitions for *Counter-Strike: Global Offensive* teams. There are also competitions offered by the *Overwatch* League, which has emerged as a premier esports league based on the model of city-based franchises that major professional sports leagues follow.[39] Third-person-shooter games (or TPS games) are similar to FPS games, except that the avatar is typically displayed from a halo-view through which the human player has a bird's-eye view over the actions of the avatar. While TPS games have existed for some time, their popularity exploded with the introduction of a subgenre of TPS called "battle royale" games, which includes titles like *Fortnite*, *PUBG*, and *Apex Legends*.[40] The battle royale format has competitors facing off as individuals against dozens of other competitors until there is a single surviving player who is declared the victor.[41] Although, in comparison to more established game-play models, battle royale games faced initial resistance, *Fortnite* game maker Epic Games committed more than $100 million to prize money for *Fortnite* competitions over a two-year period, thus heightening the popularity of the game genre.[42]

Real-Time Strategy Games

Real-time strategy (RTS) games were once the jewel in the esports crown, as games like *Starcraft II* were instrumental in establishing esports as more than just kids playing video games. Despite this, the RTS genre of game has faded from the top-level of esports. Instead of playing RTS games, consumers have focused their energy on multiplayer online battle arena (MOBA) games, which are often free to download, giving them a distinct advantage over comparatively expensive RTS games.[43] The objective of RTS games commonly centers around players playing on a PC and building infrastructure and offensive and defensive forces to conquer and repel enemies who are seeking to destroy the player's base. RTS games involve all players acting simultaneously—often hidden from opponents until a player chooses to launch an attack.[44] While the RTS genre has lost

---

39. *See* Tho Salaun, *Overwatch and the NBA: Basketball's Involvement in the World's First City-Based Team Esport*, The Overguard (Aug. 18, 2018), https://theoverguard.com/overwatch-and-the-nba-basketballs-involvement-in-the-worlds-first-city-based-team-esport/.

40. Holden, Edelman & Baker, *supra* note 12, at 525.

41. *Id.*

42. *Id.* at 526.

43. *Id.*

44. Holden, Edelman & Baker, *supra* note 12, at 526.

popularity amongst esports fans, there have been efforts to revive popular games like *Starcraft II*, and there are still competitions for games like *Halo Wars 2* and *Command & Conquer 3: Kane's Wrath*.[45]

Sports Video Games

In the United States, traditional sports media entities have tried to foster a connection between esports and traditional sports. Nowhere is this connection better realized than with sports-based video games. Sports video games (SVGs) are electronic games based on actual sports.[46] *NBA 2K* is the video game representation of NBA basketball, whereas the *FIFA* series is the video game version of professional and international soccer. The NBA, in particular, has sought to garner a connection with esports through establishing the *NBA 2K* League. The *2K* League features esports teams representing numerous actual NBA franchises.[47] While the NBA has grown in popularity, the *NBA 2K League* has not seen the success carry over, and it struggles with fairly dismal viewership numbers.[48] *FIFA*, by contrast, which is the most played video game series in the sports genre worldwide, had more than six million people enter its "Ultimate Team Championship" to compete for $400,000 in prize money.[49] Those six million were whittled down to thirty-two players, with the winner crowned *FIFA's* best gamer.[50] While SVGs are growing the popularity of esports among American fans of traditional sports, their success pales in comparison to that of the more popular game genres worldwide.

Multiplayer Online Battle Arena (MOBA) Games

MOBA games are the world's most popular type of video game and esport. MOBA games spawned from a modification to *Warcraft III*.[51] MOBAs

45. *See* Callum McCole, *Esports Hasn't Ruined RTS*, GAMECLOUD (Dec. 6, 2018), https://gamecloud.net.au/features/opinion/esports-hasnt-ruined-rts.

46. Holden, Edelman & Baker, *supra* note 12, at 526.

47. *Id.*

48. Ed Dixon, *'Esports Has Lessons For The Entire Industry': NBA 2K League's Brendan Donohue Talks Expansion*, SPORTS PRO MEDIA (Jan. 8, 2020), https://www.sportspromedia.com/interviews/nba-2k-league-china-esports-gen-g-brendan-donohue-interview (noting that Dallas Mavericks owner, Mark Cuban, cited the lack of viewership as a reason not to own an esports team).

49. Holden, Edelman & Baker, *supra* note 12, at 527.

50. *Id.*

51. *Id.*

typically feature two teams of five players each, with each player on a team possessing a specific role.[52] In addition to different roles for players, each player typically holds a distinct skill or ability that can help the team in its objective of defeating an enemy's base before the enemy can defeat theirs.[53] The avatars who are controlled by human players are often accompanied by spawned characters, but the spawned characters typically behave in a predetermined and known way.[54] *League of Legends* and *Defense of the Ancients 2* (*DOTA 2*) are the two most popular MOBA games, with *League of Legends* being the most popular esports title across all game genres. Released in 2009, *League of Legends* has more than 80 million monthly users.[55] *DOTA 2* has more than 100 million registered users[56] and is the subject of the most lucrative esports tournament in the world, The International, which offered a prize pool of more than $30 million in 2019.[57]

Other Games

While most of the top esports titles fit neatly into the five aforementioned categories, there are a handful of games that stand on their own because of their unique sequences of gameplay. These games have a large following, and many consider the highest levels of play of these games to be esports. A long-standing game in the "other" category is *Tetris*—a famous puzzle game featuring falling blocks.[58] But, there are also (virtual) card-based games, like the extremely popular *Hearthstone*, that have carved a unique spot in the esports world. *Hearthstone* is a game where players use cards to summon and direct minions attempting to defeat their opponent's health before they succumb to an opponent's attacks.[59] In spite of the contrast to the superfast pace of MOBAs, cerebral games like *Hearthstone* draw large numbers of fans, both online and in person.[60]

---

52. *Id.*

53. *Id.*

54. *Id.*

55. Richard Heimer, *How Many People Play League of Legends–Updated 2019*, Unranked Smurfs (Oct. 29, 2019), https://www.unrankedsmurfs.com/blog/players-2017.

56. Holden, Edelman & Baker, *supra* note 12, at 527.

57. Mike Stubbs, *The International 9 'Dota 2' Tournament Prize Pool Breaks $30 Million,* Forbes (Jul. 27, 2019), https://www.forbes.com/sites/mikestubbs/2019/07/27/the-international-9-dota-2-tournament-prize-pool-breaks-30-million/#118a9fd92c07.

58. Holden, Edelman & Baker, *supra* note 12, at 528.

59. *Id.*

60. *Id.*

The Esports Stakeholders

The esports industry touches various aspects of society, and the stakeholder groups can be broadly organized into four categories: (1) players; (2) teams, sponsors, and investors; (3) leagues and game makers; and (4) streamers.

Players

Players are the lifeblood of the esports industry—without professional players and recreational players, the industry cannot exist. Most of the top-tier esports games have premier divisions as well as lower-tier divisions that serve as training grounds for aspiring professionals. As such, there are some variations in the levels of esports competition. As a whole, the system of esports competitions is comparable to the minor league systems used in many European soccer leagues, minor league baseball, or even the Challenger Tour in tennis, where players effectively "rank up" by playing well in tournaments.[61]

On average, esports players tend to be younger than professional athletes in more traditional sports, although there is some variation across different game titles. For example, in esports, the average player is approximately 22 years old, whereas, in professional basketball, football, and hockey, the average player is 27.[62] Much attention has been paid to some of the prodigious competitors, like Jun 'TY' Tae Yung, who signed a professional esports contract at the age of twelve and made his debut the following year.[63] Despite the apparent age differences between esports and traditional sports competitors, because esports remains a relatively new industry, it is difficult to read too much into this demographic data.

The compensation of esports players varies. Some professional players make their entire esports earnings from tournament prize winnings, and many of the more established leagues now offer salaries, with a scale that includes minimum salaries for players.[64] While recent improvements have

---

61. *Id.*

62. Sok Min Yun, *A Comparative Overview of ESports Against Traditional Sports Focused in the Legal Realm of Monetary Exploration, Cheating, and Gambling*, 37 Cardozo Arts & Ent. L.J. 513, 530 (2019); Nick Summers, *The esports elders defying their age*, Engadget (Mar. 9, 2020), https://www.engadget.com/2020-03-09-the-esports-elders-defying-their-age.html.

63. Holden, Edelman & Baker, *supra* note 12, at 528.

64. *See, e.g.*, Kevin Webb, *Eight Teams Paid More Than $30 Million Each to Join The Overwatch League—Here's Everything You Need To Know Before The New Season Starts*, Bus. Insider (Dec. 29,

been made, as a whole, the esports industry has faced criticism over the working conditions that some players have endured, either directly or as a result of competitors looking to make or maintain a professional spot.[65] The video gaming consumption rate by adolescents in South Korea became such a national concern that the country imposed a ban on children under sixteen to prevent them from playing video games between midnight and 6:00 a.m.[66]

While esports has been celebrated for its universal appeal, there is a paucity of top female athletes in the esports space. This is despite reports that male and female interest in esports is nearly equal and there being no physiological advantage for males to participate in esports at a competitive or professional level.[67] Indeed, esports represents a rare opportunity for the sporting world to truly have gender equity.[68] Despite the opportunity esports presents for a level playing field between male and female athletes, the industry continues to experience difficulties rectifying issues of sexism that permeate parts of the video gaming community.[69]

Teams, Sponsors, and Investors

A second important category of stakeholders are the teams, sponsors, and investors, who are essential to the commercial viability of esports. While discussed separately below, there is frequent overlap between teams, sponsors, and investors. Many of the prominent esports organizations like FaZe Clan, Team Liquid, and Cloud9 field teams in a variety of esports titles, much like the system in some European countries where organizations field teams in multiple sports.[70] Not all organizations field teams for all games or even genres, although many of the bigger organizations field teams for most of the top-level esports, such as *League of Legends, DotA 2,* and *Counter-Strike: Global Offensive.*[71] The relationship between individual teams and the leagues that they compete in can vary greatly. Some

---

2018), https://www.businessinsider.com/overwatch-league-season-2-2018-9 (noting that Overwatch League offers a minimum salary of $50,000).

65. Holden, Edelman & Baker, *supra* note 12, at 529.

66. *Id.*

67. *Id.*

68. *Id.*

69. *See* John T. Holden, Thomas A. Baker III & Marc Edelman, *The #E-Too Movement: Fighting Back Against Sexual Harassment in Electronic Sports*, 52 Az. St. L.J. 1 (2020).

70. Holden, Edelman & Baker, *supra* note 12, at 530.

71. *Id.*

leagues, such as the ESL Pro League, allow teams significant autonomy and effectively regulate their teams as they see fit.[72] Leagues like the *Overwatch* League, on the other hand, impose a number of minimum standards on teams, including minimum salaries, and in some cases, more detailed protections with regard to working conditions.[73] The size of teams is both game title- and genre-specific, with fighting games requiring far fewer players (as they are played by a single player) than MOBAs.[74]

Esports sponsor is a term that represents a wide range of activities. Sponsors can choose varying levels of engagement, ranging from sponsorship of events like the ESL Intel Extreme Masters to team and uniform sponsorships like we have seen in more traditional sports for a number of years.[75] Sponsors have also sought out individual esports competitors to sponsor.[76] While commercial esports are still gaining a foothold, especially in the United States, some brands have already seen their sponsorships increase brand recognition and purchase intentions.[77]

The excitement around esports has also led to clamoring from investors of all sizes and net worths. While the recreational investor can capture a piece of the esports industry by purchasing shares of video game makers like Activision Blizzard (NASDAQ: ATVI) or Take-Two Interactive Software (NASDAQ: TTWO) through almost any retail brokerage account, high-net-worth and institutional investors have sought to make more direct investments in the industry. The purchasing of individual teams, or stakes in teams, has been a prominent investment, with high-net-worth individuals like New England Patriots owner Robert Kraft even purchasing a team.[78] Even companies like Amazon have invested in the industry, although they have done so through more elaborate means, such as buying the streaming site, Twitch.[79] There are also a number of individuals who have sought to garner a piece of the esports industry by creating startups, either in the form of teams themselves or organizations

72. John T. Holden & Thomas A. Baker III, *The Econtractor? Defining the Esports Employment Relationship*, 56 AM. BUS. L.J. 391, 407 (2019). *See also* Holden, Edelman & Baker, *supra* note 12, at 530.

73. Holden, Edelman & Baker, *supra* note 12, at 530.

74. *Id.*

75. *Id.*

76. *See* Trent Murray, *TEO Picks: The Top 10 Non-Endemic Sponsorships of 2018*, THE ESPORTS OBSERVER (Dec. 27, 2018), https://esportsobserver.com/top10-nonendemic-spons-2018/.

77. Holden, Edelman & Baker, *supra* note 12, at 531.

78. Kevin Webb, *The 23 investors pouring millions into Overwatch esports teams—from Patriots owner Robert Kraft to Chinese conglomerates*, BUS. INSIDER (Mar. 2, 2020, 8:27 AM), https://www.businessinsider.com/overwatch-league-esports-investors-owners-team-cost-vc-2020-2.

79. Holden, Edelman & Baker, *supra* note 12, at 530.

that provide an ancillary support system to the industry.[80] Additionally, the average recreational investor can now invest in esports via exchange-traded funds (ETFs), which hold baskets of gaming stocks.[81]

Leagues and Game Makers

The esports leagues and game makers are two irreplaceable stakeholders in the esports industry, as, without either one, the industry would not exist. Indeed, a number of prominent esports leagues, such as the *League of Legends* League Championship Series (LCS), are owned by the game makers themselves.[82] Some have argued that esports have historically served as marketing arms for game makers,[83] but the tide on that may be changing as leagues develop more of a footprint. Not all game makers own leagues. In fact, some game makers like Valve, which manufactures *Counter-Strike: Global Offensive* (CS:GO), have a very permissive approach. For example, Valve's games serve as the basis of the ESL Pro League's existence, and Valve gives the ESL Pro League permission to operate.[84] At one time, Major League Gaming (MLG) was the most prominent esports league in the United States. However, since MLG's acquisition by Activision Blizzard, other leagues, such as the *NBA 2K* League and *Overwatch* League have taken MLG's place in the market.[85]

There are seemingly more game makers emerging every year, but several have established a significant presence in the industry already, including Riot Games, which is the producer of *League of Legends* and is a subsidiary of the Chinese company Tencent.[86] Activision Blizzard, who makes *Overwatch* and operates the *Overwatch* League, in addition to making the *StarCraft* and *Hearthstone* franchises, is another prominent game maker. Additionally, there is Valve, a company that manufactures both *CS:GO* and *DotA 2*, but chooses to sponsor rather than operate a number of leagues and tournaments themselves.[87] In addition to these

---

80. *Id.*

81. Nathan Reiff, *Best Gaming ETFs for Q2 2021*, Investopedia (Feb. 2, 2021), https://www.investopedia.com/articles/investing/010616/top-4-entertainment-etfs-2016-pej-xly.asp.

82. Holden, Edelman & Baker, *supra* note 12, at 530.

83. *See* Ferguson Mitchell, *The LCS Isn't Profitable Because Riot Doesn't Want It To Be Profitable*, The Esports Observer (Sep. 13, 2016), https://esportsobserver.com/lcs-isnt-profitable-riot-doesnt-want-profitable/.

84. Holden, Edelman & Baker, *supra* note 12, at 531.

85. *Id.*

86. *Id.* at 532.

87. *Id.*

established and prominent game makers, there are a number of other game makers who do have a presence in the industry, including Epic Games, which makes *Fortnite,* Electronic Arts, which manufacturers both the *Madden* and *FIFA* series and Take-Two Interactive, the creator of *NBA 2K.*[88] Overall, the game makers of titles in the esports realm have great control over what games become esports because of the intellectual property ownership that they have over the underlying product—a factor that is not present in traditional sports.

Streamers

The fourth stakeholder group relevant to the esports discussion are streamers. Streamers are the individuals who provide commentary to esports consumers and regularly stream their gameplay on platforms such as Twitch and YouTube. Much like traditional sports have well-known broadcast personalities such as Verne Lundquist and Dick Vitale, esports has a number of streaming personalities who have risen to prominent positions within the industry.[89] Unlike traditional sports, almost anyone can be an esports streamer with the assistance of a microphone, webcam, computer, and subscription to a streaming site. There are a number of popular streaming sites around the world. In the United States, Twitch and YouTube are amongst the most trafficked, with Twitch ranking among the 20 most heavily visited websites in the world.[90] Similar to a number of broadcasters of traditional sports, many streamers played competitive esports prior to live streaming their play and commentary. Interestingly, a number of streamers are better compensated and more well-known than actual professional esports competitors.[91]

---

88. *Id.*
89. *Id.* at 533.
90. *Id.*
91. *Id.*

Chapter 3

Esports and Federal Intellectual Property Rights

Introduction: Owning the Sport

Intellectual property is a term that refers to creations of human intellect, such as artistic and literary work or inventions.[1] Intellectual property law exists to incentivize invention and creativity by providing originators with limited monopolistic protection that permits them to control the use and reproduction of the fruit of their ingenuity.[2] In the United States, intellectual property law has a constitutional foundation.[3] Traditionally, federal intellectual property law functions through the provision of rights via copyrights, patents, and trademarks, which delineate ownership and protect the owner against third-party infringement.[4] Intellectual property systems (often referred to as "regimes") are designed to balance the interests of innovators against the general public's interest in accessing and replicating technological advancements and creative expression.[5] In terms of public interest, a well-balanced intellectual property regime serves

1. *What is Intellectual Property*, World Intell. Prop. Org., https://www.wipo.int/publications/en/details.jsp?id=4528 (2020).

2. *Id.*

3. U.S. Const. Art. I §8 cl. 8.

4. Lindsey Shuler, *Modern Age Protection: Protecting Indigenous Knowledge Through Intellectual Property Law*, 21 Mich. St. Int'l L. Rev. 751, 755 (2013).

5. World Intellectual Property Org., *supra* note 1.

society by protecting creators in a way that stimulates, rather than restricts, creativity.[6]

Because esports and electronic gaming rely heavily on underlying computer code, the need for balanced applications of federal intellectual property law is particularly pertinent to the operation, participation in, and enjoyment of these activities. Esports, in particular, can easily be distinguished from just about any other sport activity in that the games that constitute esports are also intellectual property that belongs to game producers.[7] Each game title within the esports universe was developed, distributed, and maintained by a game producer with the intent to generate profits.[8] The profit-generating function of video game creation holds true even for game titles that do not require upfront costs or registration fees and instead focus on in-game purchases (e.g., "skins").[9] Additionally, the proprietary nature of esports games permits game producers to redesign the games and rewrite the rules for play so as to spark greater consumer interest in them. Further, the game producers have the authority to prevent non-partner leagues and tournaments from building events around the games they design.[10]

Overall, the control that video game producers enjoy over their games is bolstered by consent requirements like End User Licensing Agreements (EULAs).[11] EULAs require a player to consent to various terms and conditions before playing the developer's game.[12] Thus, game producers not only have the power to prevent others from profiting off of their games, but they also control who is permitted to play them and can restrict how the games may be played. For these reasons, the rights of game manufacturers, based on intellectual property law, create a dynamic within esports that is distinguishable from that of any other sport context.[13]

---

6. *Id.*

7. Veli-Matti Karhulahti, *Reconsidering esport: Economics and executive ownership,* 74 Physical Culture & Sport Stud. & Rsch., 43, 46 (2017).

8. *Id. See also*, Andreas Rahmatian, *Cyberspace and Intellectual Property Rights, in* Research Handbook On International Law and Cyberspace 72, 76 (Nicholas Tsagourias & Russell Buchan eds., 2015) (stating that individuals and companies as actors within the cyberspace can blur the divisions between sovereignty and property, providing a quasi-proprietary power to exert quasi-sovereignty over people).

9. Skins are items that gamers can purchase through the games that allow for customization of on-screen characters/avatars.

10. Karhulahti, *supra* note 7, at 46.

11. *See, e.g.*, Elizabeth Brusa, *Professional Video Gaming: Piracy That Pays,* 49 J. Marshall L. Rev. 217, 255 (2015). EULAs, for our purposes are catch-all term encapsulating traditional EULAs as well as other Terms of Use and Terms of Service agreements, which are frequently used by game makers.

12. *See id.* at 255.

13. Karhulahti, *supra* note 7, at 46.

The primary reason that intellectual property in esports differs from other sports contexts is that no single person or entity owns sports such as basketball, baseball, or football.[14] Accordingly, traditional sport activities like basketball or football may be played freely by participants, and tournament organizers need not compensate anyone in order to host an event for the privilege of playing the underlying game. Additionally, traditional sports leagues at both the amateur and professional levels may be constructed without organizers first having to seek approval from those who rightfully own or created the games that are to be played. As a result, those who desire to play a pickup game of basketball on a public court are not restricted in any way in terms of how they play the game because there is no EULA with terms that must be agreed to prior to the pickup game. Further, the continuation of traditional sport activities (e.g., basketball and baseball) are not subject to the business purpose of any single entity. While it is possible that those who manufacture products essential to the operation of a sport may decide to cease their production, the underlying games and sports do not also cease to exist based on that business decision. This is distinguishable from esports because the cessation of a once popular esports game title will likely also end the sport that has been constructed around it. For these reasons, the influence of intellectual property law is more pronounced in the world of esports than it is in traditional sports.

Esports and Copyright Law

In terms of influence, the area of intellectual property law that has the most impact on esports is copyright. The ownership rights granted through copyright law permit game producers to exert exclusive proprietary rights to control reproductions,[15] distributions,[16] public performances,[17] and creations of derivative works[18] that involve or stem from

14. *See* John T. Holden & Thomas A. Baker III, *The Econtractor? Defining the Esports Employment Relationship*, 56 Am. Bus. L.J. 391, 397–99 (2019).

15. 17 U.S.C. §106 (2018).

16. 17 U.S.C. §106(3) (2018).

17. 17 U.S.C. §106(5) (2018) (listing the copyright owner's exclusive rights to public display of their copyrighted work).

18. 17 U.S.C. §106(2) (2018). There are limitations to this right in that derivative works must be capable of independent copyright protection and the new creation must be substantially similar to the original work in order for it to quality as derivative.

their own copyrighted video games.[19] The concept of copyright law was first introduced in the United States as a common law right and was later codified with the enactment of the federal Copyright Act of 1976. The Copyright Act provides protection to the creators of original creative works that are affixed to tangible mediums of expression, and these rights exist for the life of the owner plus seventy years.[20] By way of this protection, the Copyright Act encourages game developers and other creators to continue creating new and original works.[21]

There are three basic requirements for copyright protection: (1) that the work to be protected is a work of authorship; (2) that the work is original, and (3) that the work is in a tangible medium of expression.[22] Under the Copyright Act, the types of "works of authorship" protectable under copyright law include literary works, dramatic works, music, poetry, novels, movies, songs, computer software, and architecture.[23] Video games qualify for protection as audiovisual works,[24] which are defined to include works that involve a series of related images and sounds intended to be shown and heard through the use of machines such as projectors, viewers, or electronic devices.[25] Additionally, as computer software, video games likely also qualify for copyright protection through the writing of code that is treated as similar to a literary work under Section 101 of the Copyright Act.[26]

In addition to the games themselves, the creative elements incorporated into video games, like the characters and storyline, also deserve copyright protection.[27] For example, Mario and his brother Luigi—from the eponymous *Super Mario Bros.*—are characters who are featured in

---

19. For more on the rights afforded to game producers under copyright law, see Brusa, *supra* note 11, at 255.

20. 17 U.S.C. §101 et seq. (2018). Congress has periodically extended the length of Copyright protection, most recently in 1998. *See* Josh H. Escovedo, *Disney's Influence on United States Copyright Law*, IP Law Blog (Feb. 17, 2016), https://www.theiplawblog.com/2016/02/articles/copyright-law/disneys-influence-on-united-states-copyright-law/#::text=In%201998%2C%20Congress%20passed%20the,from%20the%20year%20of%20creation.

21. *See* Walthal v. Rusk, 172 F.3d 481, 484 (7th Cir. 1999) (citing 17 U.S.C. §201(a) (2012)).

22. *See* 17 U.S.C. §102(a) (2020).

23. Copyright Act of 1976, 17 U.S.C. §102 (2012) (outlining the subject matter of copyright).

24. Atari, Inc. v. Amusement World, Inc., 547 F. Supp. 222, 226 (D. Md. 1981).

25. 17 U.S.C. §102 (2019).

26. 17 U.S.C. §101 et seq. (2018).

27. The Supreme Court and lower courts have been consistent in the view that video games are expressive creations that deserve First Amendment protection. *See, e.g.*, Brown v. Ent. Merch. Ass'n, 564 U.S. 786 (2011); ESS ENTERTAINMENT 2000 v. Rock Star Videos, 547 F.3d 1095 (9th Cir. 2008); Candy Lab Inc. v. Milwaukee Cnty., 266 F.Supp.3d 1139 (2017).

the popular esports title *Super Smash Bros.* While the software designed for the game qualifies for copyright protection, the expressive creations resulting from that coding such as the characters of Mario and Luigi, also deserve protection under the Copyright Act.[28] Thus, non-game products like T-shirts and other merchandise that reproduce characters or stories from video games will also be subject to the application of copyright law.

The next and second requirement for copyright protection is the need for the work to be original. The creative elements discussed above could all provide the required evidence of originality within a video game. Originality is "[t]he *sine qua non* of copyright,"[29] meaning that protecting originality is central to copyright law's purpose, and without originality, there is nothing to protect. With originality at the heart of copyright's purpose, it is natural to assume that plaintiffs in copyright actions must establish a significant degree of originality in their creative works to prevail on claims asserted to protect their property. However, this would be a false assumption. In *Feist Publications v. Rural Telephone Service Co.*, the Supreme Court defined "originality" to mean that "the work was independently created by the author ... [with] some minimal degree of creativity."[30] Thus, a video game developer need only establish that they created the game and that there are some (even if minimal) elements within the game that are genuinely creative and original. For example, although the incorporation of the characters Mario and Luigi, who were made famous by Nintendo in *Super Mario Bros.*, into the newer esports title *Super Smash Bros.* may seem unoriginal, this is not the case. Specifically, the use of those characters in settings diverse from those in the original *Super Mario Bros.* games and for purposes and play different from the original games easily satisfies the minimal degree of creativity and originality needed to qualify for copyright protection.[31] Overall, the holding in *Feist Publications* requiring only a "minimal degree of

28. *See also*, Star Athletica, L.L.C. v. Varsity Brands, Inc. (demonstrating where the Supreme Court held that pictorial or graphic features can be protected by copyright even when found on useful articles, 137 S. Ct. 1002, 1004–05 (2017)).

29. Feist Publ'ns, Inc. vs. Rural Tel. Ser. Co, 499 U.S. 340, 345 (1991).

30. *Id.*

31. Mario's first video game appearance was actually in Donkey Kong in 1981, although he was identified as "Jumpman." His brother joined in him in game titles starting with *Super Mario Bros.* in 1983. *See* Tom Huddleston, Jr., *'Super Mario Bros.' Debuted 33 Years Ago—Here's How Mario Accidentally Became A Gaming Superstar*, CNBC (Sep. 13, 2018), https://www.cnbc.com/2018/09/13/super-mario-bros-how-shigeru-miyamoto-created-mario-for-nintendo.html.

creativity" reflects the reality that courts are not the proper venue for discerning creativity or for judging the artistic value of creative works.[32]

Lastly, in addition to the requirement that works must be creative and original, the Copyright Act also requires that they be affixed to a tangible medium for expression in order to be protected under copyright law.[33] For arcade games and video games loaded onto compact discs, there is little debate as to the tangibility of the medium for expression as the discs themselves satisfy the tangibility requirement. In the modern age of technology, however, many popular games exist only online. Despite games not existing in a tangible CD form as often as in the past, online-only games still satisfy the requisite need for tangibility in the mode for expression.[34]

International Enforcement of Copyright Law

Esports is an international industry with revenues in excess of $1 billion and more than 443 million interested consumers across the globe.[35] Unlike most of the traditional sports that have spawned professional sports leagues in the United States, esports, since the time of their inception, have been an international phenomenon with a strong following of consumers across Asia, North and South America, and Europe.[36] The global appeal of esports has fueled investment that has increased industrial growth but also necessitates a discussion on international copyright law. The Copyright Act is not the only legal protection afforded to video game companies in the United States, as domestic copyrights can be enforced based on international treaties. Internationally, video game producers receive transnational protection provided by the World Intellectual Property Organization (WIPO),[37] the WIPO

32. Feist Publ'ns, Inc., 499 U.S. at 345.

33. 17 U.S.C. §102(a) (2015).

34. Atari, Inc. v. Amusement World, Inc., 547 F. Supp. 222, 226 (D. Md. 1981).

35. James Ayles, *Global Esports Revenue Reaches More Than $1 Billion as Audience Figures Exceed 433 Million*, Forbes (Dec. 3, 2019), https://www.forbes.com/sites/jamesayles/2019/12/03/global-esports-revenue-reaches-more-than-1-billion-as-audience-figures-exceed-433-million/#177dab021329.

36. Newzoo, Free 2018 Global Esports Market Report, 1–15 (2018), https://asociacionempresarialesports.es/wp-content/uploads/newzoo_2018_global_esports_market_report_excerpt.pdf.

37. *See generally*, World Intell. Prop. Org., https://www.wipo.int/portal/en/index.html (last visited Dec. 31, 2020).

Copyright Treaty (WCT),[38] and the United States Digital Millennium Copyright Act (DMCA).[39] The WCT requires member countries to protect works from other member countries that are not in the public domain. A similar treaty (WIPO Performances and Phonograms Treaty) exists to protect foreign copyrights for performances and recordings. The DMCA amended the Copyright Act of 1976 to reflect needs made necessary by the ever-changing digital age.[40]

Copyright Defenses

There are a number of possible defenses to copyright that could be asserted in cases brought by video game owners against esports stakeholders and rival game manufacturers. The defenses most applicable to esports include: (a) fair use, (b) the merger doctrine, (c) scènes à faire, and (d) joint authorship. The fair use doctrine allows for the reproduction of copyrighted work for the purpose of criticism, comment, news reporting, teaching, scholarship, or research.[41] For example, the fair use defense has been utilized in copyright defenses asserted by influencers on the streaming services YouTube and Twitch.[42] Likewise, the fair use defense has also been asserted, with mixed success, in copyright actions challenging the use of reverse engineering for the creation of new video games.[43] The Supreme Court established a four-step approach to applying the fair use doctrine in *Campbell v. Acoff-Rose Music.*[44] It includes the following elements:

---

38. *World Copyright Treaty (WCT)*, https://www.wipo.int/portal/en/index.html (last visited Dec. 31, 2020); *see also Summary of the WIPO Copyright Treaty*, https://www.wipo.int/treaties/en/ip/wct/summary_wct.html (last visited Dec. 31, 2020).

39. Amends U.S. copyright law so that it complies with the WIPO Copyright Treaty so that domestic copyright law fits internationally agreed upon policies for copyright enforcement of digital works. For more on the DMCA, *see generally*, Kenneth Hwang, *Blizzard Versus Bnetd: A Looming Ice Age For Free Software Development?*, 92 Cornell L. Rev. 1043 (2007).

40. Brusa, *supra* note 11, at 223.

41. 17 U.S.C. §107 (2019).

42. *See* John T. Holden, Marc Edelman & Thomas A. Baker III, *A Short Treatise on Esports and the Law: How America Regulates Its Next National Pastime*, 2020 U. Ill. L. Rev. 509, 540 (2020)

43. *See* Sony Computer v. Connectix Corp., 203 F.3d 596 (9th Cir. 2000), in which the Ninth Circuit Court of Appeals held that the use of non-infringing emulator software for game creation was protected by fair use; *see also*, Atari Games Corp. v. Nintendo of Am. Inc., 975 F.2d 832 (7th Cir. 1992), in which the Federal Circuit Court of Appeals held that Atari's reverse engineering did not qualify for fair use because the game used for the reverse engineering was wrongfully obtained by Atari.

44. Campbell v. Acuff-Rose Music, Inc., 510 U.S. 569, 577 (1994).

> (1) the purpose and character of the use, including whether such use is of a commercial nature or is for nonprofit educational purposes;
> (2) the nature of the copyrighted work;
> (3) the amount and substantiality of the portion used in relation to the copyrighted work as a whole; and
> (4) the effect of the use upon the potential market for or value of the copyrighted work.[45]

Another utilized defense, the merger doctrine, prohibits a copyright owner from using copyright law to attain monopoly power over an idea or concept for which there are limited ways of expressing that idea.[46] For example, the merger doctrine would block a video game developer from gaining exclusive copyright control over the use of standard game features such as health and control points or the perspective of a first-person in a shooting game.[47] Similar to the merger doctrine, the *scènes à faire* (i.e., scenes that must be done) doctrine also protects against the monopolization of ideas through the recognition that some cultural references and settings are important to society, and no single person or entity should have the exclusive right to prevent their use in subsequent creative works.[48] For example, the producers of a game called *PlayerUnknown's Battlegrounds* (*PUBG*) filed an action against fellow game producer Epic Games for Epic's use of a "battle royale" style of gameplay in the hit esports title *Fortnite*. As discussed in chapter 2, Battle royale is a genre of online multiplayer video game that forces players to compete in a last-person-standing mode of play.[49] At one time, *PUBG* was the only esports title that incorporated a battle royale format. However, the concept or idea behind the battle royale can be found in a variety of settings, including the novel by Koushun Takami and in the film based on that novel that was directed by Kinji Fukasaku.[50] Thus, the idea behind the battle royale is not something that one producer can own in exclusivity of others. Instead, it is a concept that predates PUBG in artistic use, and other creators, including

45. *Id.*

46. 4 Melville B. Nimmer & David Nimmer, *Nimmer on Copyright* §13.03 (B)(3) (1998).

47. Brian Casillas, *Attack of the Clones: Copyright Protection for Video Game Developers*, 33 Loy. Ent. L. Rev. 137, 149 (2012). For example, see Data East USA v. Epyx Inc., 862 F.2d 204 (9th Cir. 1988), a case in which the Ninth Circuit rejected a game producer's attempt to use copyright law to obtain a monopoly over the use of specific fighting moves in video games.

48. Thomas Baker, *What We Know and What We Don't About PUBG's Legal Fight with 'Fortnite' in Korea*, Forbes (Jun. 5, 2018), https://www.forbes.com/sites/thomasbaker/2018/06/05/what-we-know-and-what-we-dont-about-pubgs-legal-fight-with-fortnite-in-korea/#3310e6293901.

49. Holden, Edelman & Baker, *supra* note 14, at 525.

50. Baker, *supra* note 48.

game producers, should have the freedom to make new creations that incorporate the genre.

Finally, joint authorship is a defense to copyright infringement, in which there is more than one author for the protected work, with each author enjoying equal and undivided interests in copyright law.[51] The joint authorship defense is typically asserted by those accused of infringing on another's copyright interests. If the person or entity asserting the defense owns an interest in the copyright-protected work, then there is no infringement. Within the context of esports, joint authorship may be raised as a defense by content creators who stream live gameplay of copyright-protected games on media platforms.[52]

Esports Tournaments/Leagues and Copyright

When we think of esports, it is important to remember that the sports that qualify as esports are video games, which all enjoy copyright protection.[53] There has been a push to recognize the genre of the game as the actual sport rather than the game title. The problem with that recognition is that to be successful in esports a player must train for countless hours on a specific game, which provides that player with expertise in that specific game title. Because of this, professional players rarely switch between games—even games of the same type or genre—when playing at an elite level. Thus, the video games used for esports operate as independent sports with the leagues and tournaments being built around each individual game title. Since the Copyright Act provides game makers with the exclusive right to control the use and reproduction of their games, that control extends to the power to permit or reject the use of the protected video game by third parties in the development of tournaments and leagues.[54]

Accordingly, third parties interested in developing a league or tournament should start with an effort to obtain a license from the video game producer that permits the use of the copyright-protected video game in the development of the tournament or league. For example, the developers of

---

51. 17 U.S.C. §201(a) (2019).

52. Brusa, *supra* note 11, at 227.

53. Thomas A. Baker III & John T. Holden, *College Esports: A Model for NCAA Reform*, 70 S.C. L. Rev. 55, 60 (2018).

54. Tina L. Taylor, Raising the Stakes: Esports and the Professionalization of Computer Gaming 18 (MIT Press 2012).

the 2013 Evo tournament in Las Vegas, Nevada, did not receive permission from Nintendo before they incorporated *Super Smash Bros.* into the tournament.[55] Unfortunately for the tournament developers, Nintendo asserted its right to block the use of *Super Smash Bros.* from inclusion in the event.[56] In this instance, it took pressure from consumers to force Nintendo from its position against the use of its copyright-protected work from being the featured sport in the Evo tournament.[57] While this example demonstrates the right of game producers to control the use of their video games in esports tournaments, the resulting permission granted to the developers of the Evo tournament (as a result of fan pressure) also reveals the tremendous influence that video game consumers and esports enthusiasts have in influencing game producers.

Returning to the control that copyright affords game producers that allows them to restrict third-party competitions that utilize the copyright-protected work, this power must be distinguished from other types of games such as board games. In *Allen v. Academic Games League of America Inc. 25*, the Ninth Circuit held that "playing a game is not a 'performance' within the meaning of the Copyright Act."[58] This holding was in relation to board games, and the result prevented the makers of popular board games like *Scrabble*, *Trivial Pursuit*, and *Dungeons & Dragons* from asserting exclusive control under copyright law to restrict gamers from playing those games in front of spectators.[59] One important caveat to the *Allen* decision is found in the fact that the case was decided in 1996, before the emergence of the first professional esports league. Another caveat is that the defendants in *Allen* had not commercialized their play through relationships with corporate sponsors and media partners. Thus, it is crucial to recognize that organizers of tournaments or leagues built around video games will have to work with the game producers, whereas recreational tournaments for board games may be able to operate without the need for a license. The reason for this may seem arbitrary, but

---

55. Tori Allen, *What's in a Game: Collective Management Organizations and Video Game Copyright*, 8 UNLV Gaming L.J. 209, 211 (2017), citing, Jenna Pitcher, *Nintendo Wanted to Shut Down Super Smash Bros. Melee Evo Event, Not Just Stream*, Polygon (Jul. 11, 2013, 1:59 AM), https://www.polygon.com/2013/7/11/4513294/nintendo-were-trying-to-shut-down-evo-not-just-super-smash-bros-melee.

56. *Id.*

57. Will Partin, *With the Switch, Nintendo is finally taking esports seriously*, The Meta, https://killscreen.com/themeta/switch-nintendo-finally-taking-esports-seriously/ (last visited Jan. 25, 2021).

58. Allen v. Academic Games League of America, Inc., 89 F.3d 614, 616–17 (9th Cir. 1996).

59. *Id.* at 614.

(technically) the fact that video games exist on screens qualifies them for exclusive protection as audiovisual works.[60]

In addition to the power to directly control the use of their products for competitive play, game producers also can influence competitions built around their games by making substantive changes to the way the games are played.[61] In this regard, esports are distinct from traditional sports, as the manufacturers of sports equipment tailor their products to fit changes instituted by those in charge of the competition. As esports continue to grow in commercial value, the importance of tailoring game development for competitive play will intensify. At this present stage of industry development, however, game producers still perceive esports as a means for selling products more than as a driver of game development.[62] And this brings to the surface another concern—what will happen to a successful esports tournament or league if the video game for it is discontinued by the game producer?

In practice, many of the most commercially successful tournaments and leagues are operated by the producers of the games used for the tournaments.[63] Game producers have been best positioned to absorb the costs associated with starting new tournaments and leagues (e.g., renting space for the event, personnel costs, advertising), and promoting the actual video games to consumers has provided the incentive for investment.[64] And it is that incentive to sell games that has provided game producers with the patience needed to absorb the types of financial costs that have buried upstart leagues for traditional sports in the United States.[65] With commercial success, however, there will be new challenges that tournament and league operators will need to address, and copyright law will likely influence the resolution of many of those situations. For example, it is foreseeable that copyright law will affect the outcomes of potential

60. Atari, Inc. v. Amusement World, Inc., 547 F. Supp. 222, 226 (D. Md. 1981).

61. Holden, Edelman & Baker, *supra* note 42, at 539.

62. Haydn Taylor, *The State of Esports: Radical Growth and Inevitable Failure*, Game Industry Biz (Dec. 14, 2018), https://www.gamesindustry.biz/articles/2018-12-14-the-state-of-esports-radical-growth-and-inevitable-failure.

63. Laura L. Chao, *You Must Construct Additional Pylons: Building a Better Framework for Esports Governance*, 86 Fordham L. Rev. 737, 744 (2017).

64. David Segal, *Behind League of Legends, E-Sports's Main Attraction*, N.Y. Times (Oct. 10, 2014), https://www.nytimes.com/2014/10/12/technology/riot-games-league-of-legends-main-attraction-esports.html.

65. Katherine E. Hollist, *Time to be Grown-Ups about Video Gaming: The Rising eSports Industry and the Need for Regulation*, 57 Ariz. L. Rev. 823, 829 (2015). For example, despite being the nation's most-popular professional sport, there have been six failed sports leagues for professional football in the U.S.

conflicts that arise as tournaments and leagues work towards ways to better monetize the media rights to broadcast and stream events, which are also subject to protection under copyright law.[66]

Copyright and Streaming

When discussing the commercial success of esports, conversations should not be limited to topics related to tournaments and leagues. A significant segment of the esports industry involves the live streaming of gameplay by professional players and other gamers on Twitch and YouTube.[67] For the professional players, live streaming play affords fans the opportunity to watch their favorite players train and interact in a more casual setting than the intense nature of tournament and league play. At present, there is no existing counterpart within traditional sports that provides an open, online window for fans to consistently watch their favorite athletes train and play pickup games with or against other professionals.[68]

The strong consumer appeal of streaming has produced commercial opportunities for both the content creators and the game producers. The most popular streamers can make millions of dollars from subscriptions alone, with even more to be made from deals with sponsors.[69] For game producers, the content creators serve as unofficial (or in some cases, official) promoters for the video game products.[70] By streaming gameplay, often between 6-12 hours per day, the content creators keep the producer's games in front of the public.[71] In particular, Epic Games has taken a more active approach to cultivate interest in its *Fortnite* game by working with

66. See Baltimore Orioles, Inc. v. Major League Baseball Players Ass'n, 805 F.2d 663 (7th Cir. 1986), in which the Seventh Circuit recognized broadcasts of baseball games qualify for copyright protection.

67. The term "gamers" in this context is used to describe anyone who does not actively compete in esports tournaments. Many of the most popular streamers of gameplay are not professional esports competitors.

68. Holden, Edelman & Baker, *supra* note 42, at 540.

69. Jordan Smith, *The Top 10 Highest Paid Streamers in the World (and How They Make Money)*, FILTERGRADE (Nov. 11, 2019), https://filtergrade.com/top-10-highest-paid-streamers-in-the-world/ (noting top streamer Tyler "Ninja" Blevins reportedly earns nearly $500,000 per month from his live streaming).

70. For example, Adidas is one of Ninja's official sponsors and produces a "Ninja" shoe. *See NINJA ZX 2k Boost Shoes,* ADIDAS, https://www.adidas.com/us/ninja-zx-2k-boost-shoes/FZ0454.html (last visited Dec. 31, 2020).

71. Holden, Edelman & Baker, *supra* note 42, at 540.

content creators and celebrities. For example, Epic Games held a virtual concert inside *Fortnite* that featured musician and avid gamer (and sometimes streamer) Marshmello and drew 10.7 million attendees.[72]

The growing popularity of streaming, however, has also created unique challenges with regards to the policing of copyright infringement.[73] To address problems related to copyright infringement on their platform, YouTube developed a copyright strike system, which was updated in February of 2019.[74] YouTube's three-strike system increases penalties with each offense, starting with warnings on the first infraction and culminating in video removal and termination of the infringer's account on the third offense.[75] This system permits copyright holders to file strikes with YouTube for content that needs to be investigated.[76] The process can result in content creators paying off those who send them notices of copyright infringement so as to avoid strikes on their account, thereby making irrelevant the question of whether or not the streamer actually violated copyright law with their streamed content.[77]

In addition to the Copyright Act, the Online Copyright Infringement Liability Limitation Act, which is a component of the DMCA, grants copyright owners the power to remove infringing content from the internet promptly.[78] The Act also creates a "safe harbor" for online service providers like YouTube, which shields them from liability in copyright for the individual acts of streamers who use their platforms for content creation.[79] The safe harbor for providers, however, does not apply if the provider (a) has actual knowledge of the facts constituting the infringing activity; (b) receives benefits from the infringing activity; or (c) does not respond after being notified of the infringement by expeditiously removing or disabling access to the infringing material.[80] Accordingly, game

72. Andrew Webster, *Fortnite's Marshmello Concert was the Game's Biggest Event Ever*, The Verge (Feb. 21, 2019), https://www.theverge.com/2019/2/21/18234980/fortnite-marshmello-concert-viewer-numbers.

73. Jenny Park, *Copyright and the Esports Industry*, Colum. Bus. L. Rev. (Dec. 15, 2019), https://journals.library.columbia.edu/index.php/CBLR/announcement/view/252#_ftn2.

74. *Id.*

75. *Making Our Strikes System Clear and Consistent*, YouTube Creator Blog (Feb. 19, 2019), https://youtube-creators.googleblog.com/2019/02/making-our-strikes-system-clear-and.html.

76. Park, *supra* note 73.

77. *Id.*

78. For a detailed discussion on the relationship between the Online Copyright Infringement Liability Limitation Act and the DMCA, see generally, Kenneth Hwang, *Blizzard Versus Bnetd: A Looming Ice Age For Free Software Development?*, 92 Cornell L. Rev. 1043 (2007).

79. 17 U.S.C. §§512 (1998).

80. *Id.*

producers have the legal authority under both the Copyright Act and the DMCA to enforce their interests by filing strikes with YouTube or notifying other streaming service providers of infringing content. If a streaming service or content host does not expeditiously respond to the game producer's complaint and request, then that failure would disengage the safe harbor provision that insulates the service provider from copyright liability.[81] And yet, it is rare for a video game producer to assert their rights under the Copyright Act against streamers. This fact brings to light the question of whether video game producers should enforce their rights against streamers who use their intellectual property by streaming live gameplay.

In determining whether producers should enforce their rights against streamers who use their intellectual property by streaming gameplay, it is first necessary to note that it is unlikely that a reviewing court will find that a video game provider has abandoned its rights to the intellectual property under copyright law simply by failing to assert them against streamers. After all, the protections provided by the Copyright Act attach to qualifying creative works at the point that they are fixed to their tangible mediums for expression and do not release for the life of the owner, plus seventy years.[82] Judge Learned Hand proposed a test for determining whether copyright has been abandoned that turns on findings of both their (a) intent to abandon the property by placing it into the public domain and (b) an overt act that makes public their intention to do so.[83] Additionally, authority exists for the position that mere inaction from the copyright holder does not evidence an intent to abandon the copyright-protected property.[84]

In fact, there exists a classic case challenging what is needed for copyright abandonment in esports that involves the ownership of one of the most commercially successful video game properties, a game that is also the technological foundation for the "sport" used by the most popular esports tournaments.[85] The property at issue in the *Lilith Games* case was *Defense of the Ancients* (*DotA*), a modified version (mod) of *Warcraft III*, which was created by gamer Kyle Sommer. In a September 23, 2004, post

---

81. *Id.*

82. 17 U.S.C. §101 et seq. (2018).

83. Nat'l Comics Publ'ns v. Fawcett Publ'ns, 191 F.2d 594, 598 (2d Cir. 1951); *see also* Micro Star v. Formgen Inc., 154 F.3d 1107, 1109–1114 (9th Cir. 1998).

84. Dodd, Mead & Co., Inc. v. Lilienthal, 514 F.Supp. 105 (S.D.N.Y. 1981).

85. *See* David Nathaniel Tan, *Owning the World's Biggest ESport: Intellectual Property and DOTA*, 31 Harv. J. L. & Tech. 965 (2017).

on the message board forum, Sommer made known his intent to abandon his rights to the mod *DotA*.[86] In the post, Sommer stated that "[w]hoever wishes to release a version of *DotA* may without my consent, I just ask for a nod in the credits to your map."[87] In deciding whether Sommer abandoned his interests in the *DotA*, Judge Breyer recognized that an author could surrender some rights to protected work while retaining others.[88] In Sommer's case, Judge Breyer found that his requesting a "nod" from those who continue his work, as well as the fact that he "aimed" his post at only a few fellow teenagers, rather than sophisticated software companies, could lead a reasonable trier of fact to conclude that Sommer's post may not have effectively functioned as an overt act of intent to abandon all of his copyright interests in *DotA*.[89]

As *Lilith Games* demonstrates, copyright interests are generally not abandoned without an overt act that indicates a clear intent to relinquish the protected interest(s) completely. Further, the fact that copyright-protected content is regularly shared on social media platforms against the rights and interests of owners does not normalize infringement in a way that removes the rights of the copyright owners.[90] Thus, inaction on the part of game producers in failing to enforce their rights against streamers likely will not, by itself, evidence the requisite intent to abandon their respective rights to end unauthorized streams of their video games. Accordingly, the copyright interests of game producers pose a direct threat to the livelihood of content creators who stream their gameplay for a living.

At the present moment, there are two checks on the threat the copyright interests of game producers pose for content creators that preserve the status quo within professional streaming. The first is the fact that any attempt from a game producer to shut down a popular streamer could be met with strong resistance from the gaming community. The second

---

86. Kyle Orland, *Does Valve Really Own Dota? A Jury Will Decide*, Arstechnica (May 18, 2017), https://arstechnica.com/gaming/2017/05/does-valve-really-own-dota-a-jury-will-decide/.

87. *See id.*

88. Blizzard Ent. Inc. and Valve Corp. v. Lilith Games, Ltd. and Uncool, Inc., No. 3:15-cv-04084-CRB, Order Denying Motion for Partial Summary Judgment and Denying Motion for Rule 11 Sanctions, 21 (N.D. Ca. 2017); citing, *Micro Star v. Formgen Inc.*, 154 F.3d 1107, 1114 (9th Cir. 1998).

89. *Blizzard Ent. Inc. and Valve Corp., v. Lilith Games, Ltd. and Uncool, Inc.*, No. 3:15-cv-04084-CRB, Order Denying Motion for Partial Summary Judgment and Denying Motion for Rule 11 Sanctions, 21 (N.D. Ca. 2017).

90. *See* Mark Iantosca v. Elie Tahari Ltd., *1:19-cv-04527 (S.D.N.Y. 2020),* a case involving copyright action brought against a fashion brand that reproduced a photographer's protected work on Instagram and the court rejected the brand's assertion that the practice is so common that it should not result in copyright liability.

involves the recognition that streamers often serve as quasi-brand ambassadors for the producer's games, and by streaming gameplay, the streamers keep the games relevant for their subscribers (sometimes numbering in the millions). Still, with so much money involved in professional streaming, the possibility remains that the game producers will eventually attempt to find ways to profit from the practice. For example, some game producers are already working to develop their own online platforms for streaming gameplay, and there exists a concern that eventually the game producers will restrict the streaming of their games on rival platforms.[91] With that concern noted, it is necessary to recognize that streamers are also content creators, and their creative work may qualify for copyright protection.

Those who operate streaming channels create expressive and original content in the form of commentary and through demonstration of their style or techniques for gameplay. Since streamers infuse their own creative content into the channels they populate, an argument could be made that their creations should qualify for protection from copyright as fair use. As stated in the copyright defense subsection of this chapter, the fair use doctrine is an affirmative defense to copyright infringement that permits reproductions in the form of criticism, comment, news reporting, teaching, scholarship, or research.[92]

In addition to the four factors for fair use discussed above, there exists a quasi and fifth factor known as the transformative use doctrine. The transformative use doctrine qualifies reproductions for protection as fair use when the appropriated work serves as the raw material for generating new, expressive content, which is infused with new meanings and functions so as to manufacture a new creation independent of the original work.[93] Streamers may assert that their sessions qualify as transformative works because the video games serve as the raw materials used by the streamers in creating something new and original. Gamers could point to the time and energy that goes into building their channels and defend themselves on the grounds that their streams include content that qualifies as criticism, comment, and in some cases, teaching or instruction for their viewers. After all, popular content creators infuse in-game commentary into their play that may include criticism of aspects of the game or even tips for other gamers for how to improve their play.

---

91. Holden, Edelman & Baker, *supra* note 11, at 541.
92. 17 U.S.C. §107 (2018).
93. Castle Rock Ent. v. Carol Publ'g Grp., 150 F.3d 132, 142 (2d Cir. 1998).

There are, however, some hurdles that streamers would need to clear to convince a reviewing court that their channels include transformative work rather than infringing appropriations of the copyright-protected video games. The first hurdle involves the fair use factor that requires courts to delve into the purpose and character of the use. In the case of professional streamers, the evidence points to a commercial purpose for their use of the copyrighted work. Another hurdle is found in the fair use factor that delves into the amount and substantiality of the copyrighted work used in the new creation. Live streaming of gameplay often involves the use of the game in its entirety. The content creators, in this case, are literally playing games online for their subscribers, and the expressions and commentary they add to the experience may be too minimal to qualify as a new creative work that warrants copyright protection. Furthermore, there is reason to question whether the live streams should be treated as new and expressive works. After all, the video games themselves are not "raw material" that are somehow transformed by the streamers into something new and expressive—the games are instead used for play, as was intended by the game developer.

In resolving transformative use cases, courts remain consistent in requiring some form of transformation of the copyrighted work. Unfortunately, such transformation of copyrighted work does not occur in the case of streaming.[94] Additionally, live streams may be too impermanent to qualify as new derivations of the original product and instead more closely resemble public performances. Since streamers lack a license from game producers to perform video games, their public performance of gameplay may be found to closely resemble the performance of a musician singing another's song more so than a creator who has developed a new product that is distinct from the original that served as its inspiration.[95] The issue of whether streaming gameplay qualifies as transformative has not yet been tested by a court. As a result, the applicability of the fair use doctrine in this context remains unresolved.

The other possible defense available to streamers is the joint authorship defense. This defense is available when there is more than one author for the copyright-protected work.[96] For the purpose of streaming, the joint

94. *See* Mirage Editions, Inc. v. Albuquerque ART Co., 856 F.2d 1341 (9th Cir. 1988); Ryan v. Editions LTD. W., INC., No. C-06-04812 PSG (N.D. Cal. 2012).

95. *See* 17 U.S.C. §501 (2018); 17 U.S.C. §101 (2018) (offering definitions of public performance). *See also* Am. Broad. v. Aereo, Inc., 134 S. Ct. 2498, 2510 (2014) (holding that streaming copyrighted work is a form of public performance).

96. 17 U.S.C. §201(a) (2019).

authorship defense could potentially protect a streamer from liability under copyright law for the use of the protected video game in live streams if the court determines that the streamer and the game producer function as co-authors of the streamed content. Similar to the transformative use defense, the joint authorship argument posits that the streamer makes use of the video game in authoring a new expressive work, over which the streamer is a co-creator and owner. It is important to note that joint ownership and authorship are different in that joint authors share equally in the ownership of the work, even if the contributions in creating that work were not equal.[97] By contrast, a transferee of a copyright-protected work would only take ownership over that which the transferor provided to them.[98]

The requirement of intent, however, may serve as a more difficult barrier to joint authorship protection for streamers. The Copyright Act defines joint work as that which was prepared by two or more authors with the intention that their contributions would be combined into parts of one production.[99] While there is little doubt about the streamer's intent to use a copyright-protected video game in the creation of streamed content, the requisite intent is likely missing for the video game producer. Additionally, since the establishment of joint authorship may provide the video game producer with a right to their share of the revenue generated from the streams, joint authorship may not be a desirable defense for streamers.

Moving Forward: New Problems and New Applications

As the esports industry continues to mature, one could reasonably expect that the large power brokers within the industry—most notably the game publishers and tournament organizers—will seek to continue to use federal intellectual property law to curb market competition. With video game publishers enjoying at least some copyright protection over their work, they will have the choice of whether to try to monopolize control over esports competitions in their given games or to alternatively license these rights for a fee to one or more other entities. At the same time, much as

97. Cmty. for Creative Non-Violence v. Reid, 846 F.2d 1485, 1496 (D.C. Cir. 1988).

98. Scott C. Brophy, *Joint Authorship Under the Copyright Law*, 16 Hastings Comm. & Ent. L.J. 451, 452 (1983).

99. 17 U.S.C. §101 (2018).

with so many other areas where copyright protection exists, prospective users of copyrighted material such as streamers and prospective organizers of rival esports contests will likely try to argue that their unlicensed use is protected by doctrines of fair use. Based on the foregoing, it would not be surprising to find a number of intellectual property disputes related to purported esports copyright infringement making their way through the federal courts in the years that lie ahead.

CHAPTER 4

ESPORTS GAMERS' RIGHT OF PUBLICITY

The Right of Publicity and Esports

Whereas video game publishers and contest organizers are likely to rely upon federal intellectual property protections, including copyright law, to protect their contributions to the egaming space, professional gamers are likely to turn to a different set of laws to preserve the control over their value of their own identities. These alternative laws, which derive primarily under state statutory and common law, are often described as right of publicity laws. And, these laws allow for the most famous gamers to earn substantial sums of money through product endorsements–largely supplementing what they already earn through theoretical salaries or contest prize pools.

Overview of the Right of Publicity

The right of publicity is often described as one of the newest of U.S. intellectual property rights, and the individual celebrity's counterpart to what trademark is for brands. This right protects a celebrity from the commercial misappropriation of their names, images, likenesses, or other "indicia of identity" (e.g., voice, signature, nickname, or *nom de plume*).[1] Technically, the right of publicity is grounded in state tort law and grew out of the invasion of one's right to privacy. In some states, the right to privacy is protected through the law of unfair competition.[2] Since its first application, the right of publicity has been linked to the sports industry, which makes sense because celebrity athletes have long since been used for endorsements based on the athlete's potential to generate favorable attitudinal and behavioral consumer responses.[3] In fact, the very first right of publicity case evidences both the history of sports sponsorships and the creation of the right of publicity.

The right of publicity can be traced to *Haelan Laboratories, Inc. v. Topps Chewing Gum, Inc.*, which involved the unauthorized use of names, images, and likenesses (NILs) belonging to professional baseball players on playing cards packaged for purchase with chewing gum.[4] In *Haelan*, it was not the players who initiated the legal action against the chewing gum company that misappropriated player likeness. Instead, the lawsuit was filed by a rival chewing gum company that had purchased from the players the exclusive right to use their images on baseball cards.[5] In effect, the court in *Haelan* put to the test the enforceability of a practice common in the sports industry—celebrity endorsements. The defendant in *Haelan* argued against the enforceability of exclusive publicity deals, claiming that for them to be liable, the action would need to have been filed by the players, and even then, that the players could only recover for violations for invasions of their right to privacy—a right not implicated in this specific case.[6] The *Haelan* court rejected the contention that the plaintiff could not enforce exclusive rights of publicity conveyed to them, and in doing so, also recognized that in addition to a person's right to privacy, "a

---

1. White v. Samsung Electronics America, Inc., 971 F.2d 1395, 1399 (9th Cir. 1992) (providing a discussion on what the right of publicity covers and a description of "indicia of identity" that used a hypothetical example to demonstrate the extent of identifying elements that would satisfy the requirements set by the right of publicity).

2. Beth A. Cianfrone & Thomas A. Baker III, *The Use of Student-Athlete Likeness in Sport Video Games: An Application of the Right of Publicity*, 20 J. Legal Aspects Sport 35, 38 (2010).

3. For a discussion on the value of athlete endorsements, see generally, Vanessa Ratten, *The Dynamics of Sport Marketing: Suggestions for Marketing Intelligence and Planning*, 34 Mktg. Intel. & Plan., 162 (2016).

4. Haelan Lab'ys v. Topps Chewing Gum, 202 F.2d 866 (2d Cir. 1953).

5. *Id.* at 867.

6. *Id.* at 868.

man has a right in the publicity value of his photograph, i.e., the right to grant the exclusive privilege of publishing his picture."[7]

In the decades following the *Haelan* decision, other states began to recognize a common-law right of publicity,[8] and twenty-two states have since enacted a statutory right of publicity.[9] During this same time period, the right of publicity evolved through each legal decision that put it to use, with extensions of it reaching beyond appropriations of NILs in literal depictions to include the appropriation of any "indicia" of a person's identity.[10] Another sport-focused case provides the perfect example for what is intended by indicia of identity. In *Motschenbacher v. R.J. Reynolds Tobacco Co.*, a plaintiff successfully pointed to the distinctive or "peculiar" markings on his race car to establish that his publicity rights had been misappropriated in an advertisement.[11] The Ninth Circuit held that the markings identified Motschenbacher in a way that violated his right to publicity.[12] A similar interpretation of "indicia of identity" can be found in *White v. Samsung Electronics America, Inc.*, a case in which the Ninth Circuit found that a Samsung advertisement that made use of a robot wearing a wig and evening gown while turning letters on a gameboard identified Vanna White in a way that infringed upon her right of publicity.[13]

The application of the right of publicity in *White* provides particular relevance for the esports industry because the advertisement that sparked the legal controversy used an avatar-like reference to identify Vanna White. Within video games, there are often representations of real people or entities that also enjoy protection under the right of publicity. Additionally, video games may provide consumers with features that allow players to modify in-game characters in very distinctive ways that could identify particular esports players.[14] Accordingly, potential conflicts implicating both the right of publicity and copyright could emerge concerning whether characters used by esports players are the intellectual property of the game producer that designed them or whether they are

7. *Id.*

8. At least 28 states have a judicially recognized right of publicity.

9. For the list of states that have codified the right of publicity, see *State Law: Right of Publicity*, Digital Media L. Project (Oct. 13, 2020).

10. Motschenbacher v. R.J. Reynolds Tobacco Co., 498 F.2d 821, 827 (9th Cir. 1974).

11. *Id.* at 827.

12. *Id.* at 828

13. White, 971 F.2d at 1399.

14. Modifications to characters often involve the use of "skins." Skins are cosmetic components for character design that can be purchased within the game for the purpose of customizing characters.

both the property of the game developer and the third-party creator who modified the avatar and made it famous through their gameplay. After all, if Motschenbacher could be identified by distinctive markings on his car and Vanna White could be identified by a robot wearing a wig and dress while turning letters on a gameboard, then it seems possible that modified game characters could also function as indicia of identity that trigger the right of publicity when misappropriated.

Another potential publicity problem within esports involves the question of whether celebrity status is required for plaintiffs to recover based on unauthorized use of their names, images, and likenesses. To recover based on the right of publicity, plaintiffs must have incurred some identifiable economic harm that results from the appropriation.[15] Yet, the average person does not possess much, if any, commercial value in their identities. Thus, the economic injury requirement seemingly restricts the right of publicity to celebrities. The right of publicity, however, has been applied in ways that extend protection to individuals and not just celebrities, even though it may be more difficult for non-celebrities to proffer the required evidence of an economic injury.[16] For example, the defendant in the only right of publicity case to reach the Supreme Court was a human cannonball performer who was, by no means, a household name when his case was argued before the Court.[17] Yet, the Court in *Zacchini v. Scripps-Howard Broadcasting Co.* identified an economic injury when the performer's act was broadcast in its entirety.[18] In its written opinion in *Zacchini*, the Court hit on the right of publicity's central aim, with the statement that "no social purpose is served by having the defendant get some free aspect of the plaintiff that would have market value and for which he would normally pay."[19]

The economic injury requirement to recover under the right of publicity is an essential issue within professional esports because the majority of players are not well known outside of esports communities. Additionally, professional esports players are, in a way, hidden behind their

15. *See* Cianfrone & Baker, *supra* note 2, at 39–40 (examining California's common law right of publicity that requires proof of an injury in order for plaintiffs to recover). See also §46 of the Restatement (Third) of Unfair Competition, which describes the right of publicity as protecting the economic value of a person's identity.

16. For a discussion on the need for the right of publicity to apply for all, see generally, Melville B. Nimmer, *The Right of Publicity,* 19 L. & Contemporary Problems 203 (1954).

17. Zacchini v. Scripps-Howard Broad. Co., 433 U.S. 562 (1977).

18. *Id.* at 565.

19. *Id.* at 576.

monitors while the focus is placed on their avatars during competitive play.[20] Still, even lesser-known esports professional players may be able to recover under the right of publicity if their identities are misappropriated in a way that causes them to suffer economic harm.

The Right of Publicity, Transformative Use and Esports

There exists an inherent tension between the right of publicity and the First Amendment because the works that misappropriate celebrity likeness may constitute expressions that also qualify for First Amendment protection.[21] In its decision in *Zacchini*, the Court recognized the conflict between the First Amendment and the enforcement of state publicity rights.[22] Instead of resolving the matter based on use of the preemption doctrine, the Court in *Zacchini* directed lower courts to balance the interests protected by the First Amendment against those secured by the right of publicity on a case-by-case basis.[23]

Following the Court's instruction, several tests emerged across several states for balancing the First Amendment against publicity right violations. Even now, there is no uniform approach across the United States, although one test has taken root in the majority of jurisdictions—the transformative use test. The transformative use test is the preferred means for resolving conflicts involving the right of publicity and the First Amendment in the State of California and the Ninth Circuit—the two venues that have decided the majority of right of publicity cases.[24] In application to right of publicity cases, the transformative use doctrine works the same way as it does in resolving copyright cases—by requiring courts to determine whether the appropriated content served as the raw materials for the

20. John T. Holden & Thomas A. Baker III, *The Econtractor? Defining the Esports Employment Relationship*, 56 Am. Bus. L.J. 391 (2019)

21. ETW Corp. v. Jireh Pub., Inc., 332 F.3d 915, 931 (6th Cir. 2003).

22. Zacchini, 433 U.S. at 573.

23. *Id.*

24. *See* Gloria Franke, *The Right of Publicity vs. The First Amendment: Will One Test Ever Capture the Starring Role* 79 S. Cal. L. Rev. 945 (2005); *see also* Thomas A. Baker III, et al., *Simplifying the Transformative Use Doctrine: Analyzing Transformative Expression in EA's NCAA Football Sport Video Games*, 7 Elon L. Rev. 467 (2015).

creation of a new and sufficiently transformed expression.[25] The only meaningful difference between the two contexts is found in the fact that one involves appropriations of copyright-protected material, whereas the other involves the commercial misappropriation of another's likeness.

There have been a number of cases involving both traditional sports and video games through which courts have explained how the transformative use doctrine should be balanced against interests protected by the right of publicity. For example, in *ETW v. Jireh Publishing*, the Sixth Circuit used the transformative use test in finding that an artist's literal depiction of Tiger Woods in a painting of a historic moment in golf did not violate the First Amendment.[26] In *Kirby v. Sega of America*, a California Court of Appeals found sufficient transformative content in the creation of a video game character who was allegedly inspired by a former pop star.[27] In reaching its decision, the California Court of Appeals focused on the fact that Sega had built into its character distinctive features that made it a new expression, rather than a literal depiction of the plaintiff.[28]

Conversely, in *No Doubt v. Activision Publishing*, a California appellate court held that Activision's Guitar Hero misappropriated the likenesses of the band No Doubt, even though Activision had incorporated game features that permitted players to alter the avatars that represented No Doubt.[29] The court held that Activision had a commercial purpose for its use and that its game features were not sufficiently transformative because the band was featured in the game in the same setting for which it became famous.[30] Similarly, both the Ninth Circuit in *In Re NCAA Student-Athlete Name & Likeness (Keller)*[31] and the Third Circuit in *Hart v. Electronic Arts*[32] found that a video game producer's use of college athlete likeness in the commercially successful *NCAA Football* franchise did not qualify as transformative as a matter of law. Following the reasoning in *Kirby*, the courts in *Keller*[33] and *Hart*[34] each found that EA had made use of college

---

25. Comedy III Prods. v. Gary Saderup, Inc., 21 P.3d 797, 809 (Cal. 4th 2001). Comedy III was the first decision to use the transformative use test in balancing the right of publicity against the First Amendment.

26. ETW Corp., 332 F.3d at 925.

27. Kirby v. Sega of America, Inc., 50 Cal. Rptr. 3d 607, 618 (Ct. App. 2006).

28. *Id.* at 616–17.

29. No Doubt v. Activision Publ'g, Inc., 192 Cal. App. 4th 1018, 1035 (Ct. App. 2011).

30. *Id.* at 1034–35.

31. In Re NCAA Student-Athlete Name & Likeness, 724 F.3d 1268, 1276 (9th Cir. 2013).

32. Hart v. Electronic Arts, Inc., 717 F.3d 141, 170 (3d Cir. 2013).

33. In Re NCAA, 724 F.3d at 1279.

34. Hart, 717 F.3d at 170.

athlete likeness in the same setting for which the players were known—playing college football.[35] Of particular importance to the resolution of both cases was a determination reflected by the court in *Hart* that it would not "credit elements of [the game] that do not, in some way affect the use of Appellant's identity."[36]

The decisions in both *Keller* and *Hart* may prove important for resolving future right of publicity problems involving esports matters related to sports video games. Sports video games are a popular segment of both the video game and sports merchandising industries.[37] Several sports video games also serve as the basis for popular esports leagues and tournaments.[38] Yet, EA is not alone in manufacturing sports video games and in working with traditional sport partners in the development of esports around their products. In particular, *NBA2K* is a very successful sports video game franchise produced by Take-Two Interactive Software (Take-Two), which works together with the NBA in ownership and operation of the *NBA2K* League.

Esports leagues like the *NBA2K* League, and tournaments like the FIFA eWorld Cup, present interesting issues involving the right of publicity and intellectual property law. After all, the esports events using sport video games implicate multiple levels of identity use, each of which could potentially produce right of publicity problems. Specifically, sports video games incorporate the identities of professional athletes from the traditional sports that are replicated in the video games, and the avatars for these athletes are then used by professional esports players, who also possess publicity rights, during league or tournament play.

The *Keller* and *Hart* cases were not the only legal actions asserting the right of publicity that have been filed by former professional athletes concerning the unauthorized use of their identities in sports video games.[39]

---

35. In Re NCAA, at 1277–79.

36. Hart, at 169.

37. Thomas A. Baker, Kevin K. Byon, K., Beth A. Cianfrone, & John Grady, *Conceptualizing and Measuring the Use of Student-Athlete Likeness in EA's NCAA Football*, 28 J. Sport Mgmt, 3, 281 (2014).

38. David Hoppe, *EA Leads the Competition in Sports Video Games, So Why Don't They Lead in Esports?*, Gamma Law (Jul., 7, 2019), https://gammalaw.com/ea-leads-the-competition-in-sports-video-games-so-why-dont-they-lead-in-esports/. EA's competitive gaming division works with approximately 30 partners in the production of esports built around their titles and its list of its sport industry partners includes professional sports leagues such as the English Premier League, La Liga, League One, the Eredivisie, and Major League Soccer.

39. Electronic Arts has had to defend against multiple lawsuits filed by former players concerning the incorporation of their identities into the Madden NFL video games. The most recent of which involved a case brought by nearly 6,000 former players that was ultimately settled by Electronic Arts after the Ninth Circuit rejected its transformative use defense. For more on the settlement. *See* Kyle

Legal actions that challenge the use of traditional sport likenesses in sport video games are problematic because they threaten the existence of the games that form the basis for the sports leagues and tournaments that are built around them. The *Keller* and *Hart* litigations ultimately led to the NCAA making the decision to end its relationship with EA, and that caused the cessation of the commercially successful video game franchise *NCAA Football*. The right of publicity reasoning in *Motschenbacker* could create a potential dilemma in that if a driver's consistent use of a car with distinctive markings in races could result in that driver being identified by a different car with those same markings,[40] then the possibility exists that avatars of traditional sports stars could be used to identify an individual professional esports player who regularly utilizes those avatars in competition.[41] In such a case, controversies involving the misappropriation of the avatars by third parties will implicate the publicity rights belonging to both the professional esports player and the athletes featured in the games, as well as implicate the copyright interests belonging to the game producer.

Practical Considerations for Esports Gamers Pertaining to Publicity Rights

Given that the most famous esports gamers in the world have the potential to pull in millions of subscribers to their social media accounts and channels,[42] one would expect esports gamers easily be able to monetize their celebrity status by accumulating endorsement deals from brands across product categories based on the protection of their publicity rights. Arguably, the potential for market-based influence may be greater for celebrity athletes within esports than for their traditional sports counterparts. The reason for this is that esports celebrities have a more significant amount of exposure by streaming directly to fans. After all, it is not

---

Jahner, *'Madden' Video Game Maker Settles Ex-NFL Players' Lawsuit*, Bloomberg Law (Mar. 29, 2019), https://news.bloomberglaw.com/ip-law/madden-video-game-maker-settles-ex-nfl-players-lawsuit-1.

40. Motschenbacher, 498 F.2d at 828.

41. This possibility is particularly relevant if the esports league or tournament permits players to modify the avatars for the in-game characters with which they consistently play in competition.

42. For a list of the most famous professional esports players on social media, see *The Most Famous Professional Esports Players*, Esports Mktg Blog, http://esports-marketing-blog.com/most-famous-professional-esports-players-in-league-of-legends-counter-strike-global-offensive/ (last visited Jan. 1, 2021).

uncommon for an esports star to stream online play on a platform such as YouTube or Twitch for twelve or more hours each day.[43]

Yet a sponsorship concern exists within esports in that, while endorsement deals have provided a very meaningful source of income for a select few, very few professional esports players have secured endorsement deals for themselves that are in excess of five figures.[44] The lack of lucrative sponsorship deals becomes more pronounced when comparisons are made between esports stars and traditional sports stars who are of similar celebrity status.[45] The contractual relationship between professional esports players and their respective teams plays a significant role in the lack of lucrative sponsorship deals for esports stars.[46] Specifically, it is common for professional teams within esports to restrict players from endorsing products that are competitors of the brands that sponsor the player's team. For example, if a player's team is sponsored by Mountain Dew (owned by PepsiCo), then a common constraint to player contracts would prohibit that player from being sponsored by Coca-Cola or another competing brand. Additionally, the standard player contracts of many, if not most professional esports teams require the team's approval of all player sponsors, even in the absence of an apparent conflict.[47] Compounding the problem is the fact that these standard form agreements are often adhesive in nature, in that the terms are not subject to alteration based on negotiation. Additionally, there is no collective bargaining in esports as players have no labor group to represent their interests. Thus, while similar restraints on athlete endorsements exist within player agreements for traditional sports leagues such as the NBA or NFL, the players in those leagues play a role in the incorporation of those restrictive terms through the collective bargaining process.[48]

For this reason, the restraints on sponsorship imposed on players within esports more closely resemble the restraints imposed on college athletes than those placed on professional players within traditional sports

---

43. Ben Fisher, *Esports Players Have Less Endorsement Freedom*, Sport Bus. J. (May 28, 2018), https://www.sportsbusinessdaily.com/Journal/Issues/2018/05/28/In-Depth/Endorsement.aspx.

44. *Id.*

45. *Id.*

46. *Id.*

47. *Id.* The present situation, however, is still preferable to what existed previously in that former versions of the player agreements standard to esports included language that granted the team control over player publicity rights in perpetuity and prevented players from sponsoring any brands.

48. Adam Levy, *PWNED or Owned? The Right of Publicity and Identity Ownership in League of Legends*, 6 Pace Intell. Prop. Sports & Ent. L.F. 163, 166 (2016).

leagues.[49] As the restraints on college athlete endorsement deals begin to undergo increased scrutiny under both antitrust law and general doctrines of public policy and fairness, one could reasonably presume that some of the restraints placed on sports gamers exercising their publicity rights will similarly face public scrutiny. In the absence of the controversial contractual restrictions, the right of publicity would permit esports players, like any other celebrity athlete, to fully control the commercial value that they have built into their identities.[50] And, when that time comes, one can reasonably expect esports gamers to become not only increasingly wealthy, but also increasingly recognized within mainstream society.

49. *Id.*
50. *Id.* at 166–67.

CHAPTER 5

ESPORTS LABOR AND EMPLOYMENT ISSUES

A Brief Overview of the Labor and Employment Environment in Traditional Team Sports

While there are some differences in terms of the intellectual property rights enjoyed by traditional sports leagues and esports leagues,[1] the labor and employment issues in esports vary to an even greater extent. Most notably, labor and employment law issues persist in esports because of conflicts that arise at both the team and league levels.

In America's four premier traditional sports leagues (MLB, NBA, NFL, and NHL), the relationship between players and teams is stable and well fortified. Players in the MLB, NBA, NFL, and NHL are employees of the teams for whom they play, and in each of these leagues, almost all players have attained the age of majority (18 in most states).[2] Further, players in each sport are members of a union and they play under the terms and

1. With the obvious exception that esports leagues revolve around games which are capable of being owned by the game maker. *See* John T. Holden & Thomas A. Baker III, *The Econtractor? Defining the Esports Employment Relationship*, 56 AM. BUS. L.J. 391, 397 (2019).

2. Even the most prodigious athletes in the four major American leagues have reached the age of majority before their professional debuts in the modern era. *See* Matthew Jussim, *The Youngest Pro Athletes and Most Impressive Sports Prodigies of All Time*, MEN'S J. (last visited Sep. 14, 2020), https://www.mensjournal.com/sports/youngest-pro-athletes-and-most-impressive-sports-prodigies-all-time/.

conditions agreed upon between their union representatives and management (a collective voice bargaining on behalf of all teams in the league).

On top of union representation, most players also hire their own contract advisor ("agent") to help them negotiate salaries above and beyond the league's collectively bargained minimum amount. Agents who represent players in negotiating their player contracts with teams must be approved by their league's players' union, and agents who engage in bad acts risk union decertification. Agents also help players to earn additional sums of money by individually endorsing products outside the scope of their team-related activities, and unions often disperse additional sums of money to players who agree to engage in collective or group endorsement deals, such as through the use of players' names and pictures on sports cards and in video games. As such, players in traditional sports leagues understand their value to the overall sports enterprise.[3]

Most labor disputes that arise in the traditional sports context between players and teams are addressed in the scope of their collectively bargained labor agreement. These disputes generally are settled under the auspices of labor law. On rare occasions, however, players will also file antitrust disputes against their league for engaging in collective conduct that restrains trade. However, most antitrust lawsuits filed by players fail based on what is known as the "non-statutory labor exemption to antitrust law"—a doctrine that protects agreements reached in collective bargaining from labor law's reach so long as they involve mandatory subjects of bargaining that primarily affect the parties to the bargaining relationship and are agreed upon in an arm's-length fashion.[4] Indeed, since the early 1990s, antitrust disputes between players and teams pertaining to the competitive effects of certain league-wide restraints have been on the wane, whereas labor disputes and negotiation have been on the rise.

The lawyers who handle most of the major disputes in the labor and employment context of traditional professional sports are limited in number, come from a few large law firms, and frequently interact with one

---

3. Professional athletes within traditional sports have long since discovered and acted on their ability to commodify the value they have built into their reputations through the formation of product brands built around their individual identities (e.g., Brand Jordan for Michael Jordan or the brand Beast Mode for Marshawn Lynch). For more information on this phenomena, see Akiko Arai, Yong Jae Ko, Y.J. and Stephen Ross, *Branding Athletes: Exploration and Conceptualization of Athlete Brand Image*, 17 Sport Management. Rev. 97 (2014).

4. Marc Edelman, *Are Commissioner Suspensions Really Any Different From Illegal Group Boycotts? Analyzing Whether the NFL Personal Conduct Policy Illegally Restrains Trade*, 58 Cath. U. L. Rev. 631, 654 (2009).

another. In the context of collective bargaining negotiations in professional sports, it is almost expected that a team from the law firm Proskauer Rose, including notable labor attorney Bob Batterman, will be representing league ownership, likely alongside veteran attorneys from firms such as Skadden Arps, and Covington & Burling. In most cases, the players are represented by a team led by Jeffrey Kessler, currently of Winston & Strawn—perhaps America's most famous union-side sports attorney. Outside of a select few union representatives, the players themselves are rarely involved in the selection of counsel or the specific litigation and negotiation strategies. However, almost all of the players have reached the age of majority and thus have standing to enter into contracts and to choose their own representatives.

How the Esports Paradigm Is Different

While this general paradigm for labor and employment relationships is followed nearly identically by each of the four premier traditional sports leagues, the labor and employment relationship in esports is a bit more complex. Much like in each of the four professional sports leagues prior to 1970, there are few, if any, lawyers on either the employer or worker side with extensive experience in esports. Moreover, while lawyers who worked in traditional team sports might have skill sets that easily translate to resolving labor and employment matters in esports, their hourly fees often place them outside of the budgets of all but the top esports players.

Despite the owners of several esports teams being traditional business professionals with ties to traditional team sports,[5] many are reticent to offer large salaries and ideal working conditions to esports participants. The reasons for this are threefold. First, as it is a new industry, the longstanding sustainability of esports is uncertain. As such, owners of esports teams may be more risk averse. Second, there is a lack of league structure and governance in esports when juxtaposed with traditional sports, which require players to be paid a premium. Unlike the NFL and NHL, and similar to individual sports such as tennis, many esports titles have lower-level tournaments for professionals that are not quite ready for

5. Kevin Webb, *The 23 investors pouring millions into Overwatch esports teams—from Patriots owner Robert Kraft to Chinese conglomerates*, Bus. Insider (Mar. 2, 2020, 8:27 AM), https://www.businessinsider.com/overwatch-league-esports-investors-owners-team-cost-vc-2020-2.

the top echelons of competition.[6] Third and finally, not all esports organizations follow the team-within-league hierarchy present within other traditional team sports. On account of this, esports players are not offered the same protections, such as the ability to unionize and acquire union representation, as competitors in traditional sports leagues. Overall, these three factors underscore why esports is not yet on the same playing field as the NFL, NBA, NHL, and MLB.

Exploring how different esports leagues are structured and looking at the role of teams and players is critical to understanding the labor and employment issues and concerns present in professional esports. This chapter will discuss these roles and concepts in turn to highlight some of the issues the industry currently faces.

Leagues

The top four traditional sports leagues in the United States each focus on a particular sport. At the end of each season, within these leagues, various teams battle for the final championship title. Unlike traditional sports, esports leagues are not always confined to a single, end-of-season winning title like the Lombardi Trophy or the Stanley Cup.[7] In addition, unlike traditional sports where a rival league occasionally emerges within a given sport, there is typically only one esports league pertaining to each video game. And, within a given esports league, the participants are both male and female.[8] To date, the three most successful esports leagues are the ESL Pro League (ESL), the *Overwatch* League (OWL), and the *League of Legends* Championship Series (LCS).[9] The *Call of Duty* League (CDL), launched in January 2020, will likely join the ranks of these other prominent esports organizations.[10]

---

6. *See League of Legends Challenger Series Overview*, https://lemonly.com/work/league-of-legends-challenger-series-overview (last visited Nov. 4, 2018).

7. *See* Rebecca R. Rosenthal, *A Tough Pill to Swallow: Making the Case for Why eSports Leagues Must Adopt Strict Banned Substance Policies to Prevent Disability Discrimination*, 2021 Va. Sports & Ent. L. J. (2021); Holden & Baker, *supra* note 1, at 393.

8. While no women currently compete in the four major American leagues, Manon Rhaume played goalie for the Tampa Bay Lightning for one exhibition game in 1992. Mike Commito, *Manon Rhaume Still Inspiring Young Women to Pursue Hockey Dreams*, NHL (Mar. 3, 2020), https://www.nhl.com/kings/news/manon-rheaume-still-inspiring-young-women-to-pursue-hockey-dreams/c-315598612.

9. Rosenthal, *supra* note 7.

10. Kevin Webb, *I attended the launch event of the $300 million Call of Duty League and it was a wild three-day whirlwind showcasing the potential of the esports industry*, Bus. Insider (Feb. 1, 2020, 7:00 AM), https://www.businessinsider.com/call-of-duty-league-esports-launch-kickoff-minneapolis-

The ESL (formerly known as the Electronic Sports League) was founded in 2000 and is the world's largest esports league.[11] The ESL specializes in hosting events surrounding the popular games *League of Legends* and *Counter-Strike*.[12] Currently, the ESL does not compensate its players.[13] The OWL has twenty teams based in cities around the globe ranging from Houston to Hangzhou.[14] Just like in the NBA or NFL, OWL teams play one another, hoping to secure a coveted spot in the playoffs.[15] In 2019 alone, the average OWL player earned $114,000[16] and received free housing. Players who play in the LCS earned roughly double this in 2018—a figure bringing them in close competition with Major League Soccer players.[17] Unlike the OWL, the LCS does not provide its players with housing, although it does allow them to use a dedicated training facility where they typically spend in excess of forty hours per week practicing.[18] Lastly, thus far, the recently launched CDL is providing its players with a guaranteed base salary of $50,000.[19]

On top of salary disparities between the top esports leagues, these leagues do not share the same structures. For example, teams within the OWL must abide by league rules that dictate minimum contract

---

minnesota-rokkr-2020-1; Kevin Webb, *Twelve teams reportedly paid $25 million each to join a new esports league around one of the biggest games in the world—here's everything you need to know about Call of Duty League*, Bus. Insider (Nov. 9, 2019, 9:31 AM), https://www.businessinsider.com/call-of-duty-league-teams-schedule-salary-rules-format-2019-11#the-call-of-duty-league-schedule-is-an-international-tour-with-two-stops-in-each-city-4.

11. *About Us*, ESL, https://about.eslgaming.com/about-us/.

12. Ed McCambridge, *Anti-doping efforts still in their infancy in eSports*, DW (Jul. 21, 2017), https://www.dw.com/en/anti-doping-efforts-still-in-their-infancy-in-esports/a-39783790.

13. Holden & Baker, *supra* note 1, at 426.

14. Mustafa Gatollari, *How Does 'Overwatch' League Work and How Can You Join? Here Are the Basics*, Distractify, https://www.distractify.com/p/how-does-overwatch-league-work (last visited Oct. 29, 2019).

15. *Id.*

16. *Blizzard reveals Overwatch League player salaries and contract status*, Millennium (Oct. 8, 2019), https://www.millenium.us.org/news/6789.html.

17. Darren Heitner, *A Look Inside Riot Games, From $320,000 Player Salaries To Using Esports As A Catalyst For Sales*, Forbes (May 2, 2018, 8:00 AM), https://www.forbes.com/sites/darrenheitner/2018/05/02/a-look-inside-riot-games-from-320000-player-salaries-to-using-esports-as-a-catalyst-for-sales/#43802f292c6a.

18. Harrison Jacobs, *Here's the insane training schedule of a 20-something professional gamer*, Bus. Insider (May 11, 2015, 12:05 PM), https://www.businessinsider.com/pro-gamers-explain-the-insane-training-regimen-they-use-to-stay-on-top-2015-5; Noah Smith, *Esports training facility brings gaming another step closer to traditional pro sports*, Wash. Post (May 10, 2018, 10:30 AM), https://www.washingtonpost.com/sports/esports-training-facility-brings-gaming-another-step-closer-to-traditional-pro-sports/2018/05/10/c102e684-4e2f-11e8-84a0-458a1aa9ac0a_story.html.

19. Webb, *Twelve teams reportedly paid $25 million each to join a new esports league around one of the biggest games in the* world, *supra* note 10.

guarantees. In contrast, the ESL has little direction over its teams, and ESL teams may enter into various tournaments without exclusivity.[20] Further, esports leagues differ from one another in that some, like the ESL, are largely independent of game makers, while others, like the LCS and OWL, are wholly owned subsidiaries of game makers—in this case, Riot Games and Activision Blizzard, respectively.[21] Still, there is a third type of league structure—one best exemplified by the *NBA 2K* League—a league operated as a joint venture by a traditional sports league (the NBA) and a game maker (Take-Two Interactive).[22] While the *2K* League's popularity does not parallel the success achieved by leagues such as the ESL, OWL, or LCS, the *2K* League was the first official league operated by one of the four premier traditional sports leagues.[23] As such, the *2K* League demonstrates a potential paradigm shift—blurring the lines between the traditional sports leagues and the world of esports. Overall, there appears to be a relationship between the involvement of the game maker in the operation of the league and the restrictions on teams and players.[24]

Teams and Team Ownership

The ownership structure of esports has evolved since its inception. Historically, esports teams were established by players themselves, with these players often recruiting friends to play alongside them and then jointly raising funds to enter tournaments.[25] At this time, players were compensated by the prize pools associated with various competitions. But, as esports began to grow in popularity, there were an increasing number of opportunities for players to earn money via sponsorships and other branding opportunities.[26] The recent influx of money to esports has brought with it more professional ownership groups.[27] While ownership

20. John T. Holden, Marc Edelman & Thomas A. Baker III, *A Short Treatise on Esports and the Law: How America Regulates Its Next National Pastime*, 2020 U. Ill. L. Rev. 509, 530 (2020).

21. *Id.* at 531–32.

22. Peter A. Carfagna, *Exploring the Esports Approach of America's Three Major Leagues*, 11 Harv. J. Sports & Ent. Law 115, 125 (2020).

23. *Id.* at 125–26.

24. *See* 2018 Official Rules NA LCS and NA LACS, https://esports-assets.s3.amazonaws.com/production/files/rules/2018_LCS_LACS_Rules.pdf (last visited Feb. 4, 2019). *Cf.* ESL Global Rules, https://play.eslgaming.com/rules (last visited Feb. 4, 2019).

25. Steve Van Sloun, *Esports Franchise Economics*, Loup Ventures (Mar. 9, 2018), https://loupventures.com/esports-franchise-economics/.

26. *Id.*

27. *Id.*

groups can be traced back more than twenty years, within the last decade, there has been exponential growth in esports investment.[28] Two major esports teams, Evil Geniuses, and Alliance, became player-owned teams in 2016, breaking from the industry trend of associating with investor-ownership groups. The advantage is that the players are now shareholders, taking a piece of team profits. It is uncertain how sustainable player-owned teams are in the esports universe, as new money continues to flow to the industry, and there are always new incentives bringing top players to the teams with the most resources.[29]

The question of how valuable esports teams are is one that remains uncertain, despite organizations selling for tens of millions of dollars.[30] However, what is certain, is that prices are rising for esports organizations. For example, as of late 2018, some teams sold for more than thirteen times the revenue they were generating—a figure that can be juxtaposed with tech companies that frequently sell for ten times revenue, and professional sports teams that are often valued at five times their revenue.[31]

Esports team revenue can be broken down into sponsor revenue, advertising revenue, merchandise sales revenue, prize pools, and related revenue sources.[32] However, esports are distinct from professional sports in a few ways that raise questions about current valuations. First, there is no traditional ticket sales revenue for esports competitions, and second, few leagues have managed to monetize the sale of media rights so that teams are able to take a share of the league contracts with broadcasters.[33] While there is great excitement regarding esports and esports team ownership, the current league model leaves many unanswered questions about the ability of team owners to exploit value from their investments.

Players

In addition, on the whole, esports players are younger than many of the professionals playing the four major American sports leagues. In esports,

---

28. *Id.*

29. Joss Wood, *Esports Teams Evil Geniuses And Alliance Go Independent As Player-Owned Brands*, The Lines (Dec. 14, 2016), https://www.thelines.com/evil-geniuses-alliance-go-independent/.

30. *See* Josh Chapman, *Esports Teams: Valued as Tech Companies*, Medium (Nov. 27, 2018), https://medium.com/konvoy/esports-teams-valued-as-tech-companies-79d134a3e00d.

31. *Id.*

32. *Id.*

33. *How Do eSports Teams Make Money*, The Versed (Mar. 28, 2017), https://www.theversed.com/3554/how-do-esports-teams-make-money/#.Hs99JKhvZL.

the average player is approximately five years younger than the average athlete in one of the four traditional American sports leagues, with the average age falling around twenty-two.[34] Despite the fact that most professional esports players are legal adults, esports competitions such as those centered around Epic Games's *Fortnite* generally allow players to participate in their competitions starting at age sixteen.[35] In fact, the eligible age of competitors is trending even younger, as the 2019 *Fortnite* World Cup allowed eligible players aged thirteen and older to compete.[36] With some players debuting in professional esports in their pre-teen and early to mid-teenage years, it is debatable whether certain esports gamers have the sophistication to engage in their own representation. Moreover, as a strictly legal matter, it is questionable as to whether contracts signed by these individuals would be voidable.

Further, absent a players' union, the entirety of esports player salaries are negotiated on an individual basis rather than through a collectively bargained process. Without a union to play a role in determining player salaries, the wages of individual esports players vary greatly, with some top players earning more than a million dollars a year[37] and others earning far less than what one would expect for a professional athlete.[38] To date, some of the major esports leagues do not directly compensate their players—players can only earn a salary through prize winnings.[39]

Additionally, the hours that esports players work (including in practice) often exceed what one would expect from players who compete in premier, traditional sports. In some cases, esports players participate in 12- to 15-hour practice sessions in team dorms.[40] A player on Team Liquid,

---

34. Sok Min Yun, *A Comparative Overview of ESports Against Traditional Sports Focused in the Legal Realm of Monetary Exploration, Cheating, and Gambling*, 37 Cardozo Arts & Ent. L.J. 513, 530 (2019); Nick Summers, *The esports elders defying their age*, Engadget (Mar. 9, 2020), https://www.engadget.com/2020-03-09-the-esports-elders-defying-their-age.html.

35. Steven Asarch, *'Fortnite' World Cup Will Let 13-Year-Olds Compete for the Largest Prize Pool in Esports History*, Newsweek (Feb. 22, 2019, 10:00 AM), https://www.newsweek.com/fortnite-world-cup-finals-qualifiers-esports-100-million-1340015.

36. *Id.*

37. For instance, a number of members of Team Liquid have earned more than $1 million in a year. *See* Mai-Hahn Nguyen, *See how much the top eSports teams, athletes and their organizations make*, Bus. Insider (Jan. 11, 2018), https://www.businessinsider.com/top-esports-teams-players-salaries-2018-1.

38. *See id.*

39. For example, the ESL does not compensate its players while leagues such as the *Overwatch* League and *League of Legends* Championship Series do. *See* Holden & Baker, *supra* note 1, at 426.

40. Simon Hattenstone, *The rise of eSports: are addiction and corruption the price of its success?*, The Guardian (Jun. 16, 2017), https://www.theguardian.com/sport/2017/jun/16/top-addiction-young-people-gaming-esports.

which is one of the most successful teams in the LCS, shared that he and his team practice for eight hours per day during the week and then play in matches against other teams on the weekends.[41] On top of these demanding practice and match-play schedules, some players have supplemental obligations such as minimum streaming requirements to help their teams garner a bigger fan base on platforms like Twitch.[42] The hours in which some video gamers choose, or in some instances are mandated, to practice became so concerning in South Korea that the government implemented a *Cinderella Law*, which imposes a curfew on video gaming for those under sixteen years old—barring them from playing video games between midnight and 6:00 a.m.[43]

The Employment Relationship in Esports

Although there may be some variability with the analysis of players on lower-level professional or semi-professional esports teams, there is a near-consensus that, in the United States, the relationship between most professional esports teams and players is that of employer-employee.[44] As leagues continue to grow in popularity and profitability, misclassifying esports players could engender liability issues, thereby causing problems for leagues and the investors who fund them.[45] Thus, clarifying the employment status of professional esports players is necessary for purposes of examining the responsibility leagues have to their players "who make the production of esports—and any resulting profits—possible."[46]

41. Jacobs, *supra* note 18.

42. *See* Rosenthal, *supra* note 7; Noah Smith, *'It's not as awesome as people imagine': Esports players say 'dream job' is more than fun and games*, Wash. Post (Dec. 13, 2018, 9:53 AM), https://www.washingtonpost.com/sports/2018/12/13/its-not-awesome-people-imagine-esports-players-say-dream-job-is-more-than-fun-games/.

43. Hattenstone, *supra* note 40.

44. Holden & Baker, *supra* note 1, at 423; *see also* Ferguson Mitchell, *Esports Primer: Understanding Independent Contractors vs. Employees*, The Esports Observer (Jan. 21, 2016), https://esportsobserver.com/esports-primer-understanding-independent-contractors-vs-employees/; Roger Quiles, *Are Esports Players Actually Independent Contractors*?, Quiles Law (Apr. 17, 2015), http://www.esports.law/blog/are-esports-players-actually-independent-contractors; Stephen D. Fisher, *Player Contracts: Defining Expectations to Avoid Conflict League of Legends Article Series*, Foster Pepper PLLC (Aug. 2014), located at https://www.foster.com/documents/foster-pepper-white-paper/player-contracts_definingexpectionstoavoidconflict_.pdf.

45. Rosenthal, *supra* note 7 (citing Holden & Baker, *supra* note 1, at 421).

46. *See* Holden & Baker, *supra* note 1, at 415.

Determining whether professional esports players are employees or independent contractors is essential for liability purposes. It, too, is significant because, with the employee classification, a host of other issues materialize. Namely, esports leagues open themselves up to potential unionization efforts and needing to draft collective bargaining agreements, and they must be wary of suits brought under the Americans with Disabilities Act.

Determining Employment Status

The advantages of players being independent contractors as opposed to employees are numerous for team owners, as these players cost less and enjoy fewer worker protections. However, while esports leagues would undoubtedly owe fewer obligations to their players if players were classified as independent contractors, "the determination of employment status is based on application of various tests, not by voluntary declaration."[47]

Courts employ a variety of tests to determine the status of workers.[48] The tests typically focus on the degree of control that an employer exercises over employees, the nature of an ongoing relationship between the parties, and the reliance of the worker on the employer for compensation.[49] The two primary tests used to ascertain employment status are the economic realities test and the right of control test.[50] These federal law tests are likely applicable to professional esports. The reasons for this are that the *Call of Duty* League and *Overwatch* League rules clarify that the law governing all disputes shall be the law of the United States of America,[51] and the contracts created by Riot Games, the company that owns and operates the *League of Legends* Championship Series, indicate that the Federal Arbitration Act governs all disputes.[52] As such,

---

47. Rosenthal, *supra* note 7 (quoting Holden & Baker, *supra* note 1, at 422).

48. Quiles, *supra* note 44.

49. There are a variety of different tests at both the state and federal level depending on the statute that is implicated. These factors are meant to provide a broad overview of some of the factors that are common to multiple tests. Quiles, *supra* note 44.

50. Rosenthal, *supra* note 7 (quoting Holden & Baker, *supra* note 1, at 419).

51. Call of Duty World League 2019 Official Handbook, Call of Duty, https://www.callofduty.com/content/dam/atvi/callofduty/esports-new/2019-rules/2019_CWL_Handbook.pdf (last visited Jan. 19, 2020); Overwatch League Summary of Official Rules 2019 Season, Overwatch League, https://bnetcmsus-a.akamaihd.net/cms/content_entry_media/bb/BB6C3OEC530B1549590044543.pdf (last visited Dec. 7, 2019).

52. Hunter A. Bayliss, *Not Just a Game: The Employment Status and Collective Bargaining Rights of Professional ESports Players*, 22 Wash. & Lee J. Civ. Rts. & Soc. Just. 359, 367 (2016) (discussing *Riot*

determining the employment status of players who are part of the *Call of Duty League*, *Overwatch League*, and the *League of Legends* Championship Series—three of the most prominent leagues in professional esports—allows for an exploration of employment status tests under federal law.[53]

Under the economic realities test, a worker is an "employee" if the worker is "economically dependent on the employer for continued employment."[54] The idea of "continued employment" is integral to determining employment status because an independent contractor would depend on multiple employment relations, as opposed to a single employer, as their primary source of income.[55] The economic realities test looks at the totality of the circumstances,[56] but it considers explicitly factors such as how much control the employer exerts over the worker; the worker's opportunities to make a profit; the skill required to perform the job; and the extent to which the worker must supply their own equipment.[57] Alternatively, the right of control, or "common-law agency" test, considers the employer's right to control the manner and means by which the worker completes the work required.[58] Relevant factors include the skills required by the job or role, the source of the necessary instruments and tools, the location where work occurs, whether the work is part of the employer's ordinary business, and whether the employer offers benefits.[59]

Analyzing the employment status of OWL, LCS, and CDL players under both the economic realities test and the right of control test shows that the players who compete in the OWL, LCS, and CDL are employees for four main reasons. First, all three leagues directly compensate their

---

Games Terms of Service, Riot Games, https://www.riotgames.com/en/terms-of-service (last modified Jan. 15, 2020)).

53. Rosenthal, *supra* note 7.

54. Holden & Baker, *supra* note 1, at 419.

55. *Id.*

56. Brief by Employment Law Scholars as Amici Curiae in Support of Respondent at 13, *New Prime, Inc. v. Oliveira*, 139 S. Ct. 532 (2019) (No. 17-340).

57. Bayliss, *supra* note 52, at 389; U.S. Department of Labor Wage and Hour Division, *Fact Sheet #13: Employment Relationship Under the Fair Labor Standards Act (FLSA)*, Dep't of Lab. (Jul. 2008), https://www.dol.gov/sites/dolgov/files/WHD/legacy/files/whdfs13.pdf. While these factors derive from New Deal Era jurisprudence—most specifically from the United States Supreme Court cases *United States v. Silk* (1947) and *Rutherford Food Corp. v. McComb* (1947), an early and influential statement for the test also appeared in *Bonnette v. California Health and Welfare Agency*, a case from the Ninth Circuit. *See* Richard R. Carlson, *Why the Law Still Can't Tell an Employee When It Sees One and How It Ought To Stop Trying*, 22 Berkeley J. Emp. & Lab. L. 295, 318–20 (2001); Bonnette v. California Health and Welfare Agency, 704 F.2d 1465 (9th Cir. 1983).

58. Holden & Baker, *supra* note 1, at 420.

59. Rosenthal, *supra* note 7 (citing Holden & Baker, *supra* note 1, at 420). *See also* Community for Creative Non-Violence v. Reid, 490 U.S. 730, 751–52 (1989).

players[60] and provide their players with benefits like health insurance and retirement plans.[61] Second, these leagues also either provide housing or dedicated training facilities to their players.[62] Third, all three leagues supply their players with equipment, such as consoles and headsets.[63] Fourth and finally, because all three leagues are organizations focused on the business of professional competitive esports, the work of competitive gaming that OWL, CDL, and LCS players engage in is part of the "ordinary business" of these leagues.[64] Because the economic realities and right of control tests show that esports competitors are employees and not independent contractors, the federal legislation that governs employer-employee relationships likely applies to the association between these organizations and their players.[65]

Collective Bargaining and the Potential for Unionization

While teams likely have an employment relationship with their players, one of the emerging issues is the potential for unionization.[66] The desirability for esports players to unionize has two sides. On the one hand, the

60. Holden & Baker, *supra* note 1, at 428; Webb, *supra* note 10.

61. About the League, Overwatch League, https://overwatchleague.com/en-us/about (last visited Jan. 23, 2020); Kevin Webb, *I attended the launch event of the $300 million Call of Duty League*, *supra* note 10; Heitner, *supra* note 17.

62. *Overwatch League*, Wikipedia, https://en.wikipedia.org/wiki/Overwatch_League (last visited Jan. 19, 2020); Noah Higgins-Dunn, *Six-figure salaries, million-dollar prizes, health benefits and housing included—inside the Overwatch League*, CNBC (Sep. 29, 2019, 8:30 AM), https://www.cnbc.com/2019/09/29/what-its-like-to-be-a-professional-gamer-in-the-overwatch-league.html; Jacobs, *supra* note 18; Smith, *supra* note 18.

63. *See* Overwatch League Summary of Official Rules 2019 Season, Overwatch League, https://bnetcmsus-a.akamaihd.net/cms/content_entry_media/bb/BB6C3OEC530B1549590044543.pdf (last visited Dec. 7, 2019); Call of Duty World League 2019 Official Handbook, Call of Duty, https://www.callofduty.com/content/dam/atvi/callofduty/esports-new/2019-rules/2019_CWL_Handbook.pdf (last visited Jan. 19, 2020); 2020 Official Rules, League of Legends, https://nexus.leagueoflegends.com/wp-content/uploads/2020/01/2020-LCS-Rule-Set-v20.1_6bkbwz26cgp7fngeat6a.pdf (last visited Mar. 22, 2020).

64. *See generally*, *Overwatch League*, Wikipedia, *supra* note 62; *League of Legends Championship Series*, Wikipedia, https://en.wikipedia.org/wiki/League_of_Legends_Championship_Series (last visited Mar. 24, 2020); *Call of Duty League*, Wikipedia, https://en.wikipedia.org/wiki/Call_of_Duty_League (last visited Mar. 25, 2020).

65. Rosenthal, *supra* note 7.

66. Al Neal, *The eSports Union Revolution Is Coming*, Grandstand Central (Aug. 4, 2018), https://grandstandcentral.com/2018/sports/esports/esports-union-is-coming/.

players would likely see significant benefit from being able to engage in meaningful collective bargaining with ownership. On the other, teams and leagues are likely to resist efforts to unionize in order to keep costs down. To date, teams have been able to avoid many of the added costs associated with unionization and have not capitulated to non-traditional organizations like the World eSports Association (WESA), which represents player interests but is not a traditional union. However, Riot Games, the makers of *League of Legends*, launched preemptive efforts to prevent players from forming a union.[67] To do so, Riot Games has taken a two-step approach—both unilaterally raising minimum player salaries and implementing a management-funded players' association.[68]

At present, esports players do not have formal, legally recognizable union structures as found in the four premier U.S. professional sports. However, as the growth of esports has led to new sources of revenue flowing to game publishers and tournament operators, competitive esports players have begun to consider forming a legally recognizable union.[69] Indeed, the idea of esports players unionizing should not be entirely surprising, as the elite athletes in the MLB, NFL, NBA, and NFL, are all current members of players' unions.[70]

While informal players associations have begun to arise in esports, many of these associations are troubling in that they are sullied by employer-side influence in the same manner that the precursors to the players' associations in the premier U.S. professional team sports were before players formally unionized.[71] Included among these troubling employer-influenced associations of players is the organization Riot Games

67. Michael Long, *Playing the game: an insider's take on esports representation*, Sports Pro Media (Jul. 21, 2017), http://www.sportspromedia.com/analysis/playing-the-game-an-insiders-take-on-esports-representation.

68. *See* Kieran Darcy, *Riot's players' association lays groundwork for unionization*, ESPN (Jun. 15, 2017), http://www.espn.com/esports/story/_/id/19617991/riot-players-association-lays-groundwork-unionization.

69. *See* Jonathan Kogel, *State of the Esports Players Union: Drawbacks and Legal Challenges*, The Esports Observer (May 8, 2018), https://esportsobserver.com/state-of-the-esports-union (discussing some of the early talk about esports players attempting to unionize).

70. *See* Marc Normandin, *50 Years Ago, Marvin Miller and the MLBPA Changed Sports Forever*, SB Nation (Jun. 11, 2018), https://www.sbnation.com/mlb/2018/6/11/17437624/mlb-mlbpa-cba-marvin-miller-robert-cannon (recognizing that players in other sports leagues, such as the Women's National Basketball Association, similarly have unions).

71. *See* Kogel, *supra* note 69 (discussing Riot Games' efforts to create something it referred to as the "League of Legends Players Association" as a purported bargaining unit of players against which Riot Games could attempt to collectively negotiate; *see also* Normandin, *supra* note 70 (discussing the period from 1954 until 1968 when the Major League Baseball Players Association operated not as an NLRA-recognized union, but rather an entity for negotiating the players pension plans, under the

helped found for its *League of Legends* players, the LCS Players Association. On the surface, Riot's attempts to help their players form such a body may seem praiseworthy. But, to the extent such an employer-influenced organization is aimed at precluding sincere player-side representation, both legal and ethical concerns arise.

As esports leagues continue to formalize themselves and increase revenue, one can reasonably expect that esports players will attempt to form more traditional unions—perhaps turning to the same lawyers and law firms that have helped athletes in traditional sports to unionize to help them to pursue the same result. The National Labor Relations Act of 1935 (NLRA) is the federal statute that grants esports players the right to attempt to form a union without the fear of retaliation.[72] The NLRA, in pertinent part, states that private employees have the legal right to self-organize and "engage in ... concerted activities for the purposes of collective bargaining or other mutual aid or protection."[73] If a recognizable union is formed, the employer group then garners the "affirmative duty to bargain over the mandatory terms and conditions of bargaining—hours wages and working conditions."[74] Employers also must bargain with unionized employees over disciplinary procedures.[75] This could lead to important changes not only in terms of the salaries of esports players but also with regard to the rights afforded to them.

A comparison to the player unionization movement in traditional sports leagues during the late 1960s and early 1970s is apt for a number of reasons, including the increasing commercialization of the underlying activities. The unionizing of athletes in the four premier U.S. professional sports leagues led to the advent of modern free agency and the substantial increase in sport-related revenues to the players.[76] For example, prior to

leadership of Robert Cannon, a Wisconsin judge who was paid by the Major League Baseball owners and who encouraged the players not to make any demands).

72. National Labor Relations Act, ch. 372, §8, 49 Stat. 449 (1935) (recognizing under the National Labor Relations Act that it would constitute an unfair labor practice "to interfere with, restrain, or coerce employees in the exercise of the rights" guaranteed under the National Labor Relations Act, including the right to attempt to form a union).

73. National Labor Relations Act, ch. 372, §7, 49 Stat. 449 (1935) (codified as amended at 29 U.S.C. §157 (2012)). *See generally* Michael H. LeRoy, *Courts and the Future of "Athletic Labor" in College Sports*, 57 Ariz. L. Rev. 475, 504 (2015) (explaining that the National Labor Relations Act only applies to private sector employment).

74. Marc Edelman, *The Future of College Athlete Players Unions*, 38 Cardozo L. Rev. 1627, 1629 (2017).

75. *See* NLRB v. Jones & Laughlin Steel Corp., 301 U.S. 1, 33 (1937).

76. *See generally* Jon Shelton, *How Free Agency Changes the Course of Baseball Labor* History, In These Times (Dec. 23, 2015), http://inthesetimes.com/working/entry/18651/todays_baseball_salar-

the formation of the Major League Baseball Players Association in 1968, the MLB minimum salary sat at $6,000 for two decades.[77] However, after the first round of collective bargaining negotiations between MLB and its newly formed players union, the league minimum salary immediately increased to $10,000.[78] By 1980, the league's minimum salary was $30,000.[79] Today, the MLB minimum player salary for players who play a complete season on their team's Major League roster sits at $563,500.[80] If the revenues generated by commercial esports continue to grow at their current rate, it is reasonable to think that the unionization for esports players could yield the same positive effect it has for MLB players and star athletes in other professional sports. Nevertheless, when trying to form a union, esports players will face challenges in terms of organizing a group that has the sufficient "community of interest" to represent an "appropriate bargaining unit."[81]

Questions pertaining to the proper potential bargaining unit for esports participants present issues in terms of both the unit's proper depth and breadth. In terms of depth, the professional sports players' unions in traditional sports consist of all of the players who compete in the highest level of their sport, and they bargain against fellow teams in what is known as a league-wide multiemployer bargaining unit.[82] For example, the NFL Players Association (NFLPA) includes all players who compete on the 32 NFL team rosters, irrespective of whether the player is the starting quarterback for reigning Super Bowl champions or the backup long snapper on

---

ies_are_the_result_of_a_labor_struggle (discussing how the Major League Baseball Players Association brought free agency and improved salaries to their sport through bringing legal challenges to the league's reserve system).

77. *See* Normandin, *supra* note 70.

78. *See* Major League Baseball Minimum and Average Salary Chart, https://www3.nd.edu/lawlib/baseball_salary_arbitration/minavgsalaries/Minimum-AverageSalaries.pdf (last visited Feb. 12, 2018).

79. *See* Normandin, supra note 70.

80. *See* Ben Walker & Jake Seiner, *AP Exclusive: MLB raises salaries for minor leaguers in 2021*, AP News (Feb. 14, 2020), https://apnews.com/article/1512f5a4cf9a65f16a2641244e0c00fd.

81. *See* National Labor Relations Board, Basic Guide to the National Labor Relations Act, 7–8 https://www.nlrb.gov/sites/default/files/attachments/basic-page/node-3024/basicguide.pdf (last visited Feb. 12, 2019) (explaining that "[a] unit of employees is a group of two or more employees who share a community of interest and may reasonably be grouped together for purposes of collective bargaining," and that typically "[t]hose who have the same or substantially similar interests concerning wages, hours and working conditions are grouped together in a bargaining unit").

82. *See* Mark J. Cozzillio et. al., Sports Law Cases and Materials 663 (Carolina Academic Press 2007) (explaining that in most U.S. professional sports leagues "[t]he collective bargaining has been conducted on a league-wide basis (i.e., the entire sport, as in Major League Baseball, the National Football League, et. al.)").

the worst-ranked team in the league.[83] Similarly, at any point in time, the MLB Players Association (MLBPA) includes approximately 1,200 players —40 players designated by each of the 30 teams as eligible to compete at that point in time on their Major League roster (as well as eligible players who are temporarily on the team's injured list).[84]

In terms of breadth, the primary issue relates to how many different types of esports players should be a member of the same union, as well as whether the union should constitute a single-employer bargaining unit (where the players bargain against one publisher or one organizer) or a multi-employer bargaining unit (one that simultaneously consists of multiple publishers and/or organizers).[85] On one end of the spectrum, it would seem to make little sense to include all elite esports players as part of one large bargaining unit because the skill-set, popularity, and revenues of different types of esports vary substantially—thus indicating an absence of a "community of interest."[86] However, on the other end of the spectrum, if one were to propose adopting a single-employer bargaining unit in esports in which each individual team of players negotiated separately against the publisher or contest organizer (rather than all the teams of elite players), this could prove too narrow, as it may leave others with a reasonable "community of interest" on the outside of certain potential bargaining units.[87] As the efforts for esports players to unionize progress, both esports players and game publishers and organizers will need to think about the factors most important to them in the context of potential collective bargaining. On the other side of the table, potential labor organizers should look to propose bargaining units that are neither too broad, too narrow, too deep, nor too shallow to meet a reasonable test for determining "commonality of interest."[88]

---

83. *See id.*; *see also* National Football League Collective Bargaining Agreement, https://nfllabor.files.wordpress.com/2010/01/collective-bargaining-agreement-2011-2020.pdf (last visited Feb. 12, 2019).

84. *See* Major League Baseball Minimum and Average Salary Chart, https://www3.nd.edu/lawlib/baseball_salary_arbitration/minavgsalaries/Minimum-AverageSalaries.pdf (last visited Feb. 12, 2018).

85. *See generally* Brown v. Pro Football Inc., 218 U.S. 231, 240 (1996) (explaining that "multiemployer bargaining accounts for more than 40% of major collective-bargaining agreements, and is used in such industries as construction, transportation, retail trade, clothing manufacture, and real estate, as well as professional sports").

86. National Labor Relations Board, Basic Guide to the National Labor Relations Act, 7–8 https://www.nlrb.gov/sites/default/files/attachments/basic-page/node-3024/basicguide.pdf (last visited Feb. 12, 2019).

87. *Id.*

88. *Id.*

Substantive Working Terms for Esports Participants

When looking at the current labor environment in esports from a more substantive perspective, it becomes clear that despite the emerging popularity of certain esports, most esports gamers enjoy a financial status that pales in comparison to professional athletes—including even the financial status of many professional athletes who compete in sports outside of the "big four."

While most professional athletes in team sports live in their own homes,[89] many esports teams live together in team housing in order to maximize team building and practice time.[90] The living arrangements are provided with the understanding that they are conditional based on satisfactory player performance. Unsatisfactory performance in competition may result in a player's room being given to someone else.[91] Business Insider referred to gaming houses, where professional video gamers live, as "reminiscent of the MTV show, *The Real World*."[92] While the idea of teams and leagues providing houses to groups of young adults, often away from home for the first time, may seem shocking to some, the arrangement is common in the world of professional esports.[93]

Liability associated with providing housing to teams of young people is likely to have significant overlap with traditional landlord and tenant regulations, which vary between jurisdictions.[94] Additional legal considerations also stem from this unique relationship. For example, team

---

89. *See e.g.*, Keith Flamer, *20 Outrageous Mansions Owned By Modern Sports Legends*, FORBES (Mar. 23, 2016), https://www.forbes.com/sites/keithflamer/2016/03/23/20-ridiculous-mansions-owned-by-modern-sports-legends/#4b0e296236bd.

90. Vic Hood, *Life inside a pro-esports team house with Fnatic: streaming, training and burritos*, TECH RADAR (Sep. 21, 2018), https://www.techradar.com/news/life-inside-a-pro-esports-team-house-with-fnatic-streaming-training-and-burritos

91. *Id.*

92. Harrison Jacobs, *Here's what life is like in the cramped 'gaming house' where 5 guys live together and earn amazing money by playing video games*, BUS. INSIDER (May 5, 2015), https://www.businessinsider.com/inside-team-liquids-league-of-legends-gaming-house-2015-4. *The Real World* was an MTV reality television show that helped launch the reality television genre. The show ran for 32 seasons from 1992 to 2017 on MTV and featured a number of young adults from different backgrounds placed in house together for a period of months. *See* Nellie Andreeva, *'Real World' Reboot In Works By MTV & Bunim-Murray, Eyed For SVOD Platforms*, DEADLINE (Jun. 7, 2018), https://deadline.com/2018/06/real-world-reboot-mtv-bunim-murray-svod-platforms-1202404898/.

93. Jacobs, *supra* note 92.

94. *See generally* Mary Ann Glendon, *The Transformation of American Landlord-Tenant Law*, 23 B.C. L. REV. 503 (1982).

ownership groups provide the housing and oftentimes use the homes as a workplace as well as a traditional domicile.[95] This shared role of the structure may implicate various responsibilities for the team owner above and beyond the provision of a habitable environment, such as liability under workplace safety regulations.[96] Constantly being surrounded by the same individuals can also cause tensions to boil over, and as such, team management must be prepared to manage feuds in order to minimize the risk of workplace violence litigation.[97]

Moreover, while there are certainly esports millionaires,[98] there are many more professional and semi-professional players seeking to get by on very little.[99] In addition to 14-hour workdays and little job security, the young age of players has made it difficult for the competitors to achieve some uniform standards regarding pay and working conditions across leagues.[100] Leagues like the OWL[101] and LCS[102] have implemented minimum salaries for competitors, which pale in comparison to the amount of money coming into esports from outside investors.[103] Lastly, questions loom surrounding players not receiving minimum levels of compensation for the number of hours worked, especially in situations where they do not fall under exemptions to the Fair Labor Standards Act (FLSA) or other relevant state and federal legislation.[104]

---

95. *See* Jacobs, *supra* note 92.

96. *See generally* John Ridley & John Canning, Safety at Work 1-1030 (7th ed. Elsevier 2008).

97. *See, e.g.*, Joel H. Neuman, & Robert A. Baron, *Workplace violence and workplace aggression: Evidence concerning specific forms, potential causes, and preferred targets*, 24 J. Management 391 (1998).

98. Joshua Staskus, *The 25 Richest eSports Players (And How Much They Are Worth)*, The Gamer (Jun. 5, 2018), https://www.thegamer.com/25-richest-esports-players-much-worth/.

99. *See* Smith, *supra* note 18.

100. *Id.*

101. Overwatch League has a minimum salary of $50,000 per season. *See* Jessica Conditt, *Overwatch League pro players will earn at least $50,000 a year*, Engadget (Jul. 26, 2017), https://www.engadget.com/2017/07/26/overwatch-league-salary-esports-players-health-insurance-blizzard/.

102. North American LCS rules impose a minimum salary of $12,500, though the average North American LCS strategy in 2017 was $105,000. *See* The Score Staff, *ESPN Survey: Average NA LCS player salary approximately $105k, EU salary $81k*, Score Esports (Jan. 13, 2017), https://www.thescoreesports.com/lol/news/12728-espn-survey-average-na-lcs-player-salary-approximately-105k-eu-salary-81k.

103. Holden & Baker, *supra* note 1.

104. It is likely that the competitors are employees of their teams in the case of the major leagues and teams, as opposed to independent contractors. *See* Holden & Baker, *supra* note 1. It remains to be seen whether esports competitors would qualify as exempt for overtime pay under the FLSA's exemption for those engaged in a creative or artistic endeavor. *See* 29 CFR §541.302 (a) ("To qualify for the creative professional exemption, an employee's primary duty must be the performance of work requiring invention, imagination, originality or talent in a recognized field of artistic or creative

Americans with Disabilities Act Concerns

In 1990, Congress enacted the Americans with Disabilities Act (ADA) to eliminate discrimination against disabled individuals in the context of employment.[105] The umbrella of the ADA's protection covers the athletes who play for professional sports leagues because the Act does not contain a specific carve-out for professional sports leagues exempting them from liability.[106] Under the ADA, a "disability" consists of a physical or mental impairment that "substantially limits" one or more major life activities, a record of this impairment, or being "regarded as" having such an impairment.[107] Major life activities include things like performing manual tasks, thinking, seeing, and concentrating.[108]

The ADA applies to employers with fifteen or more employees and imposes an affirmative obligation on employers to provide reasonable accommodations to covered employees[109] unless doing so would impose an undue hardship.[110] To prove disability discrimination, an employee must demonstrate that (1) they have a disability, (2) they could not participate or engage in a work-related activity on account of this disability, and (3) the employer failed to reasonably accommodate their disability.[111] The employee must also establish that had he or she been given a reasonable accommodation, he or she would have been able to perform the "essential functions" of his or her job.[112] Overall, reasonable accommodations help remedy the workplace inequities that persist between individuals with disabilities and individuals without them.[113]

---

endeavor as opposed to routine mental, manual, mechanical or physical work. The exemption does not apply to work which can be produced by a person with general manual or intellectual ability and training.").

105. Melissa Ann Resslar, *PGA Tour, Inc. v. Martin: A Hole in One for Casey Martin and the ADA*, 33 Loy. U. Chi. L.J. 631, 639 (2002).

106. Michael Waterstone, *Let's be Reasonable Here: Why the ADA Will Not Ruin Professional Sports*, 2000 BYU L. Rev. 1489, 1497 (2000).

107. 42 U.S.C. §12102 (1990).

108. *Id.*

109. *Id.*

110. Resslar, *supra* note 105, at 640.

111. *Id.* at 639–40.

112. Waterstone, *supra* note 106, at 1503.

113. Rosenthal, *supra* note 7.

The ADA recognizes Attention-Deficit/Hyperactivity Disorder (ADHD) as a disability.[114] Adderall, known colloquially as a "study drug," is often prescribed to those who struggle with ADHD.[115] Medications like Adderall are popular in esports because they boost cognitive function, can lead to faster reaction times, and often reduce fatigue.[116] It, therefore, comes as no surprise that these drugs are increasingly popular in esports, where the path to victory often depends on mere fractions of seconds.[117] Even top players like Adam Sloss, the former world champion of *Call of Duty*, have discussed Adderall abuse in esports, sharing that "everyone is on it."[118]

Outright banning drugs like Adderall would engender ADA liability for esports leagues because players whose medical diagnosis necessitates the drug would be precluded from participation. Perhaps, this is the reason that there is only a single prominent esports league that publishes a banned substance list—the ESL.[119] However, unlike the CDL, LCS, and OWL, the ESL does not compensate its players.[120] Therefore, the ESL does not run into disability discrimination issues by outright banning drugs like Adderall because the ESL's players are independent contractors. Thus, due to the absence of an employer-employee relationship, these players may not bring ADA suits against the ESL.

While traditional sports leagues like the NFL and NBA ban Adderall and similar drugs, they do not violate the ADA because they offer what is known as a "Therapeutic Use Exemption" (TUE) to their players.[121] TUEs

---

114. Gregg E. Clifton, *The ESports Industry—The Top Ten Labor and Employment Law Issues*, The National Law Review, (Feb. 27, 2019), https://www.natlawreview.com/article/esports-industry-top-ten-labor-and-employment-law-issues.

115. Kaci Durbin, MD, *Adderall*, Drugs.com (Apr. 25, 2019), https://www.drugs.com/adderall.html.

116. Nick Summers, *Top 'Counter-Strike' player admits eSports has a doping problem*, Engadget (Jul. 17, 2015), https://www.engadget.com/2015/07/17/esports-adderall-doping/; John T. Holden, Ryan M. Rodenberg, & Anastasios Kaburakis, *Esports Corruption: Gambling, Doping, and Global Governance*, 32 Maryland J. Int'l L. 236, 269 (2017).

117. *See* Rosenthal, *supra* note 7; Abhimanyu Ghoshal, *Esports pros don't worry about younger competitors with 'faster reflexes'*, The Next Web (Mar. 4, 2017), https://thenextweb.com/gaming/2017/03/04/esports-pros-dont-worry-about-younger-competitors-with-faster-reflexes/.

118. Coleman Hamstead, *'Nobody talks about it because everyone is on it': Adderall presents esports with an enigma*, Wash. Post (Feb. 13, 2020, 10:27 AM), https://www.washingtonpost.com/video-games/esports/2020/02/13/esports-adderall-drugs/.

119. *Id.*

120. Holden & Baker, *supra* note 1, at 426.

121. *See* NFL Requirements for Therapeutic Use Exemption (TUE): Attention Deficit and Attention Deficit Hyperactivity Disorders (ADHD), The National Football League, https://nflpaweb.blob.core.windows.net/media/Default/PDFs/ADHD_requirements_2018.pdf (last visited Dec. 7, 2019);

are a form of reasonable accommodation under the Americans with Disabilities Act that allows disabled players to consume otherwise banned substances.[122] The use of a TUE is one way that esports leagues like the CDL, OWL, and LCS could establish general bans on drugs like Adderall without running afoul of the ADA's mandates.

Implementing banned substance policies but allowing for the possibility of TUEs would likely be beneficial for leagues like the CDL, OWL, and LCS for two primary reasons. First, such regulations would help leagues from a public relations interest by mitigating the media attention surrounding esports' burgeoning study-drug culture.[123] Second, if leagues do not enact banned substance policies that govern prescription drug abuse, they may render themselves liable to disability discrimination suits under the ADA.[124] This is because players who struggle with ADHD and need to take medication like Adderall to play at a competitive level are at a disadvantage when any of their competitors (including those without disabilities) can take the same drug to achieve a boost. If leagues create banned substance policies and give players an opportunity to apply for TUEs, this will allow players with disabilities who must take otherwise banned medication as part of their daily lives to compete at a professional level.[125] It will also ensure that other players—namely those without disabilities who have no legitimate grounds for Adderall prescriptions—do not gain a leg-up by consuming medications under false pretenses.[126]

Christopher R. Deubert et al., Comparing Health-Related Policies & Practices in Sports: The NFL and Other Professional Leagues 149 (2017), https://footballplayershealth.harvard.edu/wp-content/uploads/2017/05/08_Ch4_Drugs.pdf.

122. *See* Rosenthal, *supra* note 7 (citing Travis Tygart & Anthony R. Ten Haagen, *The Americans with Disabilities Act, The United States Anti-Doping Agency, and the Effort Toward and Equal Opportunity: A Case Study of the* United States Anti-Doping Agency v. George Hartman *Matter*, 2 Harv. J. Sports & Ent. L. 199, 219 (2011)).

123. *See* Rosenthal, *supra* note 7; Colby Stivers, *The First Competitive Video Gaming Anti-Doping Policy and Its Deficiencies Under European Union Law*, 18 San Diego Int'l L.J., 263, 269–70 (2017).

124. Rosenthal, *supra* note 7.

125. John T. Holden, Anastasios Kaburakis & Joanna Wall Tweedie, *Virtue(al) games—real drugs*, 13 Sport, Ethics & Phil. 19, 23, 26 (2019); *See generally* Hamstead, *supra* note 118 (explaining that because "obtaining a prescription for Adderall under false pretenses is relatively simple," eSports leagues face a challenge when it comes to where they draw the line).

126. *See* Rosenthal, *supra* note 7.

Recent Litigation

In May 2019, famed *Fortnite* player Turner Tenney ("Tfue") filed a lawsuit against his esports team, the FaZe Clan, in California court. Distinct from esports leagues like the CDL, LCS, ESL, or OWL, the FaZe Clan "could be called a media company, or an esports team, or an influencer marketing agency, or all of the above."[127] In sum, the FaZe Clan is essentially a conglomerate of 34 content creators, 15 professional esports players, and 11 hybrid creators who are both pro players and entertainers.[128] Tfue himself boasts 12 million subscribers on YouTube and 8.9 million on Twitch.[129]

Tfue brought suit against the FaZe Clan to undo his "oppressive" three-year contract, which allegedly "deprived him of business opportunities and failed to pay him his share of team sponsorship revenues."[130] Tfue brought the California state court case as an appellate placeholder for a proceeding he filed with the California Labor Commissioner.[131] In the administrative filing, Tfue argued that the FaZe Clan violated California's Talent Agency Act (TAA) by acting as his unlicensed talent agency.[132]

Three months later, FaZe countersued in the Southern District of New York, claiming that Tfue "disparaged the team in violation of a clause in his agreement, stole its confidential information, and interfered with other business contracts and relationships."[133] In July 2020, a California judge dismissed Tfue's original complaint, leaving only the FaZe suit outstanding. Although the trial was set for October 2020, Tfue and FaZe settled at the end of August 2020, leaving Tfue no longer eligible to receive

127. Taylor Lorenz, *Can FaZe Clan Build a Billion-Dollar Business?* N.Y. Times (Nov. 15, 2019), https://www.nytimes.com/2019/11/15/style/faze-clan-house.html.

128. *Id.*

129. Julia Alexander, *Tfue settles lawsuit against Faze Clan over 'oppressive' gaming contract*, The Verge (Aug. 26, 2020, 5:08 PM), https://www.theverge.com/2020/8/26/21403052/tfue-faze-clan-lawsuit-settled-streaming-events-competition-esports.

130. Jonathan L. Israel, *It's Not Just A Game—Addressing Employment Law Issues in Esports*, Foley & Lardner (Jun. 3, 2019), https://www.foley.com/en/insights/publications/2019/06/employment-law-issues-in-esports.

131. *Id.*

132. *Id.*

133. Christina Settimi, *Fortnite Star Tfue Settles Dispute With FaZe Clan, Ending Esports' First Major Employment Lawsuit*, Forbes (Aug, 26, 2020, 1:59 PM), https://www.forbes.com/sites/christinasettimi/2020/08/26/fortnite-star-tfue-settles-dispute-with-faze-clan-ending-esports-first-major-employment-lawsuit/#4e3760d922d8.

a paycheck from FaZe—a perk he had been receiving throughout the 15-month legal ordeal.[134]

Not only is the *Tfue v. FaZe Clan* lawsuit the first significant employment dispute in professional esports, but, according to industry attorneys, the lawsuit also highlights some of the "interesting dynamics that arise when a player shifts from being purely a professional player into a full-time content creator that also plays in some esports competitions."[135]

134. *Id.*
135. *Id.*

CHAPTER 6

ESPORTS BROADCASTING ISSUES

Since its inception, broadcasting of esports competitions has been distinguishable from broadcasting in traditional sports leagues.[1] Unlike conventional sports leagues such as the NFL and NBA that rely on multi-year broadcast contracts with television networks to deliver content to fans,[2] esports is primarily delivered via free internet platforms. Of the numerous streaming platforms that broadcast esports, the most popular are Twitch and YouTube.[3] The popularity of both platforms is evidenced by the fact that Twitch users live-streamed a total of 2.72 billion hours of esports content over three months in 2019,[4] while YouTube saw its viewers tune into roughly 735 million hours of esports content during the same period.[5] While esports distribution channels differ from traditional sports broadcasting models in that they are widely free and global, the open model for streaming also makes it possible for virtually anyone with a computer to become an esports broadcaster.[6]

---

1. John T. Holden, Marc Edelman & Thomas A. Baker III, *A Short Treatise on Esports and the Law: How America Regulates Its Next National Pastime*, 2020 U. ILL. L. REV. 509, 561 (2020).

2. *See, e.g.*, Patrick Hipes, *Update: NBC, CBS, and Fox Score Nine-Year NFL Extensions Taking Them to 2022*, DEADLINE (Dec. 14, 2011), https://deadline.com/2011/12/nbc-and-nfl-extend-deal-through-2022-205160/ (describing the NFL's extension of their television deal through 2022).

3. Holden, Edelman & Baker, *supra* note 1.

4. Sarah Perez, *Twitch continues to dominate live streaming with its second-biggest quarter to date*, TECHCRUNCH (Jul. 12, 2019, 2:14 PM), https://techcrunch.com/2019/07/12/twitch-continues-to-dominate-live-streaming-with-its-second-biggest-quarter-to-date/.

5. *Id.*

6. Holden, Edelman & Baker, *supra* note 1.

An Overview of Streaming

Although potential exists for streamers to make a significant amount of money by live streaming their gameplay and some streamers out-earn many esports competitors, the low barriers to entry for streaming have created a competitive environment that has led some streamers to burn out and suffer significant health consequences.[7] At a basic level, streaming essentially only requires five things: (1) access to a streaming platform like Twitch or YouTube; (2) a computer; (3) a microphone; (4) a video camera; and (5) some downloadable software.[8] By utilizing basic equipment, an aspiring broadcaster can begin to develop a following and earn money from fan donations.[9]

Although most streaming sites allow streamers to earn revenue, the structure of compensation varies between the platforms.[10] As Twitch now controls 76 percent of the streaming market in the United States, its acquisition by Amazon in 2014 appears prophetic.[11] Consumers of streaming content across top platforms consume billions of hours of content every month.[12] Despite the popularity of streaming sites, federal laws like the Digital Millennium Copyright Act cast a shadow over the industry.

Digital Millennium Copyright Act (DMCA)

In 1998, President Bill Clinton signed the DMCA into law.[13] The DMCA was designed to secure intellectual property rights and provide a remedy against piracy on the internet, which remained a somewhat new utility.[14] In the decades since the passage of the DMCA, the statute has remained controversial, with some asserting the DMCA to prevent things like using

---

7. Holden, Edelman & Baker, *supra* note 14.

8. John T. Holden & Mike Schuster, *Copyright and Joint Authorship as a Disruption of the Video Game Streaming Industry*, 2020 Columbia Bus. L. Rev. 942, 958 (2021).

9. Tae Kim, *Tyler 'Ninja' Blevins explains how he makes more than $500,000 a month playing video game 'Fortnite'*, CNBC (Mar. 19, 2018, 4:18 PM), https://www.cnbc.com/2018/03/19/tyler-ninja-blevins-explains-how-he-makes-more-than-500000-a-month-playing-video-game-fortnite.html.

10. Holden & Schuster, *supra* note 8, at 953–54, n. 58.

11. *Id.* at 954.

12. *Id.* at 955.

13. David Kravets, *10 Years Later, Misunderstood DMCA Is the Law That Saved The Web*, Wired (Oct. 27, 2008), https://www.wired.com/2008/10/ten-years-later/.

14. *Id.*

third-party companies selling replacement ink toner cartridges for printers and shutting down online forums that contained instructions on how to unlock cellphones.[15] The DMCA, however, poses a unique challenge for the streaming industry as streamers rely on game content in order to have material to share with fans.[16] The streaming industry needs video games, and video games have largely acquiesced to, and in many cases even endorsed, streaming of gameplay as a form of advertising. The difficulty for streamers is that while there is a long history of game makers permitting streaming, there is no guarantee that the game makers will continue to tolerate the practice.

Indeed, Valve, maker of the popular title *DotA 2*, issued takedown notices to some who sought to commercialize broadcasts of an event in direct competition with a paid stream from a tournament operator.[17] Takedown notices are widely utilized by other professional sports leagues seeking to prevent unauthorized use of league or team marks.[18] While it is relatively rare for game makers to issue takedown notices to streamers, it has been common for Twitch streamers to receive takedown notices in association with the use of background music or other media, with some notices resulting in streamers receiving a ban.[19] The DMCA shields hosting sites from liability, provided they act quickly to take down infringing third-party content when notified. The challenge for sites like Twitch, which have millions of users, is that it is inefficient to conduct detailed investigations of whether a user is infringing or whether the user's display of certain content is covered by fair use. Unsurprisingly, this has been one of the prevailing critiques of the DMCA.

While the DMCA provides an exemption for "fair use," the use must be limited and for a transformative purpose.[20] Common examples of fair use include using copyrighted material for critique, commentary, parody, or an educational purpose.[21] Fair use allows a user to avoid the penalties of the DMCA. Despite this, its scope is limited to enumerated circumstances,

---

15. *See* Kim Zetter, *Hacker Lexicon: What is the Digital Millennium Copyright Act?*, Wired (Jun. 6, 2016), https://www.wired.com/2016/06/hacker-lexicon-digital-millennium-copyright-act/.

16. Holden, Edelman & Baker, *supra* note 1, at 561.

17. *Id.* at 562.

18. *See e.g.*, Matt Goldman, *MLB Strikes Out in Marketing Baseball*, Beyond the Box Score (Sep. 26, 2015), https://www.beyondtheboxscore.com/2015/9/26/9401185/mlbam-gifs-vines-snapchat-social-media-marketing-baseball-mlb (describing takedown notices sent by Major League Baseball Advanced Media to Twitter users over the posting of Gifs).

19. Holden, Edelman & Baker, *supra* note 1, at 562.

20. *Id.*

21. *Id.*

meaning that the exemption is narrow and not all uses, such as, in particular, those with commercial objectives, satisfy the requirements. The narrow scope of the exceptions to the DMCA may engender some challenges and uncertainty for streamers as their use may not be sufficiently transformative despite the introduction of original commentary over gameplay. As such, relying on third-party games as a basis for generating income may prove precarious for some streamers. Overall, despite the threats posed by the Copyright Act and potential risks with statutory penalties reaching up to $1 million, streaming continues to be immensely popular.[22]

End-User License Agreements (EULAs)

The ability to stream games, particularly as a commercial endeavor, is largely determined by the scope of End-User License Agreements, or as they are more commonly known, EULAs.[23] The EULA serves as the contract between the game maker and the user. Despite the apparent absence of meaningful negotiation surrounding EULAs, they have been historically viewed as valid agreements.[24] Indeed, one of the exceptions to a court enforcing a EULA involved compelled arbitration by *Fortnite* game maker Epic Games, who sought to enforce the terms of a EULA against a minor who disaffirmed the agreement in a timely manner.[25] While the *Doe* case is within the exceptions to courts enforcing EULAs, it may offer some guidance, as video gamers and streamers tend to be younger, with many beginning their streaming careers before attaining the age of majority.[26]

Despite the apparent prohibition on the commercial use of game content in many EULAs, some EULAs create an exception for streaming of game content and allow for participating in compensation programs run by streaming sites like YouTube and Twitch.[27] Other EULAs are more

---

22. *See* 17 U.S.C. §506(a).

23. Holden & Schuster, *supra* note 8, at 957. For our purposes we use EULA to incorporate not only end-user agreements, but also Terms of Use Agreements and Terms of Service agreements, as Holden and Schuster did. *See id.*

24. *See* ProCD v. Zeidenberg, 86 F.3d 1447 (7th Cir. 1996); *see also* Davidson & Associates v. Internet Gateway, 422 F.3d 630 (8th Cir. 2005).

25. Doe v. Epic Games, Inc., No. 19-CV-03629-YGR, 2020 WL 376573, at *1 (N.D. Cal. Jan. 23, 2020). *See also* Holden & Schuster, *supra* note 8, at 957–58.

26. Doe v. Epic Games, Inc., at *1.

27. Holden & Schuster, *supra* note 8, at 958.

prohibitive, but nonetheless, some companies have taken a laissez-faire approach to enforcing their intellectual property rights against streamers, perhaps viewing the streaming, especially that done by popular streamers, as a form of free advertising. While there is a wide variety of permissibility across game makers and titles, it is important to note how delicate EULAs can be. Specifically, many EULAs require agreement before each log on to a game and thereby allow game makers to easily change the terms. As such, streaming careers without explicit agreement from game makers is a somewhat precarious source of employment.[28]

The Traditional Broadcasting Model

Although streaming on sites like Twitch and YouTube serves as the premier source of esports content for consumers, traditional broadcasters are making forays into esports. There have been limited attempts in the past to broadcast esports on traditional cable television networks, including an early partnership between Major League Gaming and the USA Network;[29] there has been recent interest in light of growing online viewership numbers. Sports networks, like ESPN, have begun broadcasting various esports competitions, and ESPN's partner network, ABC, was the first of the major U.S. networks to broadcast an esports competition when they aired the Overwatch League Stage 1 final in March of 2019.[30] Jacob Bogage of the *Washington Post* noted that what makes esports unique to the traditional broadcasting model is that, at least in its first broadcasts, the broadcasting rights have been non-exclusive.[31]

ESPN has signed agreements to broadcast various competitions on its subscription platform ESPN+ and has shown various contests on its broadcast channel. However, despite the fact that ESPN broadcasts both esports and traditional sports games and matches, esports broadcasting remains distinct and nascent in comparison to the broadcasting of conventional sports.[32] By virtue of the 1961 Sports Broadcasting Act, which

28. *Id.* at 961–62.

29. *See* Madison Brand, *USA Network to Air Video Gaming Competitions*, NPR (Apr. 24, 2006), https://www.npr.org/templates/story/story.php?storyId=5359394.

30. Jacob Bogage, *Esports Continue TV Push With ESPN and Turner, Sparking Enthusiasm, Ire*, Wash. Post (Mar. 28, 2019), https://www.washingtonpost.com/sports/2019/03/28/esports-continue-tv-push-with-espn-turner-sparking-enthusiasm-ire/.

31. *Id.*

32. *Id.*

allows for the pooling of league-wide rights without offending the Sherman Antitrust Act, traditional sports leagues have a tremendous advantage in their negotiation of broadcast agreements.[33] While some have criticized the Sports Broadcasting Act as a piece of special interest legislation,[34] the statute provides leagues with tremendous leverage in negotiations with broadcasters.[35] It is important to note, however, that the Sports Broadcasting Act is limited in its protection to "organized professional team sports of football, baseball, basketball, or hockey," thus falling silent on its applicability to any other sports.[36]

One of the most attractive esports properties for broadcasters is the *League of Legends World Championship*. In 2019, the *League of Legends World Championship* attracted upwards of a total of 100 million viewers, with 44 million viewers watching concurrently.[37] For context, the 2019 *Masters* golf tournament peaked at 18.3 million viewers, and the 2019 Kentucky Derby peaked at 16.5 million viewers.[38] In fact, the *League of Legends World Championships* even surpassed events like the College Football National Championship and the Daytona 500 in terms of both total and concurrent viewers, only lagging behind events like the Super Bowl and World Cup finals.[39] One of the challenges for broadcasters and esports organizers looking to scale up traditional broadcasting deals is that there remains a great deal of variability in league structures, and in some instances, a variety of elite-level tournaments offering competitions for the same game titles.[40]

Despite the apparent challenges posed by varying league structures, some esports leagues have taken to modeling themselves in a manner akin

33. Holden, Edelman & Baker, *supra* note 1, at 563.

34. *See, e.g.*, David L. Anderson, *The Sports Broadcasting Act: Calling It What It Is—Special Interest Legislation*, 17 Hastings Comm. & Ent. L.J. 945, 951–56 (1995) (detailing several prominent criticisms of the Sports Broadcasting Act).

35. *See* Robert Alan Garrett & Philip R. Hochberg, *Sports Broadcasting and the Law*, 59 Ind. L.J. 155, 173 (1984).

36. 15 U.S.C. §1291.

37. Kevin Webb, *More than 100 Million People Watched the 'League of Legends' World Championship, Cementing Its Place As The Most Popular Esport*, Bus. Insider (Dec. 18, 2019), https://www.businessinsider.com/league-of-legends-world-championship-100-million-viewers-2019-12#::text=The%20%22League%20of%20Legends%22%20World,final%20round%20on%20November%2010.

38. Alison Baker, *The Most Watched Sporting Events in the World*, Roadtrips (Feb. 7, 2020), https://www.roadtrips.com/blog/the-most-watched-sporting-events-in-the-world/.

39. *See* Angela Underwood, *Most Watched Sporting Events in the U.S.*, Stacker (May 28, 2019), https://thestacker.com/stories/2839/most-watched-sporting-events-us?page=4 (listing the most watched sporting events in the United States).

40. *See generally* Holden, Edelman & Baker, *supra* note 1.

to more traditional American sports leagues, perhaps in a way that will render them more attractive to broadcast television viewers (and executives). The *Overwatch* League (OWL), for instance, very much resembles leagues like the NBA and the NHL in that it is composed of geographically aligned divisions and is built to include a regular season of twenty weeks that is then followed by a playoff and eventual championship.[41] The attachment of OWL teams to home cities (in both the United States and abroad) is anticipated to intensify regional associations with the individual esports clubs, which the League hopes will translate into increased viewership.[42] The OWL sold concurrent rights to both Twitch and Disney (who owns ESPN) for a multi-year period and plans to split the revenue with the players.[43] In its first year, the OWL was far from a viewership hit in the United States.[44] While regular viewership was perhaps disappointing, the Grand Finals drew an average audience of more than one million concurrent viewers across all platforms.[45] The push to drive OWL viewership across a variety of platforms may be a beneficial trend, especially as studies show that younger audiences continue to "cut the cord" by disengaging from traditional cable and satellite contracts.[46]

With a few notable exceptions, the United States lags behind countries like South Korea and Japan in providing esports accessibility to consumers more broadly via traditional television broadcasting.[47] However, there are signs of change afoot.[48] Both Turner Broadcasting Systems (TBS) and ESPN have begun to establish relationships for more permanent commitments to esports broadcasting.

---

41. Holden, Edelman & Baker, *supra* note 1, at 564.

42. *Id.*

43. *Id.*

44. Hawken Miller, *For Overwatch League, the True Test Starts in 2020,* Wash. Post (Sep. 30, 2019), https://www.washingtonpost.com/video-games/esports/2019/09/30/overwatch-league-true-test-starts/.

45. *Id.*

46. Holden, Edelman & Baker, *supra* note 1, at 565.

47. *See* Holden, Edelman & Baker, *supra* note 1, at 565 (noting that in Japan Nippon TV both owns an esports team and broadcasts a show dedicated to esports). In Korea, there is a dedicated esports channel named OGN. *See* Rebekah Valentine, *South Korean Network OGN Bringing Esports Programming to North America with $100m Investment,* Games Industry Biz (Oct. 10, 2018), https://www.gamesindustry.biz/articles/2018-10-10-south-korean-network-ogn-bringing-esports-programming-to-north-america-with-usd100m-investment.

48. *Id.*

ESPN

In 2020, ESPN, the self-proclaimed "worldwide leader in sports," became the official television home of the 2020 *League of Legends*' Championship Series Spring Split Playoffs.[49] While ESPN has occasionally broadcast select esports competitions, such as the 2014 League of Legends World Championship, it has now begun acquiring more long-term interests in esports properties.[50] In 2018, ESPN and game maker Activision Blizzard entered into a contract for the broadcasting rights to Activision's *Overwatch* League matches. Under the contract, ESPN can broadcast OWL content across a variety of ESPN and Disney platforms, culminating in a live broadcast of the finals from New York's Barclay Center.[51] Indeed, in the absence of traditional sports during the COVID-19 pandemic, ESPN turned to esports to fill a programming void that was created by the lack of live events.[52] On April 5, 2020, ESPN launched its first "esports day," airing twelve hours of esports programming, including the opening round of the *NBA 2K20* tournament, which featured a number of NBA players.[53]

TBS

TBS, like ESPN, is an established U.S. broadcaster that has made strides in entering the esports broadcasting market.[54] TBS' Turner Sports entered the esports space not only by broadcasting content but also through creating, owning, and operating the network's own league, ELeague.[55] ELeague, which began in 2016, focused on game maker Valve's *Counter-Strike: Global Offensive*.[56] During the season, ELeague competitions are aired in three-hour broadcasts on TBS and streamed, with additional

49. Julia Alexander, *ESPN Becomes the Official Broadcast Home for League of Legends' Spring Split Playoffs*, The Verge (Apr. 8, 2020), https://www.theverge.com/2020/4/8/21213617/espn-league-of-legends-spring-split-playoffs-broadcast-stream.

50. Holden, Edelman & Baker, *supra* note 1, at 566.

51. Chloe Aiello, *Overwatch Hits The Big Time With ESPN Broadcast Deal*, CNBC (Jul. 11, 2018), https://www.cnbc.com/2018/07/11/espn-to-live-broadcast-activision-blizzard-esports-overwatch-league.html.

52. Brad Adgate, *Esports Is Filling the Programming Void*, Forbes (Apr. 21, 2020), https://www.forbes.com/sites/bradadgate/2020/04/21/esports-is-filling-the-programming-void/#744f6be2533b.

53. *Id.*

54. Holden, Edelman & Baker, *supra* note 1, at 567.

55. Sahil Patel, *Turner's Esports League Aims for Growth With More Tournaments, Advertisers*, Digiday (Jul. 19, 2018), https://digiday.com/future-of-tv/turners-esports-league-aims-for-growth-with-new-games-advertisers/.

56. *Id.*

content, on Twitch.[57] By 2018, however, TBS expanded ELeague to include a variety of different game titles in addition to *Counter-Strike: Global Offensive*, like Rocket League, Street Fighter, and Tekken.[58] ELeague has also switched up its broadcasting from the original live shots of gameplay to include more behind-the-scenes features, which is a concept for content that is borrowed from traditional sports.[59] While it does not compete against top-level broadcast content for the most-popular traditional sports leagues (e.g., the NFL), ELeague has engaged viewership who are younger in comparison to TBS' content that airs on other nights in the same time slots—and every major broadcast network covets attention from younger audiences based on their appeal for advertisers.[60]

Other Networks

Other broadcast networks, including NBC, CBS, and even the NFL Network, have sought to experiment with esports content.[61] In 2019, CBS began broadcasting limited esports content pre-recorded from a tournament at E3.[62] Despite its display of pre-recorded content, CBS managed to produce two of the top five most-viewed esports broadcasts of the year, averaging more than 400,000 viewers.[63] CBS and NBC have both bet that esports consumers will want to watch not only real-world esports, but also fictional esports, with both contracting for esports comedy shows to potentially air in the coming years.[64]

The popularity of esports continues to grow, such that it is now a mainstream form of entertainment. Just four years removed from sports "commentator" Colin Cowherd calling esports fans "nerds" and "booger-eaters,"[65] esports programming on TBS was outperforming various

57. *Id.*

58. *Id.*

59. *Id.*

60. *Id.*

61. *Esports TV History and 2019's Top 10 Programs*, The Next Level (Sep. 26, 2019), https://tnl.media/esportstv/2019/9/25/2019s-top-10-esports-programs.

62. *Id.*

63. *Id.*

64. H.B. Duran, *NBC Orders Script for Esports Comedy 'The Squad' Starring Johnny Galecki*, The Esports Observer (Oct. 24, 2019), https://esportsobserver.com/nbc-script-the-squad/.

65. Nick Schwartz, *Colin Cowherd Attacks eSports 'Nerds' In Another Angry Rant*, USA Today (Sep. 29, 2015), https://ftw.usatoday.com/2015/09/colin-cowherd-esports-rant-fox.

programs featuring Cowherd on Fox Sport 1.[66] There are likely to be continued efforts to bridge the gap between traditional sports fans and esports fans by the ongoing use of broadcast television as a means of enculturating esports to the masses. However, it is possible, and perhaps likely, that as esports continues to grow, its online presence will continue to outpace its viewership on television-based platforms due to the greater availability of customization online.

66. *Esports TV History and 2019's Top 10 Programs*, The Next Level (Sep. 26, 2019), https://tnl.media/esportstv/2019/9/25/2019s-top-10-esports-programs.

Chapter 7

Violent Content in Video Games

Violence in video games has long raised concerns for those who are outside of the industry. The first video game to attract widespread attention for its violent content was *Death Race*. *Death Race*, released in 1976 by Exidy games, allowed players to run over gremlins, but the technology at the time made the monsters on screen closely resemble pedestrians.[1] When a gremlin was killed by a player, a tombstone would appear.[2] The National Safety Council described the games as "'insidious,' 'morbid,' 'gross' and 'sick, sick, sick.'"[3] The director of research for the National Safety Council differentiated video game violence from television violence by arguing that violence viewed on television is passive, whereas the former was active, making it more problematic.[4] In the decades since the 1970s, video games have been a frequent target for blame—particularly in the wake of school shootings.[5]

In 2018, Polygon reported that of the thirty-three mass shootings between 1980 and 2018, four of those events were associated with perpetrators who had a known affinity for video games.[6] Despite the decades of effort to draw a causal link between video games and real-world acts of

1. Levi Buchanon, *Death Race*, IGN (May 12, 2012), https://www.ign.com/articles/2008/08/23/death-race.

2. *Id.*

3. Ralph Blumenthal, *'Death Race'* N.Y. Times (Dec. 28, 1976), https://www.nytimes.com/1976/12/28/archives/death-race-game-gains-favor-but-not-with-the-safety-council.html.

4. *Id.*

5. Colin Campbell, *A Brief History of Blaming Video Games for Mass Murder*, Polygon (Mar. 10, 2018), https://www.polygon.com/2018/3/10/17101232/a-brief-history-of-video-game-violence-blame.

6. *Id.*

violence, scientific studies have largely failed to establish a behavioral link between playing violent video games and committing actual acts of violence.[7] Following in the footsteps of the Recording Industry Association of America, which implemented a ratings system for music which featured "parental advisory" for albums containing explicit language, the video game industry implemented their own ratings system after facing mounting pressure from outside groups.[8] The Entertainment Software Rating Board established a six-tier rating system for games, with the most explicit rating being Adults Only or AO, a rating much like NC-17 or X-rated that ensures the game or film will not obtain wide distribution.[9]

Video Games and Free Speech

In 2005, the California Assembly passed bill 1179, which prohibited the sale of violent video games to minors and required that games with violent content be labeled with an "18," denoting the minimum age to purchase the games.[10] The software industry and video game manufacturers brought suit against the State of California, arguing that the restriction violates the First Amendment.[11] The Supreme Court held in 2011 that the obscenity exceptions to the First Amendment apply only to depictions of sexual conduct and do not extend to "whatever a legislature finds shocking."[12] The Supreme Court noted that California's efforts to couch the video game sale ban alongside a 1960s ban on the sale of pornographic materials to minors in New York failed because there was no longstanding history in the United States of "restricting children's access to depictions of violence."[13] The content-based restriction of the California law raised the burden on the state to a strict scrutiny standard, a level the state could not justify.[14] The Supreme Court focused on the State's inability to draw a "direct causal link between violent video games and harm to minors."[15]

---

7. *Id.*

8. Charlie Hall, *A Brief History of the ESRB Rating System*, Polygon (Mar. 3, 2018), https://www.polygon.com/2018/3/3/17068788/esrb-ratings-changes-history-loot-boxes.

9. *Id.*

10. Brown v. Ent. Merch. Ass'n, 564 U.S. 786 (2011).

11. *Id.* at 789.

12. *Id.* at 791.

13. *Id.* at 794–95.

14. *Id.* at 798.

15. *Id.*

Despite the Supreme Court's ruling in *Brown v. Entertainment Merchants Association*, there have been continued efforts to link video game consumption with the acts of deranged mass killers.[16] Indeed, one of the common challenges with studying video games and violence is that there is not a universal definition of "violent video game." In fact, some have asserted that nearly all games contain some element of violence.[17] The protection of the First Amendment notwithstanding, video game companies have continued to face challenges from advocacy groups in the years since the 2011 Supreme Court decision striking down the California sales ban. As technology has improved and game graphics have continued to become increasingly realistic, concerns over violence remain prescient. The concerns surrounding violent game content remain a major obstacle to the acceptance of esports by major traditional sporting organizations.

The Olympics Balks

In 2018, the International Olympic Committee and the Global Association of International Sports Federations hosted a forum in Lausanne, Switzerland, to discuss the potential adoption of esports within the Olympic movement.[18] Although intended as a broad discussion on various issues addressing how the esports industry and the Olympics could advance similar goals, the event followed with an announcement that the 2022 Asian Games would have esports competitions as full events with medals.[19] However, following the summit, Thomas Bach, president of the International Olympic Committee, argued against hosting esports in the Olympics, particularly games with violence.[20] Bach differentiated esports violence from traditional sports violence, stating: "But sport is the civilized

16. *See* Christopher J. Ferguson, *Violent Video Games, Mass Shootings, and the Supreme Court: Lessons for the Legal Community in the Wake of Recent Free Speech Cases and Mass Shootings*, 17 New Crim. L. Rev. 553, 554–55 (2014) (noting that there was wide speculation that the Newtown school shooter, Adam Lanza, was an avid consumer of violent video games, however, a lengthy investigation revealed that while he played video games, *Dance, Dance Revolution* and *Super Mario Brothers* were the games he played most, neither of which is associated with excessive or explicit violence).

17. *Id.* at 555–57.

18. Daniel Cooper, *The Olympics People Are Seriously Considering Esports*, Engadget (Jun. 28, 2018), https://www.engadget.com/2018-06-28-ioc-esports-event.html.

19. *Id.*

20. Vlad Savov, *Olympics Chief Rules Out Violent E-Sports*, Verge (Sep. 4, 2018), https://www.theverge.com/2018/9/4/17817238/olympics-ioc-esports-violence-thomas-bach.

expression about this. If you have egames where it's about killing somebody, this cannot be brought into line with our Olympic values."[21]

The global popularity and growth of esports has meant that despite President Bach's earlier statements, the Olympics has continued to flirt with esports joining the array of Olympic sports.[22] Indeed, esports is seen as attractive to the Olympics for the same reason a large number of investors have looked at the field as a growth opportunity, which is the demographics of the consumers.[23] But, following the 8th Olympic Summit held in 2019, the committee issued the following statement on the subject of esports and gaming:

> The Olympic Summit received a report from the Chair of the Esports and Gaming Liaison Group, UCI President David Lappartient, on the recommendations to promote the Olympic sports and the Olympic values in Esports and gaming.
>
> The Summit agreed on a two-speed approach:
>
> - With regard to electronic games simulating sports, the Summit sees great potential for cooperation and incorporating them into the sports movement. Many sports simulations are becoming more and more physical thanks to Virtual and Augmented Reality which replicate the traditional sports.
>
> The International Federations are encouraged to consider how to govern electronic and virtual forms of their sport and explore opportunities with game publishers.
>
> - With regard to other electronic games, the Summit concluded that, at this stage, the sports movement should focus on players and gamers rather than on specific games. This focus on individuals should promote the participation in sport and its benefits as well as healthy lifestyle at all levels, including a health management model for elite esports competitors including both physical and mental health.
>
> A continuous dialogue between the Olympic Movement and Esports and gaming communities should be fostered to develop strategic partnerships, including platforms and events as appropriate. The

21. Stephen Wade, *Bach: No Olympic Future For Esports Until 'Violence'Removed*, Associated Press (Sep. 1, 2018), https://apnews.com/article/3615bd17ebb8478ab534691080a9a32a.

22. Kevin Webb, *Games Like 'League of Legends' and 'Fortnite' Dominate the World of Esports, But They Won't Be Showing Up At The Olympics Anytime Soon*, Bus. Insider (Dec. 11, 2019), https://www.businessinsider.com/esports-olympics-ioc-pro-video-games-2019-12.

23. *Id.*

> participants also agreed that guidelines for sustainable relationships between sports stakeholders and Esports communities should be developed.[24]

Despite the stated opposition to esports as an event at the Olympics, discussion regarding possible inclusion continues to circulate, mainly because the Olympics has been seeking to add sports that appeal to a younger generation.[25] While the Olympics have pushed the pause button on esports, major sponsors like Intel have attempted to capitalize on an association. For example, prior to the 2020 Summer Olympics being postponed until 2021 due to COVID-19, Intel planned to host the Intel World Open esports tournament in Tokyo in the weeks leading up to the Olympics.[26] Still, however, opposition remains as some suggest that violent content may not be the only impediment to inclusion in the Olympics. Rather, they believe that a more significant obstacle will be the intellectual property and licensing concerns associated with offering competitive gaming as an event.[27]

Liability for Events

The concern about violence in certain video games, however, occasionally extends beyond just theoretical concerns. In August 2018, violence associated with video games took on a different meaning when a competitive *Madden* player opened fire at an esports event in Jacksonville, Florida, killing one of his rivals.[28] The shooter was a well-known competitor who had a history of mental illness.[29] Following the event, it became necessary for esports event operators to recognize the potential threats facing large gatherings, much like what the traditional sports world has been forced to

---

24. *Declaration of the 8th Olympic Summit*, Int'l Olympic Committee (Dec. 7, 2019), *available at*: https://www.olympic.org/news/declaration-of-the-8th-olympic-summit.

25. Brandon Byrne, *Why the Olympics Should Add Esports*, Tech Crunch (Jun. 18, 2020), https://techcrunch.com/2020/06/18/why-the-olympics-should-add-esports/.

26. Amrita Khalid, *Intel Is Hosting An Olympics-Sanctioned Esports Tournament in 2020*, Engadget (Sep. 11, 2019), https://www.engadget.com/2019-09-11-intel-is-hosting-an-olympics-sanctioned-esports-tournament-in-20.html.

27. *See* Kevin Hitt, *IOC Delivers Blow to Esports' Quest For International Legitimacy*, Esports Observer (Nov. 4, 2020), https://esportsobserver.com/ioc-no-to-esports-governing-body/.

28. *Florida Shooting: Video Gamers Killed By Rival at Tournament*, BBC (Aug. 27, 2018), https://www.bbc.com/news/world-us-canada-45319478.

29. *Id.*

grapple with in the wake of the 9/11 terrorist attacks and terrorist attacks on a soccer stadium in Paris. Many professional gaming communities tend to be tight-knit, and operators of events must now implement protective measures similar to those that have become commonplace at sports venues across the globe.[30]

In order to address the potential threats facing esports events, managers should adopt written procedures, develop emergency action plans, and train staff to identify possible unusual activity. Many of the necessary procedures can be adapted from the traditional sports and events world. However, competitors and organizations may also be better equipped to identify unusual behavior from actual competitors or spectators because of the close-knit nature of the esports community.

The rise in popularity of esports has meant that outside groups are likely to continue to seek a way to attach themselves to the activity in an effort to ride on the industry's coattails. However, esports as an industry is not necessarily a perfect fit for all organizations, particularly some traditional sports organizations. Concerns over violence have long followed video gaming, and as it is unlikely that game makers will abandon the production of violent content, the subject will remain controversial for the foreseeable future. While there may be a lack of correlation between video games and violent behavior, tournament organizers and event hosts must be prepared for a potential threat in a way similar to how the organizers of other large-scale gatherings prepare for such threats.

30. *See* Daniel Arken, *Jacksonville Shooting Puts Spotlight on Booming World of Esports*, NBC News (Aug. 28, 2018), https://www.nbcnews.com/news/us-news/jacksonville-shooting-puts-spotlight-booming-world-esports-n904161.

CHAPTER 8

COLLEGIATE ESPORTS

What Are College Esports?

College esports is the term used to describe the various electronic video game competitions that are restricted to full-time college students who represent their respective schools.[1] Like professional esports, the "sports" for collegiate esports are the actual video games used for competitive play, which are the intellectual property of game producers.[2] In most instances, the game producers are also involved in or are the primary party operating the college esports tournaments or leagues.[3] Instead of awarding cash prizes to players, however, collegiate esports tournaments typically provide players with scholarships or prizes intended to cover educational expenses.[4]

The teams competing in college esports tournaments are either (a) privately-formed recreational teams, (b) club teams, or (c) varsity programs.[5] The first type is the most informal or unofficial and typically originates from friend groups composed of those who attend the same

1. Thomas A. Baker III & John T. Holden, *College Esports: A Model for NCAA Reform*, 70 S.C. L. REV. 55, 59 (2018).

2. Dan L. Burk, *Owning e-Sports: Proprietary Rights in Professional Computer Gaming*, 161 U. PA. L. REV. 1535, 1536–37 (2013).

3. For example, see League of Legends College, which is a championship series owned and operated by Riot, the game producer for League of Legends.

4. Baker & Holden, *supra* note 1, at 60.

5. *Id.*

school and who agree to compete in tournaments together. Due to the involvement of teams that are not officially sponsored by the schools they represent, the possibility exists for multiple teams to represent the same university in the same tournament. The second type of college esports team is the club team. Club sports are those that are not varsity squads but are official teams of students who receive funding through the school to form a club around their chosen activity. The third type of college esports program involves varsity esports teams. Varsity esports programs are those that closely resemble traditional varsity intercollegiate sports (e.g., college basketball, football, swimming, etc.). The resemblance is found in how varsity esports programs recruit students to campus and provide scholarships in exchange for participation on esports teams that are resourced and operated by the institution.[6]

In 2014, Robert Morris University in Illinois became the first institution to embrace collegiate esports through the creation of a varsity program.[7] In 2016, the University of California-Irvine followed Robert Morris's lead by becoming the first public university to both establish an esports program and to open and operate a college esports arena.[8] In 2019, Caldwell University became the first to establish an esports business management degree program.[9] While Caldwell University may have been the first to implement a formal business program in esports, many of the earliest adopters of varsity college esports did so through the formation of programs developed to address declining rates in student enrollment by attracting students to campus who had an interest in electronic gaming.[10]

No matter the driving influence behind program creation, there exists a swelling wave of program expansion within collegiate esports. In 2019, ESPN estimated that approximately one hundred varsity esports programs

6. For a discussion on the traits used to distinguish varsity programs from club or recreational sports, see Thomas A. Baker III, *Recreational Sports Law*, *in* The Oxford Handbook of American Sports Law 411, 415 (Michael A. McCann ed., 2018). For cases making this distinction, see *Ochoa v. Cal. State Univ.*, 85 Cal. Rptr. 2d 768 (Ct. App. 1999); *Kyriazis v. Univ. of W. Va.*, 450 S.E.2d 649 (W. Va. 1994).

7. A.P. *Gamers to Get College Scholarships*, ESPN (Jun. 20, 2014), https://www.espn.com/chicago/college-sports/story/_/id/11113637/robert-morris-university-offers-esports-scholarships-league-legends-video-game.

8. Jess Conditt, *UC Irvine Debuts the First Public College Esports Arena in the US*, Endgadget (Sep. 14, 2016), https://www.engadget.com/2016-09-14-esports-arena-college-uc-irvine-leage-of-legends.html.

9. *The Rise of Collegiate Esports Programs*, Athletic Director U, https://www.athleticdirectoru.com/articles/the-rise-of-collegiate-esports-programs/.

10. *Id.*

were operative in the U.S.[11] In 2021, Uni Esports Group estimated that the number of varsity programs had expanded to more than two hundred.[12] Accordingly, the number of varsity esports programs ballooned from 0 to more than 200 in only seven years.

The tremendous growth of collegiate esports is evident, but there exists no uniform approach to where these programs are situated within the college or university in which they are housed. Some programs are based within the college or university's athletic department, but the majority are located in departments for student affairs or within academic departments, centers, or institutes.[13] In fact, a study conducted in 2018 of the first fifty varsity esports programs found that only twenty percent of these programs were housed within athletic departments.[14] The location of the varsity esports program matters because of the differences in how academic programs are managed and resourced in comparison to athletic departments. Another concern related to the placement of the varsity esports program within the institution involves the application of Title IX and its requirement of equity in the distribution of academic opportunities at institutions that receive federal financial assistance. Scholarships awarded by varsity esports programs positioned in academic departments are treated as merit-based and are omitted from counting towards the athletic department's athletic opportunities.[15]

Regulating Collegiate Esports

Prior to 2016, all regulation of collegiate esports occurred at the tournament or league levels. Even now, tournament and league producers such as Collegiate Starleague (CSL), College League of Legends (CLL), and Tespa continue to set both the rules for play as well as the qualifying and standards for those who participate in their competitions. For some leagues, like Riot Games with CLL, the game producers play a significant role in the

11. Sean Morrison, *List of Varsity Esports Programs Spans North America*, ESPN (May 15, 2018), https://www.espn.com/esports/story/_/id/21152905/college-esports-list-varsity-esports-programs-north-america.

12. Athletic Director U, *supra* note 9.

13. For example, Georgia State positioned its varsity esports program within its Creative Media Industries Institute.

14. Baker & Holden, *supra* note 1, at 65.

15. Derek R. Walton, Leanne M. Lower-Hoppe, and Marc Horger, *Do Esports Classify as Intercollegiate Sport? Legal Analysis of Title IX*, 13 J. Issues Intercollegiate Athletics, 94, 95 (2020).

operation of collegiate competitions.[16] While it is not uncommon for private businesses to involve themselves in the production of college competitions via official sponsorships, the game producers actually own the games that are played, and this is a level of involvement that is unique from anything that exists within other intercollegiate sports.

In 2016, the National Association of Collegiate Esports (NACE) formed with the purpose of "developing the structure and tools needed to advance collegiate esports in the varsity space."[17] The NACE presently fills a role within collegiate esports that is similar to the regulatory service provided by the NCAA. Like the NCAA, the NACE is also a member-formed and member-managed association. And like the NCAA, the NACE also operates under a constitution and has developed a set of bylaws for its Official Policy Handbook, which is similar in purpose to the *NCAA's Division I Manual*. There are, however, very significant differences between the NACE and the NCAA in terms of how each regulates its members and students.

Amateurism

First and foremost, there are critical differences between the role of amateurism in traditional sports sponsored by the NCAA and the concept's importance and application in esports. For the NCAA, amateurism is at the core of all of its sport opportunities. In fact, the organization that we now identify as the NCAA was founded, in large part, to address safety concerns within college football by imposing eligibility rules requiring that athletes be unpaid students rather than paid "ringers."[18] Thus, the importance of amateurism traces back to the NCAA's establishment. The same is not true for college esports, which initially grew out of the tournaments and leagues that, for the most part, had no concern about whether college esports participants have earned money through electronic gaming.

---

16. For more information on CLL, see, https://rsaa.riotgames.com/2021-college-league-of-legends-season/.

17. *About*, Nat'l Ass'n of Collegiate Esports, https://nacesports.org/about/ (last visited Apr. 12, 2021).

18. *See* Thomas A. Baker III., Marc Edelman, & Nicholas M. Watanabe, *Debunking the NCAA's Myth that Amateurism Conforms with Antitrust Law: A Legal and Statistical Analysis*, 85 Tenn. L. Rev. 661, 663 (2018).

Even now, NCAA bylaws mandate that only amateurs are eligible for its competitions and define what is intended by the word "amateur" based on member-approved eligibility requirements.[19] Specifically, the NCAA bylaws prohibit athletes from receiving compensation for their athletic participation that exceeds the amounts needed for room and board, tuition, fees, necessary course books,[20] and a stipend set for other costs that should not exceed the cost of tuition for the athlete's school.[21] Furthermore, with a few exceptions,[22] college athletes may be deemed ineligible by the NCAA for either their involvement in professional sports or their receipt of impermissible compensation prior to them becoming college athletes.[23] The NCAA also restricts its college athletes from profiting from commercial uses of their names, images, and likenesses (NIL).[24]

While the NCAA's concept of amateurism has never been enforced by esports leagues and tournaments, the NACE values the amateur status of its college athletes and limits the compensation that schools provide to tuition, room and board, supplies needed for class, and medical and dental expenses incurred while enrolled and on the team.[25] Note that presently, the NACE is actually *more* restrictive than the NCAA in terms of what schools may provide to their students as there is no cost-of-attendance adjustment stipend yet permitted by the NACE. The NACE, however, does not deny eligibility to those who have competed for or won prize money in esports tournaments prior to their becoming a collegiate esports player.[26] Given the nature and culture around esports, too many current college esports players would be ineligible if the NACE prohibited the participa-

---

19. Nat'l Collegiate Athletic Ass'n, 2020–2021 NCAA Division I Manual, Bylaw 12.1.1, at 61 (2017) [hereinafter NCAA Manual], http://www.ncaapublications.com/productdownloads/D118.pdf.

20. *Scholarships*, NCAA, http://www.ncaa.org/student-athletes/future/scholarships.

21. *Cost of Attendance Q&A*, NCAA, https://www.ncaa.com/news/ncaa/article/2015-09-03/cost-attendance-qa.

22. For example, college athletes are permitted to compete in the Olympics or on national teams and receive money as part of their involvement for actual and necessary expenses. NCAA Manual, Bylaw 12.2.3.2.5.

23. NCAA Manual, at Bylaw 12.01.3, at 61. Specifically, NCAA rules state that college athletes are ineligible for the loss of amateur status for doing any of the following: student-athlete compensation in any form for that sport; acceptance of a promise for future payment for performance in that sport following completion of NCAA eligibility; signing a contract to play professional sports; compensation or financial assistance provided by a sports organization based on athletic skill; competitive play for a professional team; entering a professional league draft; or entering an agreement with a sports agent. *Id.* at Bylaw 12.1.2.

24. NCAA Manual, Bylaw 12.5.2.1, at 75.

25. NAC ESPORTS HANDBOOK Bylaw art. VIII §A, at 13.

26. Bryce Blum, *The NCAA and Esports Don't Mix—But Soon, They Might Have To*, ESPN (Oct. 23, 2017), http://www.espn.com/college-sports/story/_/id/21121852/the-ncaaesports-mix-soon-to.

tion of players who had won prizes in previous esports tournaments.[27] Additionally, the NACE does not restrict its athletes from benefiting from commercial uses of their NIL, as the NCAA has historically done.[28] This difference between the NACE and the NCAA is critical because esports players are able to stream their gameplay on social media platforms such as Twitch and YouTube, and the NACE does not prohibit them from monetizing their streams.[29]

The difference between the NACE and NCAA is also significant because the NCAA's historic NIL policy has generated substantial criticism from pundits who argue that it is unfair for the NCAA and its membership to build a multi-billion dollar industry around the use of college athlete NIL while simultaneously denying college athletes their individual and collective publicity rights to the commercial value generated from the use of their NILs.[30] More significantly, the perceived unfairness within the NCAA's historic NIL restrictions has led to state legislative efforts in approximately 28 states that would render the NCAA's NIL policy powerless.[31] Additionally, Congress has responded to the state legislative efforts with interest in federal legislation that would set guidelines for college athlete NIL use as a means to render moot the state laws that are pending and have already passed.[32] In response, the NCAA created a working group—the NCAA Division I Name, Image, and Likeness Legislative Solutions Group—to develop a proposal for changing the NCAA's present policy so as to afford college athletes more economic freedom.[33] The NCAA's NIL Solutions Group returned to the members with a

---

27. *Id.*

28. *Id.*

29. Baker & Holden, *supra* note 1, at 82; Lisa K. Levine, *Jeremy Bloom v. National Collegiate Athletic Association and the University of Colorado: All Sports Are Created Equal; Some Are Just More Equal than Others.* 56 Case W. Res. L. Rev. 721, 725 (2005).

30. *See generally*, James J. Landry & Thomas Baker, *Change or Be Changed: A Proposal for the NCAA to Combat Corruption and Unfairness by Proactively Reforming Its Regulation of Athlete Publicity Rights.* 9 NYU J. Intell. Prop. & Ent. Law 1 (2019); Taylor Branch, The Shame of College Sports, Atlantic (Oct. 2011), https://www.theatlantic.com/magazine/archive/2011/10/the-shame-of-college-sports/308643/.

31. *Tracker: Name, Image and Likeness Legislation*, businessofcollegesports.com, https://businessofcollegesports.com/tracker-name-image-and-likeness-legislation-by-state/ (last updated Sep. 3, 2020).

32. Eric Olson, *Congressman: No NCAA Antitrust Exemption in Athlete Pay Bill*, U.S. News (Jun. 4, 2020), https://www.usnews.com/news/sports/articles/2020-06-04/congressman-no-ncaa-antitrust-exemption-in-athlete-pay-bill.

33. *Board of Governors Start Process to Enhance Name, Image and Likeness Opportunities*, NCAA (Oct. 29, 2019), http://www.ncaa.org/about/resources/media-center/news/board-governors-starts-process-enhance-name-image-and-likeness-opportunities.

22-page proposal that would permit college athletes to endorse products, promote private lessons or camps and their own business activities, receive compensation for autograph sessions, solicit funds through crowdfunding for non-profits or charities, and enter into relationships with agents for the purpose of seeking advice on NIL ventures and to assist in contract negotiations for those ventures.[34] A January 2021 vote on the group's proposal, however, was tabled, purportedly because the NCAA received a letter from the Department of Justice that informed the NCAA that it was being monitored "closely" by the DOJ's antitrust division for conduct related to curtailing "robust competition" for athlete services.[35] With all the controversy surrounding its NIL restrictions, the NCAA could turn to the NACE's example by adopting a similar "hands-off" approach that permits college athletes the same NIL rights that ordinary students enjoy. By doing this, the NCAA would moot any state or federal legislation on the topic.

Unfortunately for the NCAA, its legal problems extend from its historic restriction of college athlete NIL use to include the compensation limits that prevent athletes from earning more than the cost-of-attending their respective schools.[36] In fact, the extension of grant-in-aid to include the full cost-of-attendance resulted from a United States Court of Appeals for the Ninth Circuit decision in *O'Bannon v. NCAA*.[37] In *O'Bannon*, the Ninth Circuit addressed an antitrust challenge to the NCAA's amateurism rules, in part, by holding that the provision of amounts of money to athletes that is in addition to what is needed for books, fees, room and board, would not threaten the NCAA's interests in preserving its concept of amateurism.[38] The NACE, however, does not include a cost-of-attendance adjustment in its compensation restrictions, which could open the association up to antitrust liability if that specific constraint is challenged by plaintiff athletes. Nevertheless, an off-setting measure arguably exists in the fact that the NACE permits athletes to keep award money earned by students in esports tournaments and excludes the amount earned from

34. Gregg E. Clifton & Iciss Rose Tillis, *NCAA Takes Additional Steps Toward Ratification of Name, Image, and Likeness Legislation*, Nat'l L. Rev. (Oct. 15, 2020), https://www.natlawreview.com/article/ncaa-takes-additional-steps-toward-ratification-name-image-and-likeness-legislation#::text=While%20NIL%20laws%20have%20already,still%20appear%20to%20be%20more.

35. *Id.*

36. At the time of writing, the NCAA was engaged in multiple antitrust actions, each challenging its compensation limits. The most-prominent of the cases, *NCAA v. Alston*, was decided by the U.S. Supreme Court against the NCAA on June 21, 2021. *See NCAA v.* Alston, 141 S. CT. 2121 (2021).

37. *See* O'Bannon v. Nat'l Collegiate Athletic Ass'n, 802 F.3d 1049 (9th Cir. 2015).

38. *Id.* at 1079.

financial aid calculations.[39] The NACE would be wise to closely monitor what happens in NCAA-related litigation involving athlete compensation limits and be prepared to adjust its policies to match what is demanded from the NCAA by the courts.

Academic Eligibility

The basic eligibility requirement for any competitor within collegiate esports is that the person be a student at the school for the team the student represents. The tournaments and leagues are in some ways similar, but each varies from the others in terms of what is required for participant eligibility. For example, the CLL and CSL each require that college esports participants be students in good academic and disciplinary standing, and the CSL requires that all participants be full-time students at their schools.[40]

The NACE, however, provides consistency for its members by requiring more than just proof of enrollment and good standing. The NACE includes within its rules a minimum ACT score of 18 or SAT score of 860 and a minimum high school grade point average of 2.00 or higher on a 4.00 scale.[41] On top of the 2.00 GPA requirement, the NACE requires that students finish in the upper half of their high school class ranking in order to be eligible.[42] Furthermore, the NACE requires evidence of eligibility in the form of high school transcripts or an official letter written by the school's headmaster or principal.[43] The NACE also limits the duration of eligibility to compete to five seasons in esports (or ten semesters).[44]

By comparison, the NCAA has far more detailed academic eligibility requirements than what exists within esports and the NACE.[45] As with the NACE, the NCAA also requires a minimum GPA and a qualifying score on either the ACT or SAT standardized tests for college admission.[46] The difference, however, is found in how the NCAA has implemented a

---

39. NAC ESPORTS HANDBOOK, Bylaw art. VIII, §A, at 13.

40. Eligibility Rules, COLLEGE LEAGUE OF LEGENDS, https://d33jl3tgfli0fm.cloudfront.net/college-league-of-legends/2020/rules.pdf.; LOL Rules: Season Guide to CSL Fall 2018–Spring 2019, CSTARLEAGUE.COM, https://drive.google.com/file/d/1zHSpgxFeM8AuH9GGQBi7CGv_XqZ64MlQ/view.

41. NAC ESPORTS HANDBOOK, Bylaw art. II, at 9-10.

42. *Id.*

43. *Id.*

44. *Id.*

45. Baker & Holden, *supra* note 1, at 69.

46. NCAA MANUAL, Bylaw 14.3.1.1.3, at 165.

sliding-scale standard that permits students to offset lower standardized test scores with higher GPAs or vice versa.[47] The NCAA shifted to a sliding scale in reaction to claims made in *Cureton v. NCAA*, a lawsuit within which college athlete plaintiffs argued that the NCAA's previous policy, which made use of a cutoff score of 820 on the SAT, resulted in disparate impact discrimination against minority athletes in violation of Title VI of the Civil Rights Act of 1964.[48] While the NCAA ultimately prevailed in *Cureton*, the membership, nevertheless, agreed to change its policy to be more inclusive and less discriminatory.[49] In addition to a sliding scale, the NCAA also implemented an academic redshirt policy in the wake of *Cureton* that permits students who failed to academically qualify under the NCAA's rules to still practice with their teams so long as they sit out for the first year of competition.[50] Accordingly, the NACE may also want to consider adopting a sliding-scale standard for determining academic eligibility so as to avoid the potential for criticism that claims the current standards are discriminatory to minority esports players. A sliding scale permits athletes with higher GPAs to qualify despite lower scores on standardized tests that have been criticized as prejudicial to non-Asian minorities.[51]

Another component of academic eligibility where NACE may seek to look to the NCAA for guidance involves the adoption of specific high school course requirements.[52] For domestic students, NCAA rules require that college athletes must have completed ten of sixteen required core courses, seven of which involve English, math, and science subjects.[53] International students, however, are under a different standard and must qualify based on the NCAA's international student policy.[54] Once on campus, the NCAA continues with its academic oversight through rules that demand students to make progress towards degree development; including a minimum number of hours for degree and minor,[55] and a

47. *Id.*

48. *See* Cureton v. Nat'l Collegiate Athletic Ass'n, 198 F.3d 107, 108 (3d Cir. 1999).

49. See Thomas A. Baker III & Daniel P. Connaughton, *Cureton v. NCAA: A Blow-by-Blow Account of the Landmark Title VI Challenges to the NCAA and Their Recent Implications*, 13 J. Legal Aspects Sport, 145, 175 (2003).

50. NCAA Manual, Bylaw 14.3.1.1, at 164.

51. *See* Joseph A. Soares, The Scandal of Standardized Tests: Why We Need to Drop the SAT and ACT (2020).

52. Baker & Holden, *supra* note 1, at 70.

53. NCAA Manual, Bylaw 14.3.1.1, at 164.

54. *Id.*

55. NCAA Manual, Bylaw 14.4.3.1.7, at 172.

requirement that students meet a percentage of their degree by the time they reach their third year of academic/athletic eligibility.[56] The NACE might consider adding more in the way of degree requirements that go beyond merely requiring that athletes remain in good academic and disciplinary standing. The problem with adding these standards is that they are complicated to implement and enforce, and they would require substantial time and effort from not only the member institutions but also the NACE.[57] Still, the NACE may want to consider additional academic rigor in the form of course requirements for eligibility and proof that students are making progress towards their degrees as a way to ensure that collegiate esports programs adhere to their purported academic missions.

Transfers

A stark contrast exists between what is required by the NACE and the NCAA for college athlete transfers. For this subject, however, it is the NACE's more scaled-down approach that the NCAA should consider adopting. The NCAA is currently in the process of revising its policies that control athlete transfers. Currently, the NCAA allows college athletes a one-time transfer for all sports, with the exception of men's football, basketball, and hockey.[58] The NCAA requires athletes for those three sports to sit out for one season of competition before competing for their new school unless the athlete receives a waiver from the NCAA.[59] To assist college athletes with their transfers, the NCAA has developed an application it calls the Transfer Portal that manages the transfer process for college athletes across its three divisions.[60]

The NCAA's transfer policies have been the subject of multiple lawsuits[61] and have recently caught the attention of the Department of Justice, which included the NCAA's transfer policies as a subject it is monitoring

---

56. NCAA Manual, Bylaw 14.4.3.2, at 172.

57. Baker & Holden, *supra* note 1, at 71.

58. NCAA Manual, Bylaw 14.5.5.2.10, at 185.

59. NCAA Manual, Bylaw 14.5.5.2.10(a), at 185.

60. Nat'l Collegiate Athletic Ass'n, NCAA Transfer Portal User Guide Division II and III 2 (Version 2.0 2019), https://ncaa.s3.amazonaws.com/files/apps/transfer/DI_DIII_TransferPortal_UserGuide_v2.pdf.

61. *See* Deppe v. Nat'l Collegiate Athletic Ass'n, 893 F.3d 498 (7th Cir. 2018); Smith v. Nat'l Collegiate Athletic Ass'n, 266 F.3d 152 (3d Cir. 2001) (discussing the case of a college graduate who had remaining eligibility and wanted to transfer to, and play for, her graduate institution).

closely in the warning letter sent to the NCAA.[62] The NCAA defends the additional restrictions that it imposes on the transfer process for the sports of men's basketball, football, and hockey, with the justification that its policy helps transferring students acclimate to life at their new school.[63] This reasoning, however, has been criticized as a pretext for protecting team stability at the behest of NCAA coaches.[64] The NCAA is currently in the process of reconsidering its transfer rules based on continued external criticism that the regulations are too restrictive for men's basketball, hockey, and football athletes.

In reconsidering its transfer policies, the NCAA might want to look to the way transfers are regulated within collegiate esports. The only discernable transfer restriction imposed by the leading collegiate esports leagues and tournaments is one that prohibits players from competing for two different teams in the same season.[65] Accordingly, the most popular collegiate esports leagues and tournaments afford their players the same degree of mobility that is enjoyed by other students.[66]

The NACE, however, is somewhat more restrictive than the various leagues and tournaments in that it imposes on players the condition that they must complete a "permission to contact" form, which must be signed by the player's coach and submitted to the NACE ESPORTS national office prior to the player's contact with another NACE school.[67] Once that form is signed and submitted to the NACE, the player then must obtain an "Official NACE ESPORTS Transfer Player Eligibility Statement" from the NACE, which must then be presented to both the player's original and new school.[68] The NACE also places tighter restrictions on players who are transferring from programs at which they were suspended or disciplined. Disciplined athletes must sit out for two semesters at their new academic institution.[69] In terms of remaining eligibility post-transfer, the NACE has a rule that students who were credited with one season of competition for

62. Sarah Polus, *NCAA Tables Name, Image and Likeness Vote After DOJ Warns of Potential Antitrust Violations*, THE HILL (Jan. 12, 2021), https://thehill.com/business-a-lobbying/533830-ncaa-suspends-name-image-and-likeness-vote-after-doj-warns-of-potential.

63. McHale v. Cornell Univ., 620 F. Supp. 67, 68, 68 n.4 (N.D.N.Y. 1985).

64. *See generally*, Kevin May & Chad Seifried, *NCAA transfer rules: Restrictions created to benefit Division IA institutions and hinder student-athletes?*, 6 J. CONTEMPORARY ATHLETICS, 3, 159 (2012).

65. Baker & Holden, *supra* note 1, at 73.

66. *Id.*

67. NAC ESPORTS HANDBOOK, Rule E8, at 12.

68. NAC ESPORTS HANDBOOK, Rule E1, at 11.

69. NAC ESPORTS HANDBOOK, Rule E5, at 11.

one school will be charged with two years of eligibility if that student competes for another school in the same academic year.[70]

Most of the NACE's policies regarding transfer are more perfunctory than restrictive. For example, the form that must be signed by the member institution does not permit the coach for that school to block the player's transfer. If anything, the process serves as a notice requirement and allows for the transfer of information between schools and the NACE concerning any disciplinary action that is pending or controlling over the athlete's existing institution. One rule that might be overly restrictive within the NACE is the one that charges students with two seasons of eligibility for transfers made within the same academic year.[71] Yet, this rule recognizes that it is possible for there to be multiple seasons for esports competition within the same academic year.[72]

Thus, even within the more restrictive NACE, there seems to be substantially more freedom afforded to college esports players than that which is provided to NCAA athletes—particularly those competing in men's basketball, hockey, and football. After all, there is no rule requiring transferring college esports players to sit out unless they were disciplined by the university that they are leaving. This rule serves to prevent disciplined players from escaping responsibility for their misconduct by transferring to a different institution. Similarly, while there are forms that must be completed by the esport player's exiting program, the coaches for that program are unable to interfere with the player's remaining eligibility or restrict the athlete's transfer options by limiting scholarship opportunities post-transfer. In this regard, the transfer policies imposed within the NACE operate as a middle ground between the esports leagues and tournaments, with their extremely liberal rules, and the NCAA, with its hyper-restrictive and very controversial transfer rules that have historically served to prevent free market competition among NCAA member colleges to secure athletes' services.[73]

---

70. NAC ESPORTS HANDBOOK, Rule E7, at 11.

71. *Id.*

72. For example, an esports player may compete within different leagues or in different "sports," meaning that the player competes in tournaments or leagues for multiple game titles.

73. For a more detailed conversation on the controversies related to the NCAA's transfer policies, see Sarah M. Konsky, *An Antitrust Challenge to the NCAA Transfer Rules*, 70 Univ. Chi. L. Rev. 1581, 1587 (2003).

NCAA Involvement in Collegiate Esports

Whether collegiate esports will ever be brought under the broader umbrella of the NCAA, nevertheless, remains an open issue. In 2019, the NCAA confirmed that its board of governors had voted, unanimously, to table any possibility of adding collegiate esports to its offering of intercollegiate athletics.[74] In an interview, NCAA President Mark Emmert listed two primary reasons for why the NCAA had decided to pause efforts to expand into the rapidly growing industry of intercollegiate esports. The first involved the recognition that the majority of competitors within collegiate esports are male, and thus, this could create a Title IX concern for member institutions.[75] The second concern involved Emmert's description of popular video games as misogynistic and violent.[76] Meanwhile, a seemingly third, albeit unstated, concern arguably relates to the disparate economic rights currently afforded to college-age gamers and NCAA athletes, and the NCAA's desire to neither expand economic rights to traditional athletes nor to attempt to curtail them with respect to egamers.

The NCAA tabled its expansion into collegiate esports approximately two years after it issued a request for proposals (RFP) for assistance in evaluating ways, if any, in which the NCAA could involve itself in the business of collegiate esports.[77] The NCAA's RFP, however, made it clear that any move into collegiate esports would be done on the NCAA's terms and according to the NCAA's organizational values.[78] In terms of its values regarding Title IX, critics might point to the fact that the NCAA has a controversial history with regard to both the initial enactment of Title IX and its requirement of substantial proportionality in regards to sport offerings for men's and women's sports.[79] Similarly, critics of the NCAA may argue against its professed opposition to sexual violence by pointing to the NCAA's own assertion that it is not responsible for sanctioning or

---

74. Tom Shad, *NCAA Tables Possibility of Overseeing esports*, USA Today (May 21, 2019), https://www.usatoday.com/story/sports/college/2019/05/21/ncaa-and-esports-not-just-yet-organization-tables-possibility/3751122002/.

75. *Id.*

76. *Id.*

77. Kieran Darcy, *College Esports is the Next Big Thing in Varsity Athletics*, ESPN (Oct. 23, 2017), http://www.espn.com/college-sports/story/_/id/21113602/thenext-big-thing-collegiate-athletics-esports

78. Ben Fischer, *Reaching Out: NCAA Issues RFP for Help Evaluating Possible Role in Esports*, Street & Smith's Sports Bus. Daily (Aug. 31, 2017), https://www.sports businessdaily.com/Daily/Issues/2017/08/31/Colleges/Esports.aspx.

79. For an account of the history of Title IX and the NCAA, including accounts of resistance from member institutions, see Welch Suggs, A Place on the Team: The Triumph and Tragedy of Title IX (2006).

preventing sexual violence that takes place at member institution programs.[80] Thus, the NCAA's purported problems with collegiate esports are seemingly inconsistent with the organization's official positions and conduct.

Still, there is some legitimacy to the NCAA's expressed concerns with regard to the incorporation of esports into intercollegiate athletics. Esports has the potential to be a gender-neutral activity, but substantially more men are involved in competitive gaming than women, and this does pose a Title IX problem for athletic programs that need to expand their women's sports offerings.[81] Furthermore, the NCAA's focus on violence and misogynistic content in games reflect a valid concern surrounding which game titles could be used for esports without displaying mature content that is not suitable for all age groups. Emmert's comment on game content also reflects another issue that could create problems for the NCAA if it were to move into the esports space—specifically, the NCAA's lack of control over the sports it would oversee.

If the NCAA were to sponsor collegiate esports, it would be forced to work with the game producers for the titles. The reason for this is simple—game producers own the games as intellectual property and therefore control the use and reproductions of the games (including reproductions in streamcasts and broadcasts of esports competitions). Thus, unlike its other sport offerings, the NCAA has no control over the constitutive components that make up the sports used for esports (i.e., the video games). Game producers are primarily interested in selling their products, whether those products are the actual video games or items that can be purchased in-game (i.e., "skins"). Accordingly, video game producers incorporate content into their games that appeal to consumers, and this focus will likely take priority over the interests of the NCAA and its membership to make collegiate esports family friendly. Moreover, there is nothing preventing a game producer from ending its involvement in college esports or terminating its game title if doing so benefits the producer financially.

---

80. Scott M. Reid, *NCAA Argues in Sex Abuse Case it Has No Legal Duty to Protect Athletes*, The Orange County Reg. (Jun. 2, 2020), https://www.ocregister.com/2020/06/02/ncaa-argues-in-sex-abuse-case-it-has-no-legal-duty-to-protect-athletes/.

81. Lindsey Darvin, *At Colleges Nationwide, Esports Teams Dominated by Men*, The Conversation (Mar. 12, 2021), https://theconversation.com/at-colleges-nationwide-esports-teams-dominated-by-men-154793.

NACE and the NCAA: Moving Forward

There is little question that the NCAA has extensive experience in conducting intercollegiate athletics.[82] The NCAA has also proven itself capable of both cultivating consumer interest in an intercollegiate sport, and in capitalizing on that interest.[83] Accordingly, there was some degree of cautious optimism when the NCAA issued its RFP to examine how it could become involved in a rapidly-growing new sport phenomena.[84] Yet, the NCAA's decision to table its involvement in college esports might not be a bad thing for college esports. After all, it may be preferable for college esports to grow under the control of a regulatory body that *only* regulates college esports.

The NACE presently provides such an organization in that its only purpose for existence is the regulation of college esports. If the NCAA were to become involved, the interests of esports would need to be balanced against those of the ninety championships the NCAA sponsors across twenty-four other sports.[85] Under the NACE, however, whatever regulation is generated within can be specifically crafted to meet the unique needs and interests of college esports, without reference or concern for the interests of sports that are very different from college esports.

When juxtaposed with the NCAA, another benefit to the NACE may be found in the composition of its membership. The NACE is open to institutions that are members of either the NCAA or the National Association of Intercollegiate Athletics (NAIA).[86] Like the NCAA, the NAIA is also a governing body for intercollegiate sports. However, the NCAA's membership is made up of a lot of prominent research institutions, whereas the NAIA has differentiated its offerings by appealing to teaching colleges, liberal arts colleges, and historically black colleges and universities (HBCUs).[87] If the NCAA were to become involved in the regulation of collegiate esports, it might not do so in a way that is inclusive of the NAIA members within the NACE. Thus, at this point in time, it may make more

---

82. Holden, Edelman, & Baker, *supra* note 1, at 578.

83. *Id.*

84. *See* Blum, *supra* note 26.

85. *See Frequently Asked Questions About the NCAA*, NCAA, https://www.ncaa.org/about/frequently-asked-questions-about-ncaa.

86. *Why Choose NACE?*, The Nat'l Ass'n of Collegiate Esports, https://nacesports.org/get-involved/for-schools/.

87. Marvin Washington, *Field Approaches to Institutional Change: The Evolution of the National Collegiate Athletic Association 1906–1995*, 25 Org. Stud. 393, 400 (2004).

sense to grow collegiate esports under a regulatory association that is expansive enough to capture all potential varsity esports programs.

The involvement of current NCAA members within the NACE highlights that the NCAA could still influence the direction of NACE legislation moving forward. Like the NCAA, the NACE is a member-governed association. As more members of the NCAA join the NACE, the potential for influence increases as members with voting interests may elect to propose and pass legislation within the NACE that resembles what is done within the NCAA.

In sum, with or without the NCAA's direct involvement, college esports continues to grow at a rapid rate. As collegiate esports expands, the NACE will need to adopt new regulatory measures to manage the industry's growth. Accordingly, the regulatory controls over college esports in the future may be very different in both form and application than what exists now.

CHAPTER 9

WOMEN IN ESPORTS

Women's Involvement in Esports and Electronic Gaming

Since the inception of video games and esports, gaming culture has been a boys' club. For example, in 1982, scholars found that 80 percent of men played arcade video games, in comparison to 20 percent of women.[1] Scholars contend that the "larger than expected number of females" who played video games in the early 1980s was only due to the fact that one of the most popular games at the time was *Pac-Man*—a game that did not involve "violence or war."[2] In another survey from the early 1980s, of the 430 college students interviewed, a statistically significant number of women acknowledged their "lower level of skill in video game playing as compared to men."[3]

Despite the low number of female gamers at the beginning of the video game age, women have always participated in the gaming industry behind the scenes. In 1981, Atari's first female coin-operated game programmer, Dona Bailey, co-created the famous arcade game, *Centipede*.[4] The

1. Sidney J. Kaplan, *The Image of Amusement Arcades and Differences in Male and Female Game Playing*, 28 J. POPULAR CULTURE 93, 94 (1983).

2. *Id.*

3. *Id.*

4. International Center for the History of Electronic Games, *A Brief History of Women in Gaming: The 1980s*, GOOGLE ARTS & CULTURE, https://artsandculture.google.com/exhibit/a-brief-history-of-women-in-gaming-the-1980s-the-strong/CwKCGJf3HpdoIg?hl=en.

following year, in 1982, after leaving a job at Atari, Carol Shaw joined Activision, where she created the best-selling jet pilot shooting game, *River Raid*.[5] Several years later, in 1988, Nintendo hired female advertising specialist, Gail Tilden, to create a magazine called *Nintendo Power*, which provided subscribers with tips and tricks on how to master games like *Super Mario Bros*.[6] Today, although the gender gap between male and female gamers is narrowing,[7] a great gender disparity still exists in both the recreational gaming and professional esports spaces. For example, boys spend almost twice as long as girls gaming each week, and boys play games like *FIFA* using gaming consoles, whereas their female counterparts opt for mobile games like *Candy Crush*.[8]

A change in gaming gender dynamics seemed to be on the horizon in 2018, when the Pew Research Center reported an uptick in female gaming, with 83 percent of teenage girls reporting they played video games and 75 percent of these girls sharing that they had access to a gaming console.[9] Although these statistics were initially promising, the increase in gaming by teenage girls coincided with a rise in popularity of Activision's game *Overwatch* and Epic Games's *Fortnite*—both of which feature female characters.[10] At the end of 2020, despite more women playing video games than in any previous decade, the 100 top male gamers earned a total of $192.4 million, whereas the top 100 female games only earned a total of $2.8 million—roughly 70 times less.[11] Additionally, a vast gender disparity exists in the esports streaming space, with Twitch reporting that in 2019, 65 percent of its users were male, and only 35 percent were female.[12]

---

5. *Id.*

6. *Id.*

7. Amanda Lenhart, *Chapter 3: Video Games Are Key Elements in Friendships for Many Boys*, Pew Research Ctr. (Aug. 6, 2015), https://www.pewresearch.org/internet/2015/08/06/chapter-3-video-games-are-key-elements-in-friendships-for-many-boys/.

8. Jenny Anderson, *The gender gap in gaming is closing as more kids get smartphones*, Quartz (Feb. 5, 2020), https://qz.com/1796333/the-gender-gap-in-gaming-is-closing-as-more-kids-get-smartphones/.

9. Monica Anderson & Jingjing Jiang, *Teens, Social Media & Technology 2018*, Pew Research Ctr. (May 31, 2018), https://www.pewresearch.org/internet/2018/05/31/teens-social-media-technology-2018/.

10. *See* Leo Sun, *New study indicates video games aren't just for boys anymore: A Foolish Take*, USA Today (Jun. 23, 2018, 6:00 AM), https://www.usatoday.com/story/money/economy/2018/06/23/video-games-arent-just-for-boys-anymore/36143575/.

11. Danny Howard, *Women In Esports Are Getting Paid Way, Way Less Than Men*, The Gamer (Feb. 8, 2020), https://www.thegamer.com/women-in-esports-are-getting-paid-way-way-less-than-men/.

12. Christina Gough, *Distribution of Twitch users worldwide as of 2nd quarter 2019, by gender*, Statista (Jul. 2, 2020), https://www.statista.com/statistics/633937/twitch-user-gender-worldwide//.

Although still present, the gender gap in esports and recreational video gaming is undoubtedly closing. For example, in 2019, Chiquita Evans was the first female ever drafted into the *NBA 2K* League,[13] and the *Overwatch* League selected female player Kim "Geguri" Se-Yeon for its Shanghai Dragons team.[14] Likewise, in 2019, the *Call of Duty* League appointed former Vice President at the NFL, Johanna Faries, as its Commissioner.[15] That being said, women in esports are the exception rather than the rule.[16] In 2020, three women fought for an opportunity to join the *NBA 2K* League.[17] Unfortunately, none of the women made the team, and all three experienced sexism during the draft process.[18] Amber Sammons reported that male competitors tried to flirt with her, Wendi Fleming explained that the things male competitors said to her were "pretty discouraging," and Hazel Childress explained: "When they find out you're a female it goes downhill from there."[19] Overall, while the barriers of the esports boys' club are slowly breaking down and the industry has made great strides, the world of professional esports still faces many challenges that limit its ability to offer female players an equitable playing field. Namely, this chapter will explore the issues of sexual harassment, genderfication, and lack of professional play opportunities, in turn.

---

13. Brando Simeo Starkey, *Chiquita Evans is a trailblazer as the first black woman drafted in the NBA 2k League*, The Undefeated (Mar. 6, 2019), https://theundefeated.com/features/chiquita-evans-is-a-trailblazer-as-the-first-black-woman-drafted-in-the-nba-2k-league/. Unfortunately, Se-yeon no longer plays for the *Overwatch* League. *See* Cass Marshall, *Overwatch pro player Geguri leaves the Shanghai Dragons*, Polygon (Oct. 26, 2020, 11:14 AM), https://www.polygon.com/2020/10/26/21534413/overwatch-league-geguri-shanghai-dragons-2020-free-agent.

14. Kevin Webb, *A gamer tried to go pro by pretending to be a woman, and the scandal exposed an ugly truth about esports*, Business Insider (Jan. 12, 2019, 12:19 PM), https://www.businessinsider.com/ellie-overwatch-women-esports-2019-1.

15. Adam Fitch, *Johanna Faries named as Commissioner of Call of Duty Esports*, Esports Insider (Jul. 9, 2019), https://esportsinsider.com/2019/07/johanna-faries-commissioner-call-of-duty/.

16. *See* Tatiana Tacca, *Women are big—and underserved—esports fans. Here's how to market to them*, Venture Beat (Dec. 10, 2019, 3:40 PM), https://venturebeat.com/2019/12/10/women-are-big-and-underserved-esports-fans-heres-how-to-market-to-them/.

17. Noah Smith, *Three women dreamed of joining the NBA 2K League. The road to the draft was a gauntlet of abuse and adversity.*, Wash. Post (Feb. 24, 2020, 12:52 PM), https://www.washingtonpost.com/video-games/esports/2020/02/24/three-women-dreamed-joining-nba-2k-league-road-draft-was-a-gauntlet-abuse-adversity/.

18. *Id.*

19. *Id.*

Sexual Harassment Explained

Background of Sexual Harassment Claims and Title VII

To better understand the unequal treatment that female gamers in professional esports face, this section looks to the law behind claims of sexual harassment in an employment context. Congress enacted Title VII of the Civil Rights Act of 1964 to eradicate "discrimination in the workplace on the basis of race, color, religion, sex, or national origin."[20] The critical inquiry behind Title VII claims is "whether members of one sex are exposed to disadvantageous terms or conditions of employment to which members of the other sex are not exposed."[21] Title VII applies to employers with 15 or more employees and requires a plaintiff to file his or her claims with the Equal Employment Opportunity Commission (EEOC) within 180 days of the discriminatory act occurring.[22] An employee's Title VII sexual harassment claim can be brought against a supervisor, an agent of the employer, or even a co-worker.[23]

Even though it is now common to think of sexual harassment as a form of employment discrimination,[24] it was not until 1986, in *Meritor Savings Bank v. Vinson*,[25] that the Supreme Court determined that sexual harassment constituted a form of sex discrimination prohibited by Title VII.[26] In *Meritor* the Court explained that Title VII's ban on employment practices that discriminate on the basis of sex with respect to "terms, conditions, or privileges of employment"[27] extends to sex-based discrimination that creates a hostile or abusive working environment."[28] Although in *Meritor*, the Supreme Court identified two forms of sexual harassment —quid pro quo harassment and what is known as a "hostile work environment"—claims of a "hostile work environment" are more widespread.[29] Moreover, while quid pro quo and hostile work environment are

---

20. Bostock v. Clayton Cty., 140 S. Ct. 1731, 1737 (2020).

21. Marion G. Crain, Pauline T. Kim & Michael Selmi, Work Law: Cases and Materials, 639 (3d ed. 2015).

22. *Id.* at 565.

23. *Facts About Sexual Harassment*, U.S. Equal Emp. Opportunity Comm'n, https://www.eeoc.gov/publications/facts-about-sexual-harassment (last visited Nov. 9, 2020).

24. *See* Crain, Kim & Selmi, *supra* note 21, at 630.

25. Meritor Sav. Bank v. Vinson, 447 U.S. 57 (1986).

26. Crain, Kim & Selmi, *supra* note 21, at 630.

27. Meritor, 447 U.S. at 66.

28. Crain, Kim & Selmi, *supra* note 21, at 634.

29. *Id.* at 630. Quid pro quo harassment occurs "when sex becomes a condition of employment." *Id.*

two theoretically distinct claims, these two types of harassment may occur simultaneously.[30] For example, the two claims become intertwined in a situation where a supervisor abuses his or her authority over employment decisions by creating implicit threats if a subordinate refuses sexual advances or does not participate in sexual conduct.[31]

Nearly seven years after *Meritor*, in *Harris v. Forklift Systems, Inc.*,[32] the Supreme Court elaborated on "hostile work environment," explaining that when establishing a hostile environment claim, "a plaintiff need not demonstrate that she had suffered 'severe psychological injury.'"[33] Instead, determining whether behavior rises to a level that violates Title VII is a fact-intensive inquiry.[34] Relevant factors include the frequency and severity of the discriminatory conduct, whether it is physically threatening or humiliating, and whether it "unreasonably interferes with an employee's work performance."[35] Thereafter, in 2008, the First Circuit elaborated on the specific circumstances that give rise to a hostile work environment.[36] According to the First Circuit, to bring a sexual harassment claim under a theory of a hostile working environment, "[a] worker need not be propositioned, touched offensively, or harassed by sexual innuendo in order to have been sexually harassed."[37] The court also shared that "harassing conduct need not be motivated by sexual desire to support an inference of discrimination on the basis of sex."[38] The EEOC supports the First Circuit's contentions, as it similarly clarifies that harassment does *not* have to be of a sexual nature to violate Title VII.[39] Instead, according to the EEOC, sexual harassment can occur simply on the basis of "offensive remarks about a person's sex."[40]

---

30. *Policy Guidance on Current Issues of Sexual Harassment*, U.S. Equal Emp. Opportunity Comm'n, https://www.eeoc.gov/laws/guidance/policy-guidance-current-issues-sexual-harassment (last visited Nov. 10, 2020).

31. *Id.*

32. Harris v. Forklift Sys., Inc., 510 U.S. 17 (1993).

33. *Id.* at 22.

34. *See* Crain, Kim & Selmi, *supra* note 21, at 631.

35. *Id.*

36. *Id.*

37. Billings v. Town of Grafton, 515 F.3d 39, 48 (1st Cir. 2008).

38. *Id.* at 51.

39. *Sexual Harassment*, U.S. Equal Emp. Opportunity Comm'n, https://www.eeoc.gov/sexual-harassment (last visited Nov. 9, 2020).

40. *Id.*

Liability and Potential Issues in the Esports Context

In esports, the confusion surrounding the employee versus independent contractor distinction sheds light on which teams and leagues may be liable for the sexual harassment faced by their players. According to the EEOC, an employer "is automatically liable for harassment by a supervisor that results in a negative employment action such as termination, failure to promote or hire, and loss of wages."[41] In esports, it is likely that players who play for prominent leagues such as the *League of Legends* Championship Series (LCS), *Call of Duty* League (CDL), and *Overwatch League* (OWL) are employees as opposed to independent contractors.[42] As such, pursuant to EEOC guidelines, these prominent professional esports leagues would be liable if their players endured sexual harassment from coaches or league officials.[43] In the case of smaller esports leagues, however, the employer versus independent contractor distinction is ambiguous,[44] and therefore league liability for sexual harassment is uncertain.

While more minor leagues and teams may not be liable for sexual harassment based on EEOC guidelines, even an independent contractor may engender sexual harassment liability issues for these organizations.[45] For example, in a growing number of jurisdictions like New York and Maryland, state employment discrimination laws now offer independent contractors the same protections as employees.[46] In other states, such as California and Washington, independent contractors enjoy some protections, but not the same level of protection as employees.[47]

---

41. *Harassment*, U.S. Equal Emp. Opportunity Comm'n, https://www.eeoc.gov/harassment (last visited Nov. 10, 2020).

42. *See* Rebecca R. Rosenthal, *A Tough Pill to Swallow: Making the Case for Why eSports Leagues Must Adopt Strict Banned Substance Policies to Prevent Disability Discrimination*, 2021 Va. Sports & Ent. L. J. (forthcoming Spring 2021).

43. *Compare* U.S. Equal Emp. Opportunity Comm'n, *supra* note 41 (indicating that an employer is automatically liable for the negative employment actions directed by an employer's supervisors), *with* Rosenthal, *supra* note 7 (emphasizing that in professional esports, players of prominent leagues such as the LCS, CDL, and OWL, are employees of the leagues for whom they play).

44. *See* Jonathan Stoler, *10 Labor and Employment Considerations in Esports*, Sheppard Mullin (Jun. 12, 2019), https://www.mygamecounsel.com/2019/06/articles/esports/labor-employment-considerations-esports-athletes//.

45. Quinn D'Isa, *It's Groundhog Day: Esports Confronts Another #MeToo Moment*, The National Law Review (Dec. 3, 2020), https://www.natlawreview.com/article/it-s-groundhog-day-esports-confronts-another-metoo-moment.

46. *Id.*

47. *See* Cal. Gov't Code §12940(j); Marquis v. City of Spokane, 130 Wash. 2d 97, 101, 108 (1996) (explaining that under the broad protections of Washington's Law Against Discrimination (WLAD) "an independent contractor may bring an action for discrimination in the making or performance of a

New York state law is relevant to the world of professional esports because the New York Subliners—a team within the *Call of Duty* League franchise—is based in New York City.[48] California law is also applicable in the context of sexual harassment because the vast majority of leagues and game developers call California home.[49] The New York State Human Rights Law enacted in 2018 and revised in 2019, prohibits an employer from permitting "unlawful discrimination against [certain] non-employees in its workplace," if the "employer, its agents or supervisors knew or should have known" that the non-employee "was subjected to an unlawful discriminatory practice" in the workplace, and "the employer failed to take immediate and appropriate corrective action."[50] Under California civil rights law, it is unlawful for an employer . . . because of sex, gender, [or] gender identity . . . to harass . . . a person providing services."[51] In California, harassment of a person providing services "shall be unlawful if the entity, or its agents or supervisors, knows or should have known of this conduct and fails to take immediate and appropriate corrective action."[52] As a whole, despite the fact that smaller esports leagues and teams may not be subject to federal legislation surrounding sexual harassment like Title VII, depending on the state in which a team or league is located, it may be subject to liability on the basis of state statutes.

A Substantive Guide on Sexual Harassment in Esports

With a background understanding of sexual harassment law and state-specific liability, this chapter next turns to address the issue of sexual harassment in esports. On June 23, 2020, the *New York Times* reported that 70 people in the gaming industry—nearly all of whom were women—came forward alleging they had experienced gender-based discrimination,

---

contract . . . where the alleged discrimination is based on sex, race, creed, color, national origin or disability.").

48. *See* Cody Luongo, *Vindex's Belong to establish gaming venues in NYC through Andbox deal*, Esports Insider (Jul. 29, 2020), https://esportsinsider.com/2020/07/vindex-belong-andbox/.

49. *See* Matt Fernandez, *California Risks Losing Its Lead in the Video Game Industry*, Variety (Feb. 13, 2018, 5:26 PM), https://variety.com/2018/digital/news/milken-institute-california-video-game-1202697483/.

50. N.Y. Exec. L. §296-d (2019).

51. Cal. Gov't Code §12940 (j).

52. *Id.*

harassment, and sexual assault while working or playing in the world of esports.[53] While some of the harassment suffered by these women was recent, for others, it was the first time they chose to speak up and speak out against an industry long plagued by gender-based discrimination and sexual advances.[54] In sum, the *New York Times* article served as a reminder that for women in esports, inequality is endemic.[55] Female gamers experience harassment in chatrooms, on live streams, and at events from teammates, coaches, sponsors, and even game developers.[56] Likewise, women working in the esports industry for leagues and female game developers also experience sexual harassment.[57]

The foundations of the #E-Too movement[58] began in 2014—three years before the #MeToo movement sent waves through Hollywood after actress Ashley Judd accused film producer Harvey Weinstein of sexual harassment.[59] In 2014, the "Gamergate" scandal began in esports, after independent game designer Zoe Quinn released a video game in the form of interactive art called *Depression Quest*, which illustrated the story of a young adult's depression.[60] After the game experienced a surge in popularity, Quinn's ex-boyfriend published a series of blog posts suggesting that

53. Taylor Lorenz & Kellen Browning, *Dozens of Women in Gaming Speak Out About Sexism and Harassment*, N.Y. TIMES (Jun. 23, 2020), https://www.nytimes.com/2020/06/23/style/women-gaming-streaming-harassment-sexism-twitch.html.

54. *See* Keza MacDonald, *Is the video games industry finally reckoning with sexism?*, THE GUARDIAN (Jul. 22, 2020, 3:00 PM), https://www.theguardian.com/games/2020/jul/22/is-the-video-games-industry-finally-reckoning-with-sexism; Associated Press, *Female esports players face routine sexism and toxicity: 'I no longer have power'*, N.Y. POST (Jan. 3, 2019, 12:01 PM), https://nypost.com/2019/01/03/female-esports-players-face-routine-sexism-and-toxicity-i-no-longer-have-power/.

55. Liz Richardson, *Esports is having its #MeToo moment—finally*, DOT ESPORTS (Jun. 24, 2020, 3:42 PM), https://dotesports.com/culture/news/esports-is-having-its-metoo-moment-finally.

56. *See id.*; Rachel E. Greenspan, *Twitch streamer SayNoToRage denies allegations of sexual misconduct by six women, claiming that accusers 'conspired against him despite his previous apology*, INSIDER (Jul. 2, 2020, 11:22 AM), https://www.insider.com/twitch-saynotorage-apologized-for-sexual-harassment-allegations-2020-6.

57. *See* Dean Takahashi, *Sexual abuse allegations rock the game industry again*, VENTUREBEAT (Jun. 24, 2020, 5:15 PM), https://venturebeat.com/2020/06/24/sexual-abuse-allegations-rock-the-game-industry-again/.

58. *See* John T. Holden, Marc Edelman & Thomas A. Baker III, *A Short Treatise on Esports and the Law: How America Regulates Its Next National Pastime*, 2020 U. ILL. L. REV. 509 (2020)

59. Jodi Kantor & Megan Twohey, *Harvey Weinstein Paid Off Sexual Harassment Accusers for Decades*, N.Y. TIMES (Oct. 5, 2017), https://www.nytimes.com/2017/10/05/us/harvey-weinstein-harassment-allegations.html?hp&action=click&pgtype=Homepage&clickSource=story-heading&module=a-lede-package-region&region=top-news&WT.nav=top-news.

60. Caitlin Dewey, *The only guide to Gamergate you will ever need to read*, WASH. POST (Oct. 14, 2014, 5:23 PM), https://www.washingtonpost.com/news/the-intersect/wp/2014/10/14/the-only-guide-to-gamergate-you-will-ever-need-to-read/.

Quinn cheated on him by sleeping with several men in the gaming industry to get ahead in her game design career.[61] What began as a series of blog posts written by an aggrieved ex-boyfriend soon catalyzed a movement wherein anonymous gamers launched vicious attacks against other women in the gaming industry.[62] The next victim was Anita Sarkeesian—a video game critic who began receiving death and rape threats in response to posts on her blog, Feminist Frequency.[63] Sarkeesian's blog focused on the roles of female characters in video games—characters who "often occupy a dual role as both sexual playthings and the perpetual victims of male violence."[64] Shortly thereafter, Jenn Frank, a gaming journalist, and Mattie Brice, a game designer, left the esports industry on account of the harassment they faced.[65]

Four years after Gamergate, in August of 2018, a reporter wrote an article in which she detailed a history of sexual harassment at Riot Games—the company behind *League of Legends*.[66] The article described the "bro culture" at Riot Games's offices, which included a senior male leader regularly grabbing his genitals, and office-wide email chains between male colleagues discussing which female colleagues would be "a good target to sleep with and not call again."[67] Several weeks after the article was published, Riot Games issued an apology to former and current Riot Games players, fans, and employees, detailing how they would clean up the company culture and implement diversity, equity, and inclusion training.[68] In November 2018, a former and a current Riot Games employee filed a class-action lawsuit against Riot Games, alleging gender-based discrimination.[69]

Not even a year later, in August 2019, more sexual harassment allegations infiltrated the esports industry when three women accused three

---

61. *Id.*

62. *Id.*

63. Nathan Rott, *#Gamergate Controversy Fuels Debate on Women and Video Games*, NPR (Sep. 24, 2014, 4:26 PM), https://www.npr.org/sections/alltechconsidered/2014/09/24/349835297/-gamergate-controversy-fuels-debate-on-women-and-video-games.

64. *Id.*

65. *Id.*

66. Cecilia D'Anastasio, *Inside the Culture of Sexism At Riot Games*, Kotaku (Aug. 7, 2018, 3:00 PM), https://kotaku.com/inside-the-culture-of-sexism-at-riot-games-1828165483.

67. *Id.*

68. Emily Rand, *How we got here: A timeline of the Riot Games cultural controversy*, ESPN (Dec. 2, 2019), https://www.espn.com/esports/story/_/id/26686134/how-got-here-line-riot-games-cultural-controversy.

69. *Id.* In early December 2019, Riot settled the gender discrimination class action lawsuit for $10 million.

prominent men in the gaming world of sexual assault and harassment.[70] While news outlets predicted these public accusations could officially begin the #MeToo movement of the gaming industry,[71] the death of one of the three prominent industry men accused—independent game developer Alec Holowka—chilled #MeToo efforts.[72] Specifically, after Holowka committed suicide in response to the allegations leveled against him, anonymous Twitter users engaged in relentless attacks against female gamers and women in esports, threatening them that they dare not speak out and ruin the lives of additional men in the industry.[73]

The real reckoning in esports began on June 20, 2020, when JewelsVerne, a Twitch streamer, accused popular streamer Lono of sexual assault on Twitter.[74] After JewelsVerne's tweet, six other women came forward with allegations against Lono.[75] These allegations included complaints of non-consensual touching, harassment, and propositions for sex.[76] After the allegations launched against Lono, numerous other streamers came forward about the harassment they faced in the industry.[77] For example, Molly Ayala, a Twitch streamer and community development lead for *Overwatch*, tweeted that the CEO of a talent management agency that works with many streamers, the Online Performers Group, propositioned her for a threesome.[78] Ayala's allegation led to other female streamers managed by the Online Performers Group stepping away from the agency at the end of their contracts.[79]

The flurry of allegations against prominent men in the gaming industry quickly led to the formation of "Twitch Blackout" in late June of 2020. During "Twitch Blackout," Twitch streamers refrained from going live as regularly scheduled, standing in solidarity with 70 individuals who

70. Liz Lanier, *Is the Games Industry Getting Its #MeToo Movement?*, Forbes (Aug. 28, 2019, 11:44 AM), https://www.forbes.com/sites/lizlanier/2019/08/28/is-the-games-industry-getting-its-me-too-movement/?sh=4eb3f3c65202.

71. *See id.*

72. *See* Takahashi, *supra* note 57 .

73. *See* Laurie Penny, *Gaming's #MeToo Moment and the Tyranny of Male Fragility*, Wired (Sep. 6, 2019, 7:00 AM), https://www.wired.com/story/videogames-industry-metoo-moment-male-fragility/.

74. *See* Richardson, *supra* note 55; Yules Verne (@DawktaJawlz), Twitter (Jun. 19, 2020, 8:09 PM), https://twitter.com/DawktaJawlz/status/1274147280455634947.

75. Rachel E. Greenspan, *Twitch streamer SayNoToRage denies allegations of sexual misconduct by six women, claiming that accusers 'conspired against him despite his previous apology*, Insider (Jul. 2, 2020, 11:22 AM), https://www.insider.com/twitch-saynotorage-apologized-for-sexual-harassment-allegations-2020-6.

76. Lorenz & Browning, *supra* note 53.

77. *Id.*

78. *Id.*

79. *Id.*

brought sexual harassment allegations against industry leaders, game developers, and players during the first two weeks of June 2020.[80] Streamers hoped that the coordinated "Twitch Blackout" effort would send a message to Twitch and other gaming companies that they must address the ubiquitous sexual harassment in esports.[81] While, in June 2020, Twitch's CEO, Emmett Shear, vowed to look into all sexual harassment allegations, Twitch did not alter its Terms of Service until December 2020.[82] Twitch's new Terms of Service include stricter rules surrounding sexual harassment and give Twitch greater leeway to ban streamers and viewers who make offensive or derogatory remarks to female streamers or users.[83]

Twitch updating its Terms of Service is a good first step to help eradicate the pervasive culture of sexual harassment in esports. However, these new policies only scratch the surface in dealing with the toxic culture of online gaming. Specifically, the anonymity of online gaming combined with the competitive nature of games increases the likelihood that female gamers will experience toxic behavior.[84] For example, female gamers are often told: "Get back in the kitchen and make me a sandwich!"[85] and other female gamers are asked what they are wearing, with male gamers typically requesting pictures.[86] As a result of the commentary and requests female gamers face while on online chatrooms or streaming platforms like Twitch, many women choose to disguise their identity through neutral usernames and avatars and avoid using voice chat features.[87] Likewise, some women

80. Jacob Wolf, *#TwitchBlackout trends amid accusations of sexual assault in gaming*, ESPN (Jun. 24, 2020), https://www.espn.com/esports/story/_/id/29359032/twitchblackout-trends-amidst-accusations-sexual-assault-gaming; Trilby Beresford, *Amid Twitch Blackout, Calls Grow for Game Industry Culture Change*, The Hollywood Rep. (Jun. 24, 2020), https://www.hollywoodreporter.com/news/twitch-blackout-calls-grow-game-industry-culture-change-1300093.

81. *See* Beresford, *supra* note 80.

82. *See* Olivia R., *Did Twitch update its ToS to protect itself from accusations*?, Win.GG (Dec. 21, 2020), https://win.gg/news/6601/did-twitch-update-its-tos-to-protect-itself-from-accusations-question-mark.

83. Jacob Kastrenakes, *Twitch bans 'simp'*, The Verge (Dec. 16, 2020, 4:28 PM), https://www.theverge.com/2020/12/16/22179256/twitch-bans-simp-virgin-incel-new-sexual-harassment-policy.

84. Amanda Cote, *Here's what it'll take to clean up esports' toxic culture*, The Conversation (Aug. 21, 2020, 8:38 AM), https://theconversation.com/heres-what-itll-take-to-clean-up-esports-toxic-culture-143520.

85. *Id.*

86. Kate O'Halloran, *'Hey dude, do this': the last resort for female gamers escaping online abuse*, The Guardian (Oct. 23, 2017, 1:00 PM), https://www.theguardian.com/culture/2017/oct/24/hey-dude-do-this-the-last-resort-for-female-gamers-escaping-online-abuse.

87. Lavinia McLean & Mark D. Griffiths, *Female Gamers' Experience of Online Harassment and Social Support in Online Gaming: A Qualitative Study*, 17 Int. J. Mental Health. Addiction 970, 983 (2019).

only log on to online platforms if other female gamers log on at the same time[88] because gaming in groups allows female gamers to build emotional resistance and resilience to the harassment they experience online.[89] Because many male gamers hide behind keyboards when launching harassment against female players,[90] the toxic culture of gaming is able to persist, virtually unregulated, on the internet.[91]

In addition to companies like Twitch updating their Terms of Service, another way to mitigate sexual harassment in esports is to demand more respect for female players.[92] One new development on the horizon to help champion the success of female gamers is the fact that Cloud9, a Los Angeles-based esports organization that runs games for *League of Legends* and *Fortnite*,[93] created an all-women's esports team to participate in Riot Games' Valorant esports tournaments.[94] The female and male Valorant teams will play in the same league and practice with each other.[95] Vice President of Cloud9, Kristen Salvatore, explains that with the introduction of an all-female Valorant team, "the goal is parity" and to "normalize" the role of women in professional esports "so it isn't news anymore."[96] Hopefully, the combination of stricter Terms of Service surrounding permissible conduct on online streaming platforms like Twitch, as well as the advent of women-only teams in competitions sponsored by prominent game developers, are the first steps on the path toward equality for men and women in the esports space.

---

88. *Id.* at 987.

89. *See* O'Halloran, *supra* note 86.

90. *See id.*

91. *See* Associated Press, *Women in professional esports navigate hyper masculinity and harassment*, MARKET WATCH (Jan. 3, 2019, 11:43 AM), https://www.marketwatch.com/story/women-in-professional-esports-navigate-hyper-masculinity-and-harassment-2019-01-03.

92. *See id.*; Liz Clarke, *Silencing the haters*, WASH. POST (Dec. 24, 2019), https://www.washingtonpost.com/graphics/2019/sports/toxic-online-culture-women-esports/.

93. Dean Takahashi, *Esports team Cloud9 teams with Kaiser Permanente to improve mental health*, VENTURE BEAT (May 12, 2020, 9:01 PM), https://venturebeat.com/2020/05/12/esports-team-cloud9-teams-with-kaiser-permanente-to-improve-mental-health/.

94. Dean Takahashi, *Cloud9 launches first all-women esports team for Valorant*, VENTURE BEAT (Oct. 25, 2020, 11:00 AM), https://venturebeat.com/2020/10/25/cloud9-launches-first-all-women-esports-team-for-valorant/.

95. *Id.*

96. *Id.*

College Esports and Title IX

With the rapid growth in popularity of video games among both men and women,[97] esports has the potential to bridge the gender gap that segregates sports based on the sex of the participants. Not only is the interest there for both sexes, but the skills needed to be successful in esports do not involve physical attributes that are believed to provide one sex with an advantage over the other or make participation potentially less safe.[98] For the purpose of Title IX, the gender-neutral nature of competitive video gaming appeals to colleges and universities that look to add sports opportunities without violating Title IX.[99]

Congress passed Title IX in 1972 to end sex-based discrimination in education by prohibiting the use of federal funds to support discriminatory practices in educational programs.[100] Most of the Title IX-related litigation has involved claims from female students that they have been deprived of opportunities for participation in school-provided athletics.[101] In defending against a Title IX claim, the institution must demonstrate that it conforms to at least one of the factors of a three-part test established by the Department of Education: (1) athletic participation opportunities provided for male and female are substantially proportionate to the general student population; (2) a history of program expansion of opportunities for the underrepresented sex; or (3) full and effective accommodation of interests for the underrepresented sex.[102]

A gender-neutral varsity esports program seemingly has the potential to work towards making sports offerings at an institution more proportionate to the overall student body and could provide evidence of both a history of program expansion and efforts to address the interests of the underrepresented. There are, however, some concerns that constrain this potential. First, studies have found that collegiate esports participants are predominantly male, even though both men and women are eligible to

97. *See* Justin Hilbert, *Gaming & gender: How Inclusive are Esports?*, The Sports Integrity Initiative (Apr. 9, 2019), https://www.sportsintegrityinitiative.com/gaming-gender-how-inclusive-are-esports/ (stating findings of a consumer-based study which found that 57% of women between the ages of 18-29 self-identify that they play video games).

98. Holden, Baker, & Edelman, *supra* note 58.

99. *Id.*

100. 20 U.S.C. §§1682–83.

101. Elain Chamberlain, Hannah Cornett & Adam Yohanan, *Nineteenth Annual Review of Gender and the Law*, 19 Geo. J. Gender & L. 231, 242 (2019).

102. *See Clarification Of Intercollegiate Athletics Policy Guidance: The Three-Part Test*, U.S. Dep't of Educ. (Jan. 16, 1996), https://www2.ed.gov/about/offices/list/ocr/docs/clarific.html#two.

compete.[103] A second concern involves the placement of esports programs within the college or university. Title IX requires equity in the distribution of scholarship money within athletic departments, and scholarships afforded to students by esports programs that are housed outside of their respective athletic departments are treated as merit-based and are omitted from counting towards federal Title IX protections.[104]

Meanwhile, a third concern involves whether esports would be treated as a "sport" for the purpose of Title IX. However, this concern is likely more academic than actual.

Title IX & Sexual Harassment

In addition to its role in ending sex-based discrimination in the form of educational and athletic opportunities, Title IX also prohibits sexual violence and harassment as a form of sex-based discrimination.[105] The Supreme Court has held that Title IX authorizes private actions for damages based on sexual harassment.[106] In fact, Title IX sexual harassment liability parallels, in many ways, the Title VII liability for workplace harassment in that both allow for quid pro quo harassment and hostile environment sexual harassment claims.[107] As more fully described earlier, quid pro quo sexual harassment occurs when a person's employment or education-based opportunity is made dependent on the person's submission to or denial of a sex-based solicitation from a person who holds superior status within the organization or institution.[108] For Title VII, a hostile environment is one that is permeated with intimidation, ridicule, and insult that is either so severe or so pervasive in nature that it alters by making hostile the victim's workplace condition.[109] In application to Title IX, the sexual hostility in the environment must be so pervasive and objectively

103. Jeremy Bauer-Wolf, *Video Games: Entertainment or Sports?* Inside Higher Ed (Feb. 12, 2019), https://www.insidehighered.com/news/2019/02/12/new-frontier-college-athletics-video-games.

104. Derek R. Walton, Leanne M. Lower-Hoppe, and Marc Horger, *Do Esports Classify as Intercollegiate Sport? Legal Analysis of Title IX*, 13 J. Issues Intercollegiate Athletics, 94, 95 (2020).

105. Russlyn Ali, Assistant Secretary for Civil Rights, *Dear Colleague Letter: Sexual Violence,* U.S. Dep't of Educ. (Apr. 4, 2011), https://www2.ed.gov/about/offices/list/ocr/letters/colleague-201104.pdf.

106. Franklin v. Gwinnett Cnty. Pub. Sch., 503 U.S. 60, 76 (1992).

107. Anita M. Moorman, & Lisa P. Masteralexis, *An Examination of the Legal Framework between Title VII and Title IX Sexual Harassment Claims in Athletics and Sport Settings: Emerging Challenges for Athletics Personnel and Sport Managers*, 18 J. Legal Aspects Sport 1 (2008).

108. 29 C.F.R. §1604.11(a) (2020).

109. 45B Am. Jur. 2d Job Discrimination §844 (2020).

offensive that it, in effect, prevents the victim from having access to an educational opportunity or benefit.[110]

In addition to the existence of a hostile environment, for a student plaintiff to recover against an institution under Title IX, the student must establish that the school received federal funding[111] and an agent or official was given the opportunity to take corrective action in response to the discriminatory conduct, but instead acted with deliberate indifference to the known acts of harassment.[112] In such a case, it is the actions of the institution and not the harasser that matter; thus, an institution is not liable merely because someone affiliated with it harassed the plaintiff.[113] Furthermore, liability under Title IX is limited to those situations in which the school exercises substantial control over both the harasser and the context.[114] For the plaintiff to recover, they must establish deliberate indifference on the part of the institution in response to known harassment, and this indifference effectively denies the plaintiff of meaningful access to an educational opportunity or benefit.[115]

The toxicity that permeates the gaming industry will eventually seep into collegiate esports if it has not already. Accordingly, collegiate esports programs must have Title IX policies in place for reporting and response. While the failure to promulgate Title IX policies is not actionable in and of itself, once a program is put on notice of an offense, it must reasonably respond to that notice, and Title IX policies facilitate that process.[116] However, if a program has a Title IX policy that does not include adequate reporting procedures and training for those who enforce the program or institutional policy, then the policy may be found in violation of Title IX for being deliberately indifferent to the potential for Title IX concerns.[117] The same standards that mandate reporting of offenses for other programs within the institution also attach to collegiate esports programs, and those programs that fail to prepare for the addressing of harassment will run the risk of being found in violation of Title IX.[118] Title IX does not mandate a

110. Davis v. Monroe Cnty. Bd. Of Educ., 526 U.S. 629 (1999).

111. Floyd v. Waiters, 133 F.3d 786, 789 (11th Cir. 1998), *vacated*, 525 U.S. 802 (1998), *reinstated*, 171 F.3d 1264 (11th Cir. 1998).

112. Davis, 526 U.S. at 633.

113. *Id.* at 633.

114. *Id.* at 645.

115. *Id.* at 640–41.

116. Gebser v. Lago Vista Indep. Sch. Dist., 524 U.S. 274, 292 (1989).

117. *See* City of Canton v. Harris, 489 U.S. 378, 389–90 (1989).

118. *See generally*, *Intersection of Title IX and the Clery Act*, Dep't of Just. (Apr. 2014), https://www.justice.gov/archives/ovw/page/file/910306/download.

particular course of action from program administrators, but claims made by purported victims must be taken seriously in terms of both investigation, response, and remediation or sanction, if necessary.[119] For example, in *Simpson v. University of Colorado Boulder*, the school's athletic department failed to take remedial actions after being notified by a local district attorney that its methods for hosting high school recruits for the football program made the school and its students vulnerable to sexual assault, following the report of a high school student being sexually assaulted by CU recruits at a party hosted by a football player.[120] Thus, when two CU students, one of whom was on the football team, were subsequently assaulted, the institution's failure to address the initial reports of sexual violence and failure to change its policies for hosting high school recruits made the school vulnerable to Title IX liability.[121]

The key to ensuring Title IX compliance is found in avoiding the appearance of deliberate indifference to the victim's claims. When a victim alleges incidents of sexual harassment to an appropriate person within the program's administration, then the institution is put on actual notice and must act on that notification.[122] Failure by an institution to adequately respond could result in the victim being denied access to education, especially if the victim feels that they must leave the institution so as to avoid further harassment. In such a case, the institution's potential for liability under Title IX intensifies.

In terms of the level of harassment to which programs should respond, it's important for administrators to appreciate that a hostile environment can emerge in two different ways, the first of which involves pervasive harassment over a period of time. If the extent of consistent harassment is objectively offensive, that is sufficient to create a hostile environment.[123] Unfortunately, this type of hostility is commonplace within electronic gaming as online players regularly engage in sexually explicit insults or other dialogue, the type of which would not be legally tolerated in workplace or educational settings. Institutions are not expected to police all online environments or communities that are frequented by their students. In fact, schools are only responsible for harassment in which they exercise substantial control over both the harasser and the context.[124]

119. *Id.*

120. Simpson v. Univ. of Colo. Boulder, 500 F.3d 1170, 1173–74 (10th Cir. 2007).

121. *Id.* at 1185.

122. *See generally*, Dep't of Just., *supra* note 118.

123. Davis, at 650.

124. Davis, at 645.

Yet, if the toxicity that rises to the level of hostility emerges from within the program, then that conduct must be addressed in a serious manner so as to avoid Title IX liability.[125] While objectively offensive conduct may be normalized within electronic gaming, that same conduct could potentially result in liability for the institution if it is also tolerated within a varsity esports program, whether that program is housed within the athletic department or in another department or college within the institution.

Administrators must also appreciate that a hostile environment can be found even in the absence of pervasive harassment. Even a single offense can create a hostile educational environment for students if that act is so extreme in nature that it deprives the student of educational access. For example, in some instances, sexual assault and rape have been found to be so extreme in nature that they deprive the student of education in violation of Title IX.[126]

This begs the question as to what level of attention and response is necessary to avoid a finding that the institution acted with deliberate indifference? The level of response depends on the nature of the offense(s) and hostility. Using a more extreme example, the court in *Samuelson v. Oregon State University* identified measures for adoption in situations involving sexual assault or rape.[127] Those measures included: (a) end the hostile and sexually violent culture; (b) create and implement more effective sexual assault prevention policies; (c) prepare and present training programs for students, coaches, and faculty about consent and appropriate sexual conduct; (d) investigate sexual assault allegations impartially and comprehensively; (e) engage law enforcement; (f) craft discipline that matches with the severity and frequency of the acts of sexual harassment; and (g) provide ongoing emotional, psychological, and educational on-campus support and off-campus resources for victims.[128]

---

125. For example, see *Hernandez v. Baylor Univ.*, 274 F.Supp.3d 602 (W.D. Texas, 2017), in which sexual assaults were committed by athletes within an athletic department at a private university and the court found that the school exercised control over both the context and the harassers.

126. *See* Samuelson v. Oregon St. Univ., 162 F.Supp.3d 1123 (D. Oregon, 2016); Hernandez v. Baylor Univ., 274 F.Supp.3d 602 (W.D. Texas, 2017).

127. Samuelson, 162 F.Supp.3d at 1128.

128. *Id.*

Socialization and Genderfication of Esports

In June 2020, a Twitter thread included more than 70 allegations of sexism and harassment in the gaming industry.[129] That thread sparked renewed interest and conversations on the subject of a widespread culture in esports that is toxic for women and girls. The toxicity in esports consists of far more than just "harmless locker-room talk" from teenagers in their parent's basement, with accounts from the affected that include direct threats made to player safety.[130] The pervasiveness of toxicity in electronic gaming has led sociologists who study the intersectionality of sex within sport to conclude that "hegemonic masculinity"—a sociological term that describes patterns of social practices that have been normalized by tenets of "patriarch, which guarantees the dominant position of men and the subordination of women—is a problem within electronic gaming.[131]

At the professional level, an example of such as toxic culture can be found in the case of Miranda Pakozdi, a professional gamer who allowed her avatar to be killed during competitive play so as to end harassment from her coach that included taunts about her bra size and her boyfriend.[132] Pakozdi's coach also objectified Pakozdi during the competition by pointing a webcam at private parts of her body while asking her inappropriate questions.[133] Within the corporate environment, an example can be found in the May 6, 2019, public demonstration in which 100 employees at Riot Games walked off their jobs to protest a culture of sexual harassment within the company.[134]

The toxicity at the upper levels of professional play and game production can also be found in recreational play. For example, shortly after

---

129. Lorenz & Browning, *supra* note 53.

130. Brianna Wu, *Rape and Death Threats Are Terrorizing Female Gamers. Why Haven't Men In Tech Spoken Out*, WASH. POST (Oct. 20, 2014), https://www.washingtonpost.com/posteverything/wp/2014/10/20/rape-and-death-threats-are-terrorizing-female-gamers-why-havent-men-in-tech-spoken-out/?utm_term=.ebd978a57d3e.

131. *See* Anna Cameron, *No More Games: An Intersectional Approach to Geek Masculinity and Marginalization in Video Gaming Culture*, 19 GNOVIS: J. COMMC'N, CULTURE & TECH. 2, 9 (2019); Lindsey Darvin, Ryan Vooris & Tara Mahoney, *The Playing Experiences of Esports Participants: An Analysis of Treatment Discrimination and Hostility in Esport Environments*, 2 J. ATHLETE EXPERIENCE 1, 3 (2020).

132. NPR Staff, *Online Harassment Gets Real For Female Gamers*, NPR (Aug. 8, 2012), https://www.npr.org/2012/08/08/158433079/virtual-harassment-gets-real-for-female-gamers.

133. *Id.*

134. Rachel England, *Riot Games Staff Walk Out After Sexism Lawsuit Result In Forced Arbitration*, ENGADGET (May 7, 2019), https://www.engadget.com/2019-05-07-riot-games-walk-out-sexism-lawsuits-arbitration.html.

the 2018 release of *Red Dead Redemption 2*, a player uploaded a video to his YouTube channel depicting an avatar in the game punching a woman suffragist.[135] He titled the clip "Beating Up Annoying Feminist."[136] YouTube eventually closed the channel, but not before it had attained more than one million views.[137] This is just a sample of the type of sexist content that is so commonplace on social media spaces for electronic gaming. Unfortunately, the comments directed at female players during online play are often far worse, to the point that some parents have discouraged their daughters from playing video games as a means for protecting them from toxicity.[138] While it is understandable that parents of young women would not want to expose their children to toxicity and abuse, the end result is sex-based segregation that reinforces the gendered stereotype that electronic gaming is an activity for males only.

Closing the Gender Gap

Despite the rampant toxicity within electronic gaming and esports, statistics suggest that the gender gap has shrunk as more girls and women identify as gamers.[139] Already, women gamers make up approximately 45 percent of video game consumers in the U.S.[140] Video game developer Brenda Laurel addressed the growth of video game popularity among women as well the need to create safe spaces for girls and women within gaming with a speculative comment that, "[t]here's $6 billion (being left) on the table."[141] Unfortunately, the toxicity in electronic gaming does more than just cost game producers money; it also costs female players opportunities.

Statistics evidence an extremely low rate of female players involved in the major titles for esports such as *Counter-Strike: Global Offensive* (CS:

135. Jessamy Henricksen & Marika Guggisberg, *Violence Towards Women in the Video Game Red Dead Redemption 2 Evokes Toxic Masculinity*, The Conversation (Nov. 18, 2018), https://theconversation.com/violence-towards-women-in-the-video-game-red-dead-redemption-2-evokes-toxic-masculinity-106920.

136. *Id.*

137. *Id.*

138. Holden, Baker, & Edelman, *supra* note 58.

139. *2020 Essential Facts About the Video Game* Industry, Ent. Software Ass'n, https://www.theesa.com/esa-research/2020-essential-facts-about-the-video-game-industry/ (last visited Jan. 1, 2021).

140. Jen Ortiz, *She's Got Game*, Marie Claire (Dec. 5, 2018), https://www.marieclaire.com/career-advice/a25379999/female-gamers/.

141. *Id.*

GO) (24% female), *DOTA 2* (20% female), *Hearthstone* (26% female), *Rainbow 6: Siege* (23% female), and *Overwatch* (26% female).[142] Low female involvement for gameplay for those specific game titles likely explains the lack of female representation as professional esports players for those games. Professional gaming remains dominated by men, with women accounting for only five percent of all professional players.[143] And yet, accounting for 30 percent of the viewing audience, women are a significant and growing piece of the esports viewership pie.[144] With girls and women consuming both video games and esports, there exists hope for closing the gender gap in professional gaming. To facilitate this process, game producers and those who operate or manage esports tournaments and leagues need to make commitments to securing their spaces as safe for both girls and women. While it is both reasonable and manageable for stakeholders to make professional play inclusive of women and intolerant to harassment through the use of rules with sanctions for offenders, the task of curbing or removing toxicity from online recreational play is a tougher challenge. Still, those involved at every level of esports need to make a commitment to normalizing to avoid the exacerbation of a culture that is exclusionary, and arguably harmful, to women.

Those with authority within esports and electronic gaming need to adopt rules and procedures to encourage the reporting of sexual harassment and work with gamers to design and implement means for investigation and punishment mechanism for harassers. In addition, esports managers must actively engage their professional players in the process of developing procedures to detect and punish sexual harassment. There is no magic cure for ending sexual harassment in electronic gaming and esports.[145] The process for eradicating harassment from the industry will take effort and time. Accountability, however, is necessary, and the #MeToo movement represents both a shift in social norms on sex and gender and a warning to those in electronic gaming and esports who engage in toxic behavior.[146] The video game industry has no choice: it

142. *Females and Esports Progress Update*, Interpret (Feb. 21, 2019), https://interpret.la/females-gains-6-increase-in-gender-share-for-esports-viewership/.

143. Justin Hilbert, *Gaming & gender: How inclusive are eSports?*, The Sports Integrity Initiative (Apr. 9, 2019), https://www.sportsintegrityinitiative.com/gaming-gender-how-inclusive-are-esports/.

144. *Id.*

145. John T. Holden, Thomas A. Baker III & Marc Edelman, *The #E-Too Movement: Fighting Back Against Sexual Harassment in Electronic Sports*, 52 Az. St. L.J. 1, 35 (2020).

146. Rebecca Seales, *What has #MeToo Actually Changed?* BBC News (May 12, 2018), https://www.bbc.com/news/world-44045291.

must also adapt in the same way that other sectors have by taking the appropriate and necessary steps for making spaces safe for women.

Proposals for the Future of Female Gaming

To eradicate gender-based discrimination and sexual harassment in competitive, esports four central developments are necessary. First, competitive esports featuring female players must receive recognition on an international scale. Second, game publishers and streaming sites must develop new rules to manage online spaces. Third, game developers and leagues must create support mechanisms through which female gamers can report instances of bias and harassment. Fourth and finally, video game designers and game makers must reevaluate their marketing policies and internally re-evaluate their diversity, equity, and inclusion policies.

First, championing female participation in esports requires the recognition of women esports players on an international scale—not just as notable exceptions within typically male-dominated American professional esports leagues. In 2017, the International Olympic Committee (IOC) began to recognize competitive esports as a sport.[147] In 2018, as part of its Gender Equality Review Project, the IOC acknowledged its role in achieving a gender balance of Olympic athletes.[148] Specifically, in its Gender Equality Review Project report, the IOC suggested that beginning in the 2024 Olympic Games, for all team sport and events, there will be "an equal number of athletes for both genders."[149] While the inclusion of esports and the IOC's goal towards gender equity seems promising for female esports players, in March 2019, Kit McConnell, the Sports Director of the IOC, explained that due to licensing problems and violence in video games, it was unlikely that esports as an Olympic medal event would happen anytime soon.[150] Despite Mr. McConnell's comment, in April of 2020, Thomas Bach, President of the IOC, released a letter in which he suggested that the inclusion of esports in the Olympics may be closer than

147. Jacqueline Martinelli, *The Challenges of Implementing A Governing Body for Regulating eSports*, 26 U. Miami Int'l & Comp. L. Rev. 499, 503 (2019).

148. IOC Gender Equality Review Project, *IOC Gender Equality Report*, Int'l Olympic Comm. (2018) (accessible at https://stillmed.olympic.org/media/Document%20Library/OlympicOrg/News/2018/03/IOC-Gender-Equality-Report-March-2018.pdf).

149. *Id.*

150. Lisa Marie Segarra, *Why the Olympic Games Are Steering Clear of E-Sports*, Fortune (Mar. 22, 2019, 11:00 PM), https://fortune.com/2019/03/22/esports-olympic-future/.

previously expected.[151] Bach shared that due to the fallout from the COVID-19 pandemic, it is unlikely that the IOC will be able to "sustain every single initiative or event . . . plann[ed] before th[e] crisis hit."[152]As a result, Bach believes social distancing due to COVID may result in the inclusion of esports events at the Olympics because, unlike some other traditional athletics competitions, esports competitions can be held in a creative, remote manner.[153] Thus, the opportunity for the IOC to include esports as a medal event, and ensure gender parity between male and female esports players, maybe on the horizon.

Second, in addition to the need for international recognition of esports, which would place female esports players on the world stage, game publishers and streaming sites like Amazon-owned Twitch should adopt new rules to govern their online spaces. To date, game companies are becoming increasingly interested in community management strategies.[154] For example, in 2019, Electronic Arts (EA) held a community management summit[155] called the Building Healthy Communities Summit, at which over 200 gamers and gaming influencers joined together to discuss how EA should address disruptive behavior and where to draw the line between competitive banter and hurtful language.[156] Further, companies like Microsoft and Intel are also developing tools for managing online spaces.[157] Specifically, Microsoft, which owns Xbox, released a new set of community guidelines in April 2019 to govern its Xbox Live platform,[158] and Intel, which powers several major esports championships and tournaments surrounding *Counter-Strike: Global Offensive*,[159] built an artificial

---

151. *IOC President Bach Writes to Olympic Movement: Olympism and Corona*, OLYMPIC.ORG (Apr. 29, 2020), https://www.olympic.org/news/ioc-president-bach-writes-to-olympic-movement-olympism-and-corona.

152. David Wharton, *Even post-coronavirus, will esports replace real games?*, L.A. TIMES (Apr. 29, 2020, 10:21 AM), https://www.latimes.com/sports/story/2020-04-29/will-esports-flourish-in-the-post-coronavirus-world.

153. *IOC President Bach Writes to Olympic Movement: Olympism and Corona*, OLYMPIC.ORG (Apr. 29, 2020), https://www.olympic.org/news/ioc-president-bach-writes-to-olympic-movement-olympism-and-corona.

154. Cote, *supra* note 84.

155. *Id.*

156. Ian Sherr, *Gaming can be toxic toward women and minorities. Electronic Arts wants to help fix that*, CNET (Jun. 13, 2019, 9:00 AM), https://www.cnet.com/news/gaming-can-be-toxic-toward-women-and-minorities-electronic-arts-wants-to-help-fix-that/.

157. Cote, *supra* note 84.

158. Ian Sherr, *Microsoft's Xbox team has a plan to fight toxic gamers*, CNET (May 21, 2019, 5:00 AM), https://www.cnet.com/news/microsofts-xbox-team-has-a-plan-to-fight-toxic-gamers/.

159. *Transforming the Future of Esports*, INTEL, https://www.intel.com/content/www/us/en/gaming/esports.html (last visited Jan. 1, 2021).

intelligence program called Ally, which is a tool gaming companies can use to detect sexual harassment and abuse.[160]

The initiatives from leaders in the esports space like EA and Intel are significant because, according to attorney and former Microsoft user experience designer Rebecca Chui, online gaming communities are not inherently toxic.[161] Instead, the culture of harassment that persists on online platforms stems from the community norms which do not prohibit it.[162] The creation of the Fair Play Alliance, an initiative launched in 2017 that includes nearly 200 gaming companies who have agreed to work together to encourage healthy player interactions,[163] has the potential to move the needle on eradicating the harassment that occurs in esports. In December of 2020, the Fair Play Alliance teamed up with the Anti-Defamation League Center for Technology and Society to release a Disruption and Harms in Online Gaming Framework.[164] The Framework is a call to action that seeks to mitigate toxicity in online gaming and demand respect for all players.[165] The Framework's policy suggestions seek to foster an inclusive, healthier online gaming world.[166] Further, the Framework suggests that simply increasing attempts to moderate and control online behavior is not a sustainable path for game developers and leagues—there must be a "measurable pathway towards making online games respectful and inclusive spaces for everyone."[167] Hopefully, the creation of this Framework and the initiatives companies like Intel have taken will engender lasting and meaningful policy reforms to mitigate sexual harassment and toxic conduct in esports.

Third, in addition to esports needing recognition on an international stage and game developers needing to adopt new policies to limit harassment, to eradicate gender-based discrimination and sexual harassment

---

160. Michael Kan, *Intel Levels Up AI to Battle Toxicity in Online Games*, PC MAGAZINE (Mar. 22, 2019), https://www.pcmag.com/news/intel-levels-up-ai-to-battle-toxicity-in-online-games.

161. *See* Cote, *supra* note 84; Rebecca Chui, *A Multi-faceted Approach to Anonymity Online: Examining the Relations between Anonymity and Antisocial Behavior*, 7 J. VIRTUAL WORLDS RSCH. 1, 1–8 (2014).

162. *Id.*

163. *Fair Play Alliance and ADL Announce Partnership to Rally Industry to Combat Hate and Harassment in Video Games*, ANTI-DEFAMATION LEAGUE, https://www.adl.org/news/press-releases/fair-play-alliance-and-adl-announce-partnership-to-rally-industry-to-combat; *About the Fair Play Alliance*, FAIR PLAY ALL., https://fairplayalliance.org/about/

164. *Id.*

165. *See generally* FAIR PLAY ALLIANCE, DISRUPTION AND HARMS IN ONLINE GAMING FRAMEWORK (Anti-Defamation League 2020), accessible at https://www.adl.org/media/15447/download.

166. *Id.*

167. *Id.*

in competitive esports, greater support mechanisms for female players are paramount. In August 2020, Anita Sarkeesian—one of the women of the Gamergate scandal[168] and a video game critic who received death and rape threats in response to posts on her blog, Feminist Frequency, in 2014[169]—launched the Games and Online Harassment Hotline (GOHH). GOHH is a free, non-profit, text message-based service that offers confidential, emotional support to members of the gaming community.[170] The hotline features trained call center experts and volunteers who handle the influx of messages it receives and, if needed, they subsequently make referrals to outside resources such as suicide prevention organizations.[171] Overall, GOHH represents a step in the right direction as an outlet for support for those experiencing harassment and toxic treatment in the gaming industry. Hopefully, Sarkeesian's idea for this hotline will inspire individual esports leagues to create similar internal support systems, perhaps with the assistance of their Human Resources departments. Doing so would allow for league-specific autonomy over issues of harassment its players face, and in turn, greater accountability at the league level.

Fourth and finally, to mitigate sexual harassment and other toxic behavior in professional gaming, game designers and game makers should reflect on their marketing policies and analyze their diversity, equity, and inclusion efforts. For example, although the video game industry was not explicitly marketed towards a specific gender when it began in the 1970s, that changed after the video game industry crash in the early to mid-1980s.[172] Between 1983 and 1985, several low-quality games caused video game revenue in North America to fall from $3.2 billion to $100 million.[173] Eager to regain their share of the market, game developers like Nintendo realized they could no longer afford to appeal to a wide demographic and instead must re-brand their video games.[174] Thus, the Game Boy portable system was born in 1989.[175]

---

168. *See* Dewey, *supra* note 60.

169. Rott, *supra* note 63.

170. *About Us*, GAMES & ONLINE HARASSMENT HOTLINE, https://gameshotline.org/about/.

171. Dean Takahashi, *Why Anita Sarkeesian started the Game and Online Harassment Hotline*, VENTURE BEAT (Aug. 3, 2020, 9:47 AM), https://venturebeat.com/2020/08/03/why-anita-sarkeesian-started-the-game-and-online-harassment-hotline/.

172. Doug Powell, *Why Are Games Marketed Toward Boys*?, GAME LUSTER (Nov. 14, 2017), https://gameluster.com/why-are-games-marketed-toward-boys/.

173. *Id.*

174. *Id.*

175. *Id.*

By 1992, Nintendo had sold 9 million Game Boys across America.[176]

The rise in popularity of the Game Boy correlates to gaming research from the 1990s, which suggests that boys played video games more frequently than girls.[177] Video game developers took advantage of masculine stereotypes, with even Activision publishing an ad in 1995 for its game *Earthworm Jim*.[178] The ad depicts a man being pulled back into bed by a woman as he clasps his head with his hands.[179] A textbox displays the woman suggesting: "maybe if you didn't play with that worm so much . . . "—an innuendo to suggest that the man is experiencing impotence because he has played too many video games.[180]

By the early 2000s, video games seemed to grow up alongside the young boys who played Nintendo's Game Boy.[181] As a result, game developers and companies chose to market to these demographics, thereby demonstrating a "progression of the idea . . . once you're a gamer, you're always a gamer."[182] In keeping with this, magazines like *PC Zone* ran contests for readers to win a date with an actress dressed as the hypersexualized female video game figure, Lara Croft.[183] Today, the widespread marketing of esports toward men in a sometimes sexually charged manner stems from these early and consistent marketing efforts. Currently, local toy stores and even Target have one aisle targeted towards girls, which features Barbies, stuffed animals, and other dolls, and another aisle for boys. The aisle for boys features superhero action figures, toy cars, Nerf guns, and video games.[184] By reconsidering marketing campaigns and publishing gender-neutral ads, it is likely that game designers and devel-

176. Richard Moss, *How Nintendo introduced the Game Boy, Tetris, and Pokmon to the West*, POLYGON (Apr. 19, 2019, 12:00 PM), https://www.polygon.com/2019/4/19/18295061/game-boy-history-timeline-tetris-pokemon-nintendo.

177. Jenna Drenten, Robert Harrison, & Nicholas Pendarvis, *Video Gaming as a Gendered Pursuit*, *in* HANDBOOK OF RESEARCH ON GENDER & MARKETING 28, 30 (Susan Dobscha ed., (2019), accessible at https://ecommons.luc.edu/cgi/viewcontent.cgi?article=1178&context=business_facpubs.

178. *See* Jess Morrissette, *How Games Marketing Invented Toxic Gamer* Culture, VICE (Mar. 25, 2020, 8:59 AM), https://www.vice.com/en/article/5dmayn/games-marketing-toxic-gamer-culture-on-line-xbox-live-dreamcast; *Video Game Print Ads*, TUMBLR, https://vgprintads.tumblr.com/post/129871798797/earthworm-jim-maybe-if-you-didnt-play-with (last visited Jan. 1, 2021).

179. TUMBLR, *supra* note 178.

180. *Id.*

181. Tracey Lien, *No Girls Allowed*, POLYGON (Dec. 2, 2013, 12:00 PM), https://www.polygon.com/features/2013/12/2/5143856/no-girls-allowed.

182. *Id.*

183. Morrissette, *supra* note 178.

184. *See* Lien, *supra* note 181.

opers will be able to capture more of the female market share of gamers—roughly 46 percent at present—and thereby encourage greater participation from future generations of girl gamers.[185]

In sum, goals of gender equity in professional esports can likely be attained through specific three main avenues. First, recognition of female esports athletes on an international scale is imperative for establishing female gamers as serious competitors who have the skills to compete alongside and against male counterparts. Next, by fostering more inclusive online spaces and creating support mechanisms like confidential hotlines for female gamers, esports leagues and game developers can encourage female gamers to remain committed to their craft and ban toxic conduct. Lastly, game developers should take an introspective look into their advertisements and marketing endeavors to limit the hyper-masculine male stereotypes they often perpetuate. With the worst of the #E-Too movement hopefully behind the esports industry, the time is now for esports leagues to act to create positive and lasting change for female gamers.

185. *See* Marc Saltzman, *Video games: More women play now than teen boys do, millennials and boomers play, too*, USA Today (Jul. 5, 2019, 9:18 AM), https://www.usatoday.com/story/tech/columnist/2019/06/11/more-women-play-video-games-now-than-teen-boys-busting-stereotypes/1414430001/.

Chapter 10

Esports and Gambling

The rapid growth of esports is just one of two trends rapidly reshaping the contemporary, commercial sports landscape. The other recent trend relates to the massive increase in the legal betting on sports, which the United States has expedited since the Supreme Court's May 14, 2018, decision that overturned the general federal ban on sports gambling in *Murphy v. National Collegiate Athletic Association.*[1] Since that decision, a growing number of states have legalized some form of sports gambling, with legalized, licensed online betting on sports emerging as the fastest-growing segment of the sports betting market.[2]

While the relationship between esports and online sports gambling is intertwined in that both are now gaining mainstream acceptance, esports and online gambling also overlap significantly in terms of their core customer base—men under the age of 35. Many of the same desires for ongoing engagement, competition, and a tad of counterculture draw individuals to sports betting and esports. Of course, it is true these same interests have played a role in the newfound American interest in day trading, which, in January 2021, led to unusual crowdsourcing behavior and alleged improprieties when GameStop Corp., a U.S. video game retail company that was perceived by some equity analysts as already overvalued, experienced a more than four-hundred percent increase in its stock price over a one-week period.[3]

1. 1138 S. Ct. (2018).

2. *See* John Holden & Marc Edelman, *A Short Treatise on Sports Gambling and the Law: How America Regulates Its Most Lucrative Vice*, 2020 Wis. L. Rev. 907 (2020).

3. *See* Peter Eavis, *What Is GameStop, the Company, Really Worth? Does It Matter?*, N.Y. Times (updated Feb. 3, 2021), https://www.nytimes.com/2021/02/01/business/gamestop-how-much-worth.

Overall, gambling law and emerging gambling markets directly intersect with esports in three specific ways. First, there are reasonable questions as to whether esports contests in which participants pay a sum of money to enter and the victors receive a prize would constitute a form of illegal gambling under certain state laws. Second, there are questions pertaining to the legality of emerging markets to offer both online sports gambling and daily fantasy sports contests. Finally, much as in all professional sports, the hosts of esports competitions need to be mindful, especially in the face of increasing legalized sports gambling, of the risks that certain esports participants may either directly bet against themselves or share confidential information about certain competitions with betting third parties. Each of these three topics merits a separate discussion in this chapter of the book.

The Role of Gambling Laws on Primary Esports Competitions

While there are a variety of formats for hosting esports events, the predominant model for esports competition today continues to revolve around a hosting entity charging an entry fee for teams of qualifying participants to enter a given contest, with the participants being paid directly by the event host with prizes of decreasing monetary value that are based on place of finish. This structure, while distinct from that of MLB, the NBA, the NFL, or the NHL, is consistent with the way that most sports tournaments throughout the United States operate in activities including tennis, golf, NASCAR, and boxing. Recognizing this model as the dominant structure for esports competition today, one of the important sets of issues pertaining to esports leagues and their game makers relates to determining who is eligible to participate in a contest and who is ultimately declared the winner of that contest. As a general matter, the host, as a private association, has the full discretion to determine who is eligible to compete and who is declared the winner—subject, of course, to the mandate that the esports host does so in accordance with otherwise existing laws, and without violating the "basic rudiments of due process" or underlying state or federal law.[4] In this vein, one of the obligations that

html (describing the rapid rise of GameStop's share price, a value with seemingly little connection to the underlying value of the company).

4. Crouch v. National Ass'n for Stock Car Racing, 845 F.2d 397, 402 (2d. Cir. 1988).

becomes incumbent on esports hosts is to make sure their contests comply with state and federal gambling law, especially where the hosts receive sanctioning fees and pay prizes of monetary value to the winners.

State Gambling Laws

Somewhat oversimplified, state gambling laws prevent the operation of contests (unless specially licensed) that include three attributes: consideration, reward, and chance.[5] "Consideration" is typically described as a "*quid pro quo* or something in exchange for something else."[6] In the context of state gambling laws, the notion of "consideration" typically references an entry fee.[7] "Reward" is the tangible benefit that one obtains from winning a contest.[8] "Chance" is defined as "something that happens unpredictably without discernible intention or observable cause."[9] Nevertheless, the minimum ratio of chance-to-skill for an activity to constitute "chance" varies by state, with some states deeming a contest to be one of "chance" if it includes even a modicum of chance, whereas others only deeming a contest to be one of chance if the chance elements of a contest predominate over elements of skill.[10]

Much like professional leagues governing boxing, golf, and tennis, esports leagues typically pay participants prize money based on their finish position in a particular contest.[11] Because this prize money legally constitutes a "reward," the contest would need to forgo either requiring "consideration" (generally money) to enter or ensure that the underlying activity constitutes skill.[12]

---

5. *See* Ronald Rychlak, *Video Gambling Devices*, 37 UCLA L. Rev. 555, 556 (1990).

6. Marc Edelman, *A Short Treatise on Fantasy Sports and the Law*, 3 Harv. J. of Sports & Ent. L. 1, 27 (2012).

7. *See* Rychlak, *supra* note 5, at 556 (explaining that "[c]onsideration is the stake, wager, or bet that gamblers risk losing if they are unsuccessful," and that "[w]ith a traditional slot machine, for example, consideration is the coin that the gambler inserts into the machine before pulling the arm that sets the reels in motion").

8. *See* Edelman, *supra* note 6, at 28.

9. *Id.*

10. *See* Marc Edelman, *Navigating the Legal Risks of Daily Fantasy Sports: A Detailed Primer in Federal and State Gambling Law*, 2016 Illinois L. Rev. 117, 134 (2016).

11. *See* Tae Kim, *Epic Makes 'Fortnight' Biggest Esport in the World with $100 Million in Prize Money*, CNBC, (May 21, 2018), https://www.cnbc.com/2018/05/21/epic-makes-fornite-biggest-esport-with-100-million-in-prize-money.html (describing the prize pools offered for contests in games such as Fortnite and Dota 2, among others).

12. *See* Rychlak, *supra* note 5, at 556 (noting that consideration, chance and reward all must exist for conduct to constitute illegal gambling); Edelman, *supra* note 6, at 26–27 (expressing the same).

In traditional sports, the notion that the underlying activity is one of skill rather than chance has been treated as axiomatic under the law.[13] By contrast, in esports, the matter seems somewhat less settled. Jurisdictions are mixed on whether typical board games such as dominos constitute games of skill or games of chance.[14] In one relatively well-known court decision, a dissenting judge concluded that while the game of duplicative bridge might constitute a game of skill, the game of simple bridge would be one of chance.[15]

Video games, much like board games, seem to run the full gamut in terms of how they may be perceived by courts in legal analysis.[16] On one end of the spectrum, sports video games are those in which player performance is determined based upon hand-eye coordination to complete certain tasks. Accordingly, sports video games such as the *NBA 2K* video game are almost certainly the type to be considered as games of skill that could be reasonably likened to a contest between individuals in shooting physical baskets.[17] On the other end of the spectrum exist video games that are virtual versions of casino games, like the card game stud poker, and much like their real-life counterparts, the casino-themed games are almost certainly to be treated as games of chance. The movement of the game from a card table onto the internet changes nothing.[18] The shooter-oriented video games that have become common in the emerging world of esports seem likely to meet the definition for a "game of skill" in states that apply a "predominant purpose test" for skill.[19] Indeed, the underlying activities involved in these games undeniably entail a combination of both hand-eye coordination and strategic thinking, as well as, in some circumstances, cooperation among teammates. However, in states that adopt

13. Rychlak, *supra* note 5, at 558 (describing the "right to receive cash" as being one example of a reward).

14. *Compare H.L. Francis v. County of Stanislaus*, 249 Cal.App.2d 862 (Cal. Ct. of Appeal, 1967) (citing to a California municipal ordinance that treated dominoes as an illegal game of chance) *with* Iowa Code Annotated §99B.11 (2015) (describing as a carve-out from Iowa gambling law bona-fide contests, which include, among other things, "cribbage, bridge, euchre, chess, checkers, dominoes, and pinochle").

15. *See* In re Allen, 59 Cal.2d 5, 8-9 (Cal. Sup. Ct. 1962) (McComb, J., dissenting).

16. *See generally* Rychlak, *supra* note 5, at 566–67 (explaining that whether video games constitute games of chance is dependent upon the underlying nature of the specific video game).

17. *See id.* at 566 (sharing that "[v]ideo gambling devices are typically based on traditional games of chance such as poker, blackjack, craps, and horse racing").

18. *See id.* at 566–67 (1990) (implying that the fact a contest exists over the internet does not directly affect its chance-to-skill ratio).

19. *See* Edelman, *supra* note 10, at 130 (explaining that in predominant purpose tests states, a contest will comply with state law if the contest entails more skill than chance).

the "any chance" test for determining whether an activity is one of skill or chance, some of these games arguably may fall on the wrong side of the law.[20] For example, in Arizona, which is an any-chance state in which even the smallest elements of chance are present, esports operators may wish to scrutinize the underlying contests to make sure the ongoing video games do not include the sort of elements of chance that could provide a reasonable argument for an aggressive prosecutor's legal challenge.[21]

Federal Gambling Laws

With respect to federal gambling laws, two of the most notable—the Illegal Gambling Business Act and the Unlawful Internet Gambling Enforcement Act—include, as a predicate offense, some violation of underlying state gambling law. Thus, to the extent that an esports operator is able to avoid liability under the law of any state in which it operates, it simultaneously should be able to avoid liability under the Illegal Gambling Business Act. However, a third statute, the Federal Wire Act, provides a somewhat more complicated scenario, about which all esports operators should be advised. In pertinent part, this law prohibits those "engaged in the business of betting or wagering" from using a "wire communication facility" for the interstate transmission of "bets or wagers" or "information assisting in the placing of bets or wagers on any sporting event or contest."[22] The regulation is facially neutral on whether a party can be found in violation of the law if the underlying "business of betting or wagering" is legally permissible in all states of operation. Further, the act is silent on what constitutes a wager on a "sporting event or contest."

One of the many intriguing questions that pertain to applying a wide range of different statutory requirements to esports is whether esports indeed constitute "sporting events or contests" under the law.[23] Indeed, if esports are not "sporting events or contests" as the term is defined, then a recent U.S. Court of Appeals for the First Circuit decision would not find the betting on esports to be even subject to this act in the first instance.[24] However, if a court were to interpret "sporting events or contests" to include esports, then there is at least the possibility that a court could

20. *See id.* at 134 (discussing any chance states).

21. *See id.* (including Arizona among the any chance states).

22. 18 U.S.C. §1084(a).

23. *Id.*

24. *Id.*

potentially find an interstate esports competition—and especially one where the underlying video game entails some level of chance—under certain interpretations, to run afoul of the Wire Act.[25]

Esports Sports Betting and Daily Fantasy Sports

Not only do esports operators who pay out prize money to successful participants need to be careful to ensure that their underlying activities do not run afoul of state and federal gambling laws (which, in most cases, they probably do not), but there are also emerging questions surrounding the secondary markets for consumers to bet on the results of esports contests, as well as to enter into daily fantasy sports contests based on esports.

Fan Betting on Esports

With respect to traditional betting on the results of sports contests, it was never clear whether esports had constituted a "sport" under the now-defunct Professional and Amateur Sports Protection Act (PASPA). Nevertheless, the U.S. Supreme Court's striking down of PASPA in the *Murphy* decision overturned the federal law that had prevented states from legalizing and regulating sports betting.[26] Thus, states today are permitted to implement their own laws legalizing and regulating the taking of wagers on esports contests.[27] At present, 28 states have passed laws allowing for some form of sports gambling. Initially, some states that had passed laws legalizing sports gambling, such as New Jersey, disallowed bets on esports events. However, today, a number of states that allow for legalized sports betting have also moved toward allowing legalized and regulated esports betting.[28]

Since all states that have legalized sports betting (which, for our purposes, nowadays generally includes esports betting) have implemented

25. For a detailed discussion of where esports are situated as "sports" see, John T. Holden, Anastasios Kaburakis, & Ryan M. Rodenberg, *The Future Is Now: Esports Policy Considerations and Potential Litigation*, 27 J. Legal Aspects of Sport 46, 48–58 (2017).

26. Murphy v. Nat'l Collegiate Athletic Ass'n, 1138 S. Ct. (2018).

27. *See* Holden & Edelman, *supra* note 2.

28. *Legal Esports Betting*, Betting USA, https://www.bettingusa.com/esports/ (last visited Mar. 29, 2021).

a highly regulated market in which betting operators need to obtain a license, those entities that have become licensed to take bets on esports events are limited to "a few large and powerful companies."[29] In some states, the companies allowed to take these bets do so exclusively at brick-and-mortar facilities such as casinos, sports stadiums, or race tracks.[30] However, an increasing number of states are also moving toward allowing certain licensed operators also to take bets on the internet—a move that, in essence, puts a virtual casino in just about all Americans' hands at all times.[31] For sports betting operators, offering online sports betting on esports events is often considered the holy grail because both esports participants and their fans are perceived as spending large amounts of time on their portable electronic devices.

Fantasy Esports

Questions pertaining to fantasy esports are, in some ways, even more intricate. The term "fantasy sports," dating back to the 1960s, traditionally describes games with a mathematical orientation in which participants select fictitious teams of real-world athletes who they expect to produce the best real-world statistics over a period of time, and which, in doing so, the participants compete against each other for a prize.[32] However, by the late 1990s, many large sports and entertainment companies such as CBS Sports and Yahoo began to offer formally organized daily fantasy sports contests on the internet as a form of commercial enterprise.[33] And, even more recently still, companies like FanDuel and DraftKings have grown the market for a hybrid category of game somewhere between sports gambling and traditional fantasy sports that has become known as "daily fantasy sports."[34] In this hybrid category of game, participants draft players and predict their performance over very short durations of time—sometimes as short as a single day, game, or portion of a game. Nevertheless, almost all companies that operate under the "daily fantasy sports" moniker attempt to differentiate themselves from traditional sports betting by offering games that are based on more than just a single real-world event and

29. Holden & Edelman, *supra* note 2, at 940.
30. *See id.* at 940.
31. *Id.* 940–41.
32. *Id.* at 922.
33. *Id.*
34. *Id.*

which are played against other participants rather than against an odds-maker or "the house."[35]

As the daily fantasy sports marketplace has grown in size and scope, companies such as DraftKings and FanDuel have moved beyond offering their contests on traditional sports and moved into the realm of esports. Meanwhile, several newer niche-based companies, including Fantasy Owl, now offer daily fantasy websites that devote themselves in their entirety to esports.[36] At present, some states have adopted a legalized, licensed, and regulated model for daily fantasy sports that in many ways parallels the regulatory schemes that exist for sports gambling.[37] However, other states continue to regulate fantasy sports under general state gaming law. Thus, for example, in the State of California, which does not have separate fantasy sports law and adopts the "predominant purpose test" for assessing the required level of skill under state gaming law, it is legal to operate a true fantasy esports contest in the state that includes entry fees and prizes as long as the underlying contest involves more skill than chance.[38] Moreover, because it may be argued that the Wire Act, which applies to sports gambling, does not apply to true fantasy sports where the activity is legal in all jurisdictions, in all likelihood operators of daily fantasy esports contests can offer interstate players pools in states where the entry fees are not considered bets or wagers, whereas, at present, gambling on esports (much like traditional sports betting) arguably must be confined to an intrastate basis.

Preserving Esports Contest Integrity in an Era of Gambling's Proliferation

With the emergence of esports betting markets and high-stakes esports daily fantasy contests, one of the essential concerns relates to the integrity

35. *See* Marc Edelman, *Why Daily Fantasy Sports 'Against the House' is Likely Illegal and Could Destabilize the Industry*, Forbes (Apr. 16, 2015), https://www.forbes.com/sites/marcedelman/2015/04/16/why-daily-fantasy-sports-against-the-house-is-likely-illegal-and-could-destabilize-the-industry/?sh=1ef84e654eca.

36. For purposes of full disclosure, one of the authors of this book, Marc Edelman, has provided legal consulting services on certain, specific legal issues to Fantasy Owl.

37. Ryan Butler, *Where Is Sports Betting Legal? Projections for All 50 States,* Action Network (updated Apr. 19, 2021), https://www.actionnetwork.com/news/legal-sports-betting-united-states-projections.

38. In re Allen, 59 Cal. 2d 5, 6 (Cal. Sup. Ct. 1962)

of these contests and the potential of games being fixed for the benefit of gamblers. Indeed, until recently, one of the many reasons why the traditional U.S. professional sports leagues had opposed the legalization of sports betting was the fear of match-fixing. And, there are a few vivid examples in U.S. history of gamblers and others affiliated with organized crime attempting to engage in just these behaviors.[39] Perhaps most notoriously, it was alleged that, in 1919, organized-crime leader Arnold Rothstein bribed eight members of the Chicago White Sox baseball team to lose that year's World Series on purpose.[40] The White Sox ultimately did lose the World Series that year to the Cincinnati Reds—five games to three.

In more recent years, fears of athletes fixing games have declined for the most part as players' abilities to command substantial salaries and endorsement deals negate much of the incentive to engage with gamblers in this manner. However, in sports where the athletes remain uncompensated or under-compensated, the risk of gamblers, or their associates, inducing certain athletes to fix sporting events remains significant. Thus, it is unsurprising that some of the more recent examples of gamblers inducing athletes to corrupt the integrity of their sports have taken place at the collegiate level. For example, during the late 1940s and early 1950, "dozens of college basketball players from around the country were accused of working with members of organized crime to shave points in collegiate basketball games."[41] The point-shaving scandals were so serious that they played a significant role in leading the City College of New York, which had won the 1949-50 NCAA men's basketball championship, to drop out of NCAA Division I sports altogether.[42] Meanwhile, in 1981, "a Brooklyn jury convicted former Boston College basketball star Rick Kuhn of conspiracy in association with efforts to fix Boston College basketball games during the 1978-79 season."[43]

Within the realm of activities in which consumers today can legally bet, esports seems to fall at the high end of the spectrum in terms of the risk for a sports betting scandal. Indeed, esports has already been victimized by a number of match-fixing scandals.[44] This is true not only because many of the participants in esports contests are relatively young

39. *See* Holden & Edelman, *supra* note 2 at 912–13.

40. *Id.* at 913.

41. *See id.* at 915–16.

42. *See id.*

43. *See id.* at 919.

44. *See, e.g.*, Chris Godfrey, *'It's Incredibly Widespread': Why eSports Has a Match-Fixing Problem*, GUARDIAN (Jul. 31, 2018), https://www.theguardian.com/games/2018/jul/31/its-incredibly-widespread-

but also because most are not yet paid on levels nearly comparable with professional athletes in the four major sports. Moreover, at the same time, a good number of those who participate in esports remain highly involved in counterculture. Thus, it would not be a stretch to suggest that the same individuals who would go on a website such as 4Chan and seek to sexually harass female participants might also be predisposed to engaging in antisocial activities concerning contest integrity. While an integrity crisis in the world of esports may not necessarily emerge out of the efforts of organized crime families much as occurred with the Chicago White Sox in 1919, it is not hard to imagine how a small group of individuals could go onto a website like Reddit and attempt to promote a fix similar to how a group of quasi-organized individuals drove up the price of GameStop stock to the detriment of traditional hedge funds.

For these reasons, operators of esports contests need to be as vigilant, if not more so, than the four traditional professional sports leagues in the United States in seeking to combat the fixing of competition results. Reasonable mechanisms that esports contest hosts may seek to adopt range from educating all esports participants on the legal risks of engaging in match-fixing, to using mathematical experts to try to detect unusual betting patterns in advance of matches, to even paying contestants a fair market wage to seek to discourage the desire to engage in such antisocial behavior. As a growing number of investors in the esports marketplace come from the traditional sports world, some of the strategies that have been used for many years by conventional sports leagues to deter the fixing of sporting events may reasonably also carry over to the realm of esports.

Finally, it is worth noting that efforts to disallow betting on esports through either state-licensed sportsbooks or daily fantasy esports websites is probably not the answer. As the collegiate sports industry has found, in a variety of states, there is little public sympathy in today's environment to foreclose certain sports betting options in states where sports betting is otherwise legal. Thus, esports operators should perhaps reasonably come to accept that their businesses will almost certainly be inextricably intertwined with gambling and that it would be in their interest to hire attorneys well-versed in both gambling law and mechanisms for preserving contest integrity to work on matters for them, rather than against them.

---

why-esports-has-a-match-fixing-problem (describing some of the struggles that the esports industry has had with match-fixing).

In-Game Gambling

There have been several prominent scandals in the video game world that have spread into the esports universe involving wagering related to in-game features. The first instance that gained high-profile attention occurred in 2016, when *Bloomberg Businessweek* ran a story on gamers using in-game weapons "skins" (or decorative coatings) to fuel an online gambling industry.[45] The *Bloomberg* article came on the heels of an industry research report that projected esports wagering driven, in part, by skins wagering would reach a value of more than $23 billion by 2020.[46] The skins gambling industry was able to function by virtue of the software Application Program Interface (API) in the game *Counter-Strike: Global Offensive* (*CS: GO*), which allowed users to transfer these weapons between users.[47] The API allowed users to create a marketplace with the skins acting as a type of virtual currency with the value being associated with the scarcity of a particular design. The easy transferability then enabled the skins to be used just like money or a credit card.[48] Eventually, after pressure from a variety of regulators, the maker of *CS: GO* moved to shut down many of the sites taking advantage of the game's API.[49] However, *CS: GO* was hardly the only game with an API allowing for such transactions to take place. While concerns over gambling using in-game currencies remain prevalent, regulators have more recently focused on gambling related to in-game products, such as loot boxes.

Loot boxes are a purported $30 billion industry.[50] Loot boxes appear in a variety of games and allow players the opportunity to gain an item, which may provide some utility in gameplay or merely have an esthetic appeal. In-game loot boxes have historically allowed gamers to pay money to purchase additional chances, at what is similar in many cases to a virtual

---

45. Eben Novy-Williams, *Legal Sports Books Get Ready for Billions in E-Sports Betting*, Bloomberg (Aug. 26, 2016, 12:21 AM), http://www.bloomberg.com/news/articles/2016-08-26/legal-sports-books-get-ready-for-billions-in-e-sports-betting.

46. John T. Holden, Ryan M. Rodenberg, & Anastasios Kaburakis, *Esports Corruption: Gambling, Doping, and Global Governance*, 32 Maryland J. Int'l L. 236, 237 (2017).

47. *Id* at 248.

48. Chris Grove, Understanding Skin Gambling 1–9 (2016), https://www.thelines.com/wp-content/uploads/2018/03/Skin-Gambling-White-Paper-V2.pdf.

49. Staff, *Valve: CS:GO Skin Gambling Site Have 10 Days to Shut Down*, Score (Jul. 20, 2016), https://www.thescoreesports.com/csgo/news/9241-valve-cs-go-skin-gambling-sites-have-10-days-to-shut-down.

50. Sheldon Evans, *Pandora's Loot Box*, 5 (working paper), *available at:* https://papers.ssrn.com/sol3/papers.cfm?abstract_id=3733910.

slot machine.[51] The gambling similarities have attracted the attention of a variety of regulators.[52] The attention from regulators has caused some game makers to pull loot boxes from their titles.[53] It is unclear if loot boxes will remain a fixture in the future, but should they remain, one would expect increased disclosures and protections to prevent minors from accessing that feature in games.

Concluding Thoughts

The interplay between gambling law and esports is one of the many topics within the emerging world of esports that, in the authors' opinion, has not received nearly the attention it deserves in scholarship or the legal profession. Yet, the intertwining of these two activities is undeniable. Not only are both the esports and gambling industries coming of age at the same time to grow the pie of sports revenues overall, but the esports industry also presents many gambling-related concerns. Moreover, unlike in traditional sports leagues where players compete based upon their physical strength and acumen, esports contests that give prizes to the winners leave unresolved questions as to whether succeeding in the underlying video game entails certain elements of chance. Although in the infancy of the esports industry lawyers without independent experience in gambling-related matters could market themselves as esports experts, times have changed. Today, on account of the widespread popularity of esports in America and the integrity concerns that have presented themselves in recent years, it is imperative for attorneys who practice in the esports and electronic gaming space to have in-depth knowledge of gambling law at both the federal and state levels.

---

51. *Id.*

52. *See e.g.*, Nathan Birch, *Loot Boxes Targeted as a Concern by Gambling Regulators from 15 European Countries*, WCCFTech (Sep. 17, 2018), https://wccftech.com/loot-boxes-gambling-15-euro-countries/ (noting regulators from 15 European countries were examining the gambling-like elements of loot boxes).

53. Teddy Amenabar, *Video Game 'Loot Boxes' Are Going Away and It Could Crush Rocket League's Black Market*, Wash. Post (Aug. 27, 2019), https://www.washingtonpost.com/video-games/2019/08/27/video-game-loot-boxes-are-going-away-it-could-crush-rocket-leagues-black-market/.

Chapter 11

Doping in Esports

Introduction

"Nobody talks about it because everyone is on it."[1] "It's very, very, very widespread."[2] These are phrases used by professional esports players to describe the rampant doping culture in American esports. Distinguishable from what one might consider as doping in traditional sports—through the use of steroids and other performance-enhancing drugs (PEDs)—doping in esports involves the use of nootropics.[3] Nootropics are drugs designed to influence and enhance cognition,[4] and they include prescription medications like Adderall and Ritalin.[5] Adderall and Ritalin are used to treat Attention-Deficit/Hyperactivity Disorder (ADHD),[6] which

1. Coleman Hamstead, *'Nobody talks about it because everyone is on it': Adderall presents esports with an enigma*, Washington Post (Feb. 13, 2020, 10:27 AM), https://www.washingtonpost.com/video-games/esports/2020/02/13/esports-adderall-drugs/.

2. Simon Parkin, *Winners might use drugs—Does eSports have a doping problem?*, Eurogamer (Apr. 8, 2015), https://www.eurogamer.net/articles/2015-04-08-winners-might-use-drugs.

3. John T. Holden, Anastasios Kaburakis & Joanna Wall Tweedie, *Virtue(al) games—real drugs*, 13 Sport, Ethics & Phil. 19, 21 (2019)

4. John T. Holden, Ryan M. Rodenberg, & Anastasios Kaburakis, *Esports Corruption: Gambling, Doping, and Global Governance*, 32 Maryland J. Int'l L. 236, 269 (2017).

5. *Id.* at 239; Ryan M. Rodenberg & John T. Holden, *Cognition enhancing drugs ('nootropics'): time to include coaches and team executives in doping tests?*, 51 Brit. J. Sports Med. 1316 (2017).

6. *See* Rodenberg & Holden, *supra* note 5, at 1316.

presents itself in three primary forms—inattentive type, hyperactive-impulsive type, or combined type.[7]

In 2012, doctors prescribed 16 million Americans with Adderall.[8] Currently, Adderall abuse is especially prevalent among 18- to 25-year-olds—America's college-aged population.[9] For example, in a 2018 study conducted of 1,300 students, the University of Michigan found that 25 percent of students reported using Adderall or similar cognition-enhancing drugs to complete schoolwork or take an exam.[10] However, only 8.95 percent of the survey respondents actually had an Adderall prescription.[11] In total, of the Michigan students prescribed Adderall by a psychiatrist, 37 percent reported they had either given or sold the drug to another student.[12] These statistics regarding Adderall use by students without prescriptions are unsurprising because between 2017 and 2018, there were roughly 2.2 million adults aged 18 to 25 who misused stimulant medication.[13]

In professional esports, prescription stimulant abuse also runs rampant. In 2015, Timo Kettunen, a now-retired professional esports player who played on the *Overwatch* League's Dallas team, discussed taking cognition-enhancing stimulants on his Twitch live stream.[14] Kettunen shared, "there are probably 20 players who use Adderall in the League."[15] That same year, professional *Counter-Strike* player Kory Friesen admitted that he and his teammates took Adderall during a tournament.[16] Friesen

---

7. *What is ADHD?*, Centers for Disease Control and Prevention (Oct. 23, 2020), https://www.cdc.gov/ncbddd/adhd/facts.html.

8. Casey Schwartz, *Generation Adderall*, N.Y. Times (Oct. 12, 2016), https://www.nytimes.com/2016/10/16/magazine/generation-adderall-addiction.html.

9. *Adderall abuse on the rise among young adults, Johns Hopkins study suggests*, Johns Hopkins Magazine (Feb. 16, 2016), https://hub.jhu.edu/2016/02/16/adderall-abuse-rising-young-adults/.

10. Molly Norris, *Survey finds that 24 percent of University students use Adderall*, The Michigan Daily (Mar. 25, 2018, 8:06 PM), https://www.michigandaily.com/section/research/adderall-used-24-university-students/.

11. *Id.*

12. *Id.*

13. Substance Abuse and Mental Health Services Administration, *Key Substance Use and Mental Health Indicators in the United States: Results from the 2018 National Survey on Drug Use and Health* 19 (2019), https://www.samhsa.gov/data/sites/default/files/cbhsq-reports/NSDUHNationalFindingsReport2018/NSDUHNationalFindingsReport2018.pdf.

14. Emanuel Maiberg, *'Overwatch' Esports Pro Says 'Probably 20 Players' Use Adderall in the Official League*, Vice (Nov. 13, 2018, 8:50 AM), https://www.vice.com/en/article/3k9qpk/overwatch-esports-pro-says-probably-20-players-use-adderall-in-the-official-league.

15. *Id.*

16. Cody Luongo, *ESI Gambling Report: Sex, drugs and esports*, Esports Insider (Aug. 31, 2018), https://esportsinsider.com/2018/08/esi-gambling-report-sex-drugs-and-esports/.

explained, "We were all on Adderall. . . . It was pretty obvious."[17] In a subsequent interview, Friesen answered in the affirmative when asked whether Adderall is a popular drug taken by players at esports tournaments and competitions.[18] Most recently, in February of 2020, Adam Sloss, the former *Call of Duty* world champion, cited the prevalence of cognition-enhancing drug abuse in esports as the driving factor behind his choice to end his professional gaming career.[19]

The use of prescription stimulant medication is likely on the rise in professional esports due to the shorter average career length of esports players in comparison to traditional professional sports athletes. In esports, the average player is approximately 22 years old.[20] This is distinguishable from other traditional professional sports like basketball and football, in which the average player is roughly 26.5 years old.[21] For esports athletes, success in competition depends on a player's reflexes.[22] Because the brain's reaction time begin declining after the age of 24, professional esports athletes tend to enjoy shorter careers than professional athletes in the NFL or NBA.[23] As a result of the shorter average career lengths of esports players, players' income-generating incentives are high.[24] For example, from winning top competitions like the *League of Legends* World Championship or the *Fortnite* World Cup Finals, individual players stand to take home a prize of somewhere between \$2 to \$3 million.[25] Additionally, players can supplement their prize winnings by streaming on Twitch. Top

---

17. *Id.*

18. James A. Ingram, *Kicking It New School: Applying the FIFA Regulatory Model to the Esports Industry*, 51 Geo. Wash. Int'l L. Rev. 483, 503 (2019).

19. Hamstead, *supra* note 1.

20. Nick Summers, *The esports elders defying their age*, Engadget (Mar. 9, 2020), https://www.engadget.com/2020-03-09-the-esports-elders-defying-their-age.html.

21. Sok Min Yun, *A Comparative Overview of ESports Against Traditional Sports Focused in the Legal Realm of Monetary Exploration, Cheating, and Gambling*, 37 Cardozo Arts & Ent. L.J. 513, 530 (2019).

22. *Id.* at 531.

23. *See id.* at 531.

24. *See id.* at 529; Rebecca R. Rosenthal, *A Tough Pill to Swallow: Making the Case for Why eSports Leagues Must Adopt Strict Banned Substance Policies to Prevent Disability Discrimination*, 2021 Va. Sports & Ent. L. J. (forthcoming Spring 2021).

25. *See* Sam Nordmark & Jerome Heath, *The top 10 highest prize pools in esports*, Dot Esports (Sep. 2, 2020, 10:00 AM), https://dotesports.com/general/news/biggest-prize-pools-esports-14605. At the 2019 *Dota 2* tournament, The International, each player on the winning team—OG—won \$3.1 million. This prize winning was roughly \$1 million more than Tiger Woods won at the 2019 Masters, and approximately \$200,000 more than Novak Djokovic won at Wimbledon in 2019. Jon Fingas, *'Dota 2' champions won more money than top Wimbledon players*, Engadget (Aug. 25, 2019), https://www.engadget.com/2019-08-25-dota-2-the-international-2019-win-sets-records.html.

Twitch streamers earn nearly $10,000 per hour by streaming a certain sponsors' game on Twitch, and these players can simultaneously earn additional revenue through fan donations.[26] In sum, just as professional football or basketball players may turn to performance-enhancing drugs to extend their careers, esports athletes also resort to performance enhancers like stimulant medication to prolong their otherwise short windows for success.[27]

Understanding prescription stimulant misuse in esports is important for two primary reasons. First, looking at the prevalence of doping and existing drug policies in professional esports allows us to compare esports leagues with traditional American sports leagues. Drawing parallels between esports leagues and traditional sports leagues emphasizes why current doping policies in professional esports fall short and how leagues can better shield themselves from potential liability issues. Second, exploring the prevalence of esports doping and the unique relationship esports players share with their fans underscores why esports leagues have a significant role to play in mitigating prescription drug abuse across the industry. This chapter will explore the drug policies or lack thereof in esports and the role that leagues might play in eradicating prescription stimulant abuse, in turn. Lastly, this chapter will analyze potential arguments against enacting strict doping policies in esports and the challenges esports organizations may face as they seek to publish doping policies.

Esports Versus Traditional Sports: An Exploration of Doping Policies

Juxtaposing the current doping regulations in professional esports with the banned substances policies present in traditional professional sports illustrates why the world of American professional esports remains rife with prescription stimulant abuse and drug rumors.[28] To date, the *only* professional esports league with any form of doping policy is the Electronic Sports League (ESL).[29] The ESL enacted its policy in 2015, and the policy bans prescription stimulant medication like Ritalin and Adderall, as

26. Pavle Marinkovic, *Esports Pro Gamers: How Much Do They Earn?*, Medium (Jul. 8, 2020), https://medium.com/super-jump/esports-pro-gamers-how-much-do-they-earn-f03a1d047190.

27. *See* Yun, *supra* note 21, at 531.

28. *See* Hamstead, *supra* note 1.

29. *Id.*

well as drugs like cocaine and marijuana.[30] The ESL's drug policy is straightforward—the ESL official rules simply delineate: "Any kind of doping is forbidden."[31] However, for players who have prescriptions for medication like Adderall, the ESL creates an exception.[32] Specifically, the ESL requires players with an active prescription to "send proof to the tournament administration before the first day of the tournament."[33] While the ESL still may subject players with an approved active prescription to a drug test, the ESL will disregard any positive results for the prescribed substance.[34] Thus, a prescription for a stimulant medication is all that is needed for an ESL player to take an otherwise banned substance in competition—no medical clearance or psychiatric testing is required.

The ESL's doping policy, which simply requires players to provide proof of a valid prescription before taking substances such as Adderall or Ritalin, provides a low threshold for players to meet compared to the policies promulgated by traditional professional sports leagues.[35] For example, the NFL—the first professional sports league to enact a banned substance policy in 1987[36]—bans its players from taking drugs like Adderall and Ritalin.[37] However, the NFL offers players what is known as a Therapeutic Use Exemption (TUE), under which due to a medical condition like a learning disability, players may take an otherwise banned substance.[38] To obtain a TUE for a drug like Adderall or Ritalin, an NFL player must subject himself to an evaluation by an NFL-certified psychiatrist, who conducts a complete neurological evaluation utilizing two

---

30. Saira Muller, *eSports Drug Testing Update: ESL Announces List Of Banned Substances Including Adderall, Cocaine, Pot, Steroids and More*, INT'L BUS. TIMES (Aug. 12, 2015, 10:28 AM), https://www.ibtimes.com/esports-drug-testing-update-esl-announces-list-banned-substances-including-adderall-2050245.

31. *2.5 Doping*, ESL PLAY, https://play.eslgaming.com/rules#wdh_2_5-Doping (last visited Jan. 14, 2021).

32. *Id.*

33. *Id.*

34. *Id.*

35. *See* Rosenthal, *supra* note 24.

36. Maureen A. Weston, *The Regulation of Doping in U.S. and International Sports, in* THE OXFORD HANDBOOK OF AMERICAN SPORTS LAW 87 (Michael A. McCann ed., 2018).

37. *List of Prohibited Substances, Appendix A*, THE NATIONAL FOOTBALL LEAGUE PLAYERS' ASSOCIATION (Mar. 3, 2020), https://nflpaweb.blob.core.windows.net/website/Departments/Wellness/2020-Banned-Substances-List.pdf.

38. CHRISTOPHER R. DEUBERT ET AL., COMPARING HEALTH-RELATED POLICIES & PRACTICES IN SPORTS: THE NFL AND OTHER PROFESSIONAL LEAGUES 140 (2017), https://footballplayershealth.harvard.edu/wp-content/uploads/2017/05/08_Ch4_Drugs.pdf.

distinct ADHD diagnostic metrics.[39] NFL players seeking TUEs must also provide the NFL with all documentation related to their previous medical history and fill out a TUE application form.[40] According to NFL guidelines, all players who receive a TUE must seek renewal of their TUE on an annual basis.[41] The renewal involves a player submitting a new TUE application and providing all documentation of psychiatric visits and pharmacy records from the previous year.[42]

The TUE guidelines proffered by the NFL are similar to the policies enacted by the NBA. For a player to obtain a TUE in the NBA, the player must petition the Medical Director of the NBA's Anti-Drug Program for permission to use a banned substance.[43] After reviewing the player's diagnosis and medical documentation, including evidence of a validly issued prescription, the Medical Director may grant an NBA player permission to take an otherwise banned substance like Adderall or Ritalin.[44] Likewise, in the MLB, players seeking to take otherwise banned substances must apply for a TUE with the Independent Program Administrator.[45] Only after the Independent Program Administrator consults with members of the MLB's Medical Advisory panel and receives sufficient medical documentation and proof of a valid prescription from a TUE-seeking player may the player take an otherwise banned substance.[46]

While, like the NFL, NBA, and MLB, the ESL *does* drug test its players,[47] as a whole, the ESL's doping policy is less strict than the policies enacted by traditional sports leagues. Specifically, the ESL's policy—the only current doping policy in professional esports—falls short because it places few regulations on misuse of prescription stimulants. In America, Adderall prescriptions are ubiquitous,[48] and individuals can easily obtain

39. *See NFL Requirements for Therapeutic Use Exemption (TUE): Attention Deficit and Attention Deficit Hyperactivity Disorders (ADHD)*, The National Football League, https://nflpaweb.blob.core.windows.net/media/Default/PDFs/ADHD_requirements_2018.pdf (last visited Jan. 13, 2021).

40. *Id.*

41. *Id.*

42. *Id.*

43. Deubert et al., *supra* note 38, at 149.

44. *Id.*

45. *Id.* at 146.

46. Deubert et al., *supra* note 38, at 146; *Major League Baseball's Joint Drug Prevention and Treatment Program*, Major League Baseball, http://www.mlb.com/pa/pdf/jda.pdf (last visited Jan. 14, 2021).

47. Zachary Kandell, *eSports Has Its Own Doping Problem*, CBR (Feb. 28, 2020), https://www.cbr.com/esports-doping-problem/.

48. *See* Casey Schwartz, *Generation Adderall*, N.Y. Times (Oct. 12, 2016), https://www.nytimes.com/2016/10/16/magazine/generation-adderall-addiction.html.

prescriptions for stimulants without even needing an ADHD diagnosis.[49] Because the ESL's doping policy seems to permit players to obtain a TUE as long as they submit proof of a valid prescription,[50] even players who obtain prescriptions under false pretenses and do not have an ADHD diagnosis may take otherwise banned substances. Thus, unlike in the NFL, in which the number of players who receive TUEs is very small,[51] it is probable that due to the ESLs' lax regulations, there may be many players with TUEs for stimulant medication currently competing in the ESL.

The fact that the ESL proffers such a low threshold for TUE-seeking players is problematic for two primary reasons. First, Adderall presents serious health risks to players. Adderall is attractive to esports players due to the laser-like focus, energy boost, and quick reaction times it offers.[52] However, due to its advantageous effects, players often end up taking larger doses than prescribed—even snorting the drugs.[53] Taking a larger dose than prescribed or planned can lead to long-term psychiatric problems like psychosis, as well as heart attacks and strokes.[54] Second, in addition to the harmful effects of unmonitored use of prescription stimulants or taking stimulants without a medical necessity for doing so, the ESL's low threshold for TUEs is worrisome because it fosters a disparity between players. As it currently stands, the ESL's doping policy allows for non-disabled players to receive TUEs for ADHD medication as long as they have a prescription.[55] Without the high hurdles of medical documentation and psychiatric evaluations required by leagues like the NFL and NBA, the ESL cannot accurately determine which players do and do not have a diagnosis for ADHD or another learning disability. In turn, the ESL's policies give non-disabled players the ability to take Adderall to achieve a boost or competitive edge, whereas players for whom Adderall is a medical necessity are only able to achieve a normal or baseline state when

---

49. Liz Welch, *Adderall: The "Get Ahead" Drug*, Self (Mar. 12, 2013), https://www.self.com/story/adderall-the-get-ahead-drug.

50. ESL Play, *supra* note 31.

51. David Leon Moore & Jim Corbett, *Do pro sports leagues have an Adderall problem?*, Usa Today (Nov. 27, 2012, 8:46 PM), https://www.usatoday.com/story/sports/nfl/2012/11/27/adderall-in-pro-sports/1730431/.

52. Kevin Loria, *Some competitive video gamers are abusing drugs to get an edge*, Business Insider (Jan. 15, 2016, 3:44 PM), https://www.businessinsider.com/esports-doping-scandal-investigated-by-espns-otl-2016-1.

53. Hal Hodson, *Esports: Doping is rampant, industry insider claims*, NewScientist (Aug. 13, 2014), https://www.newscientist.com/article/dn26051-esports-doping-is-rampant-industry-insider-claims/.

54. Welch, *supra* note 49.

55. ESL Play, *supra* note 31.

taking these same medications.[56] Dr. Ari Tuckman, a psychologist, and an ADHD-focused author, explains that the distinction between disabled and non-disabled individuals taking prescription stimulants is "like how your friend's glasses give him 20/20 vision but don't make your 20/20 vision even better."[57] Accordingly, the ESL's current policies make the playing field between disabled and non-disabled esports players unequal. As a result, the ESL's policies could render it liable to suit under the Americans with Disabilities Act (ADA),[58] as one of the ADA's primary goals is to guarantee that those with disabilities are not at a disadvantage in the workplace.[59] Overall, the current lax doping regulations in esports allow for prescription drug abuse to run rampant despite the presence of drug testing. Further, the lack of strict regulations surrounding prescription stimulant use also engenders inequality between disabled and non-disabled players, and thereby opens the doors for potential disability discrimination suits against leagues like the ESL.

Eradicating Prescription Drug Abuse in Esports

It is likely that lack of central governance is the primary reason doping in professional esports is prevalent.[60] In keeping with this, various institutions have sought to uphold the integrity of esports. For example, a non-profit organization, the Esports Integrity Commission (ESIC, previously known as the Esports Integrity Coalition), began operating in 2015.[61] One of the Commission's primary goals is to prevent drug abuse in professional

56. *See* Rosenthal, *supra* note 24. For players who take cognition-enhancing drugs and do not struggle with a learning disability like ADHD, these drugs have the potential to influence athletic performance. *See* Rodenberg & Holden, *supra* note 5, at 1316.

57. Jody Macgregor, *Doctors explain why abusing ADHD meds won't help esports players*, PC GAMER (Dec. 2020), https://www.pcgamer.com/doctors-explain-why-abusing-adhd-meds-wont-help-esports-players/.

58. *See* Jonathan Stoler & Daniel Masakayan, *United States: 10 Labor And Employment Considerations in Esports*, MONDAQ (Jun. 6, 2019), https://www.mondaq.com/unitedstates/gaming/812750/10-labor-and-employment-considerations-in-esports (explaining that although Adderall is legitimately used to treat ADHD—a disability recognized by the ADA—some competitors seeking to gain an unfair advantage by using these drugs, and as a result, leagues must recognize their role of properly accommodating their disabled players under the ADA).

59. Holly v. Clairson Indus., 492 F.3d 1247, 1263 (11th Cir. 2007); Rothberg v. Law Sch. Admission Council, Inc., 300 F. Supp. 2d 1093, 1105 (D. Colo. 2004).

60. Atish Ghoshal, *Ethics in Esports*, 23 GAMING L. REV. 338, 339 (2019).

61. Ryan Toomey, *Upholding the Integrity of Esports to Successfully and Safely Legitimize Esports Wagering*, 1 GAMING L. REV. 12, 17 (2019).

esports.[62] In furtherance of this goal, the Commission publishes a Banned Substance Policy and an Anti-Doping Code that esports leagues and organizations may adopt.[63] Another initiative to help regulate the esports industry came about in 2016 when the ESL founded the World Esports Association (WESA).[64] WESA's mission is to help professionalize and streamline professional esports by offering options for player representation, creating revenue sharing opportunities, and standardizing rules and regulations.[65]

Despite the promising goals of the ESIC and WESA and the efforts these organizations have put forth to regulate the esports industry, the only major esports league that is part of WESA is the ESL (WESA's founder). Similarly, the ESL is also the only prominent esports league that is a member of the ESIC.[66] While leagues like the *Overwatch* League have discussed enacting a banned substance policy since 2015,[67] no major esports leagues aside from the ESL have enacted any form of doping policy to date. The only anti-drug sentiments top esports leagues currently offer include statements in their rulebooks like "The use, possession, distribution or sale of any illegal drugs is prohibited,"[68] and "The unauthorized use or possession of prescription drugs by a Player is prohibited."[69] These rulebooks make no mention of drug testing and do not include any sort of banned substance lists.

One potential avenue for esports leagues and organizations to eradicate prescription drug abuse could be to enact strict banned substance policies that mirror those published by leagues like the NFL and NBA. However, there is an argument to be made that the doping policies enacted by esports leagues should be even more stringent than those of traditional

62. Jacqueline Martinelli, *The Challenges of Implementing A Governing Body for Regulating eSports*, 26 U. Miami Int'l & Comp. L. Rev. 499, 506 (2019); *Anti-Doping Code*, ESIC, https://esic.gg/codes/anti-doping-code/ (last visited Jan. 14, 2021).

63. Toomey, *supra* note 61, at 17.

64. Martinelli, *supra* note 62, at 506.

65. *Home*, WESA, http://www.wesa.gg (last visited Jan. 14, 2021).

66. *See* Holden, Kaburakis & Tweedie, *supra* note 3, at 21; Hamstead, *supra* note 1 .

67. Hannah Dwan, *Overwatch League Commissioner Nate Nanzer on diversity, player unions and where the league's rules are,* The Telegraph (Jan. 24, 2018, 5:15 PM), https://www.telegraph.co.uk/gaming/features/overwatch-league-nate-nanzer-rules-diversity-player-unions/.

68. Call of Duty World League 2019 Official Handbook, Call of Duty, https://www.callofduty.com/content/dam/atvi/callofduty/esports-new/2019-rules/2019_CWL_Handbook.pdf (last visited Jan. 14, 2021).

69. Overwatch League, Rules of Competition and Code of Conduct, Blizzard Entertainment (Feb. 9, 2019), https://overwatchleague.com/en-us/news/21568602/rules-of-competition-and-Code-of-conduct.

sports leagues due to the unique demands of esports.[70] Specifically, the length and level of concentration professional esports demands are distinguishable from what is required of a professional football player.[71] For example, NFL players may put in fifty hours a week of work for sixteen weeks of a year,[72] whereas top esports players practice their game somewhere between eight to fifteen hours a day, even outside of competition season.[73] Due to the rigorous demands placed on top esports competitors, which require long hours of focus and extreme mental acuity, it is understandable why cognition-enhancing drugs should be closely monitored and policed.

Further, perhaps esports leagues seeking to enact doping policies might also consider implementing stricter regulations than traditional sports leagues because of the strong influence esports athletes have on adolescent fans. Due to the "grassroots nature" of professional esports, a great deal of success in esports stems from interactions with fans.[74] Fan interaction is significant because the more accessible a player is online via streaming platforms like Twitch, the easier time the player has building his or her personal brand.[75] According to Kyle Souder, a coach for the *Overwatch* League Paris team, personal brand building is important for esports athletes because the brands of gamers can "outlast their careers as players."[76] Unfortunately, because prescription stimulant abuse is so ubiquitous in professional esports, it is regularly discussed on platforms like Twitch and Reddit.[77] In keeping with this, Adam Sloss, the former *Call of Duty* World Champion, suggests that many kids now realize that "some of the best players in the world are taking Adderall," so they too want to "experiment and see if it helps."[78] To limit the next generation of gamers from procuring stimulant medication prescriptions in the hopes of attaining fame and fortune in the world of esports, leagues could consider

70. *See* Rosenthal, *supra* note 24.

71. *See* Katherine E. Hollist, *Time to be Grown-Ups about Video Gaming: The Rising eSports Industry and the Need for Regulation*, 57 Ariz. L. Rev. 823, 834 (2015).

72. *Id.*

73. Graham Ashton, *What is the Optimum Training Time for Esports Players?* The ESports Observer (Dec. 28, 2017), https://esportsobserver.com/optimum-player-training-time/.

74. Noah Smith, *'It's not as awesome as people imagine': Esports players say 'dream job' is more than fun and games*, The Washington Post (Dec. 13, 2018, 9:53 AM), https://www.washingtonpost.com/sports/2018/12/13/its-not-awesome-people-imagine-esports-players-say-dream-job-is-more-than-fun-games/.

75. *Id.*

76. *Id.*

77. *See* Hamstead, *supra* note 1.

78. *Id.*

enacting strict banned substance policies that require extensive testing before players can take stimulant medication. Doing so would lessen the chances that professional players discuss stimulant medication on their Twitch live streams, and in turn, influence their young fans to experiment with these dangerous drugs.

Finally, another potential option for doping regulation in professional esports may stem from the International Olympics Committee (IOC) recognizing esports as a sporting event in the upcoming Olympics.[79] The reason for this is that the IOC was the first organization to create a Prohibited List of drugs in 1967.[80] In 1992, the IOC created the concept of therapeutic use exemptions.[81] If professional esports do occur at the next Olympics or in future Olympic Games, any esports athletes will be subject to drug testing and the IOC's rigorous TUE policies.[82] As a result, players who typically play using medication under false pretenses or who play for a league that does not test for drugs will face difficulty obtaining clearance to use the prescription stimulant medication in competition. Consequently, the drug policies American professional esports players will likely face for the first time at the Olympics may inspire American esports leagues to enact doping policies that mirror those present at the highest level of competition.

Potential Limitations and Future Challenges to Doping Reform in Esports

Perhaps professional esports leagues have yet to enact doping policies because, due to the rising number of ADHD diagnoses each year in America, leagues fear that their policies will either exclude too many players who have a legitimate need for cognition-enhancing drugs or risk

79. Martinelli, *supra* note 62, at 503.

80. Alan Vernec & David Healy, *Prevalence of therapeutic use exemptions at the Olympic Games and association with medals: an analysis of data from 2010 to 2018*, 54 Brit. J. Sports Med 920 (2020). The responsibility of publishing the list, which included both stimulants and narcotics, was adopted by the World Anti-Doping Agency (WADA), in 2004. As the years passed, both the IOC and WADA recognized that certain athletes needed medical exemptions. *Id.*

81. George G. A. Pujalte et al., *Considerations in the Care of Athletes with Attention Deficit Hyperactive Disorder*, 29 Clinical J. Sports Med. 245, 251 (2017).

82. Int'l Olympics Comm., Anti-Doping Rules Applicable to the Games of the XXXII Olympiad Tokyo 2020 10–11 (2019), https://stillmedab.olympic.org/media/Document%20Library/OlympicOrg/Games/Summer-Games/Games-Tokyo-2020-Olympic-Games/Anti-Doping-and-Medical-Rules/IOC-Anti-Doping-Rules-Tokyo-2020.pdf.

player abuse of the TUE system.[83] However, if professional esports continues to be plagued by drug-taking rumors, leagues will struggle to attract and maintain major corporate sponsors.[84] Additionally, a lack of doping regulations in esports not only poses integrity concerns but also encourages recreational use of cognition-enhancing drugs, which, in turn, can influence children to experiment with various substances.[85]

Although the need for doping regulations in professional esports seems apparent, there are several arguments against enacting banned substance policies in professional esports. First, enacting doping regulations in esports could be prohibitively expensive for esports leagues. For example, the infrastructure needed to drug test all players can cost upwards of $40,000 per season.[86] Second, a common argument, and one that was offered by former *Overwatch* League Commissioner Nate Nanzer in 2018, is that there is little to no proof that drugs like Adderall make players better at esports.[87] Third, there is a slippery slope argument often made regarding where to draw the line. For example, if esports leagues ban Adderall, might they also need to ban energy drinks and nootropics made of natural ingredients?[88] Having too broad of a banned substance policy could be problematic because some more minor esports leagues are beginning to partner with nootropics manufacturers,[89] and industry giants like Monster Energy sponsor prominent esports teams.[90]

Despite the presence of three main arguments against implementing doping regulations in esports, each of these arguments can be refuted. First, with regard to doping tests being cost-prohibitive, while smaller esports leagues might struggle to absorb costs of $40,000 to administer

---

83. Holden, Kaburakis & Tweedie, *supra* note 3, at 23.

84. *See* Jake Tucker, *eSports Has to Grow Up, and Drug-Testing Its Players Is an Important Step*, VICE (Aug. 3, 2015, 11:45 AM), https://www.vice.com/en_us/article/9bgz97/esports-has-to-grow-up-and-anti-doping-measures-are-an-essential-step-930.

85. John T. Holden, Anastasios Kaburakis & Ryan M. Rodenberg, *Esports: Children, stimulants and video-gaming-induced activity*, 54 J. PAEDIATRICS & CHILD HEALTH 830 (2018).

86. Zachary Kandell, *eSports Has Its Own Doping Problem*, CBR (Feb. 28, 2020), https://www.cbr.com/esports-doping-problem/.

87. Hamstead, *supra* note 1.

88. *See* Hamstead, *supra* note 1; Lara Heintz, *Do Nootropics Give Esports Gamers an Edge?*, VICE (Sep. 1, 2016, 1:39 PM) https://www.vice.com/en/article/vv7yv4/do-nootropics-give-esports-gamers-an-edge-1.

89. Jody Macgregor, *'Nootropics' marketed to esports viewers aren't necessarily safe, says doctor*, PC GAMER (Dec. 9, 2020), https://www.pcgamer.com/nootropics-marketed-to-esports-viewers-arent-necessarily-safe-says-doctor/.

90. H.B. Duran, *A guide to: Energy drinks in esports*, ESPORTS INSIDER (Dec. 29, 2020), https://esportsinsider.com/2020/12/energy-drinks-esports-guide/.

doping tests,[91] for larger professional esports organizations like the *Overwatch* League, this price-tag would pose few, if any, issues.[92] Second, despite contentions from former *Overwatch* Commissioner Nate Nanzer and other esports industry figures that Adderall has no effect on gaming success, esports scholars argue that cognition-enhancing drugs *do*, in fact, have some potential to enhance sports performance—specifically due to their ability to reduce fatigue, increase reaction times, and improve endurance.[93] Third and finally, even though banning drugs like Adderall seems similar to banning things like Red Bull, a 2019 scientific study of the effect of energy drinks on professional esports players found that energy beverages do not influence or boost the cognitive abilities of those who consume them.[94] Therefore, if leagues chose to ban stimulant medication, they would not also need to consider banning things like caffeine or energy drinks.

While esports leagues may face various challenges in creating and adopting doping policies, two recent developments in the world of esports make it imperative for esports leagues and organizations to strongly consider adopting doping policies in the near future. First, during the COVID-19 pandemic, esports has experienced a boost in popularity, with platforms like Twitch experiencing a 50 percent increase in online traffic.[95] Further, traditional sports teams who had tournaments and matches canceled due to the pandemic quickly pivoted to esports as an alternative opportunity to engage audiences and garner revenue.[96] For example, after the NBA announced the suspension of its season, the Phoenix Suns began to simulate their regular season events using the *NBA 2K* video game and streaming the games on Twitch.[97] On account of this recent surge in popularity of esports, esports leagues "have a public-relations interest in making games fair because fans do not like cheaters."[98] Second, in June of

---

91. Kandell, *supra* note 86.

92. *See* Olga Kharif, *Activision Launces Call of Duty League for Boost in Esports*, Bloomberg (Jan. 24, 2020, 6:30 AM), https://www.bloomberg.com/news/articles/2020-01-24/activision-launches-call-of-duty-league-to-gain-lead-in-esports.

93. *See* Rodenberg & Holden, *supra* note 5, at 1316.

94. Casey J. Thomas, et al., *The Effects of Energy Drink Consumption on Cognitive and Physical Performance in Elite League of Legends Players*, 7 Sports 1 (2019), https://www.mdpi.com/2075-4663/7/9; Rosenthal, *supra* note 24.

95. *The pandemic has accelerated the growth of e-sports*, The Economist (Jun. 27, 2020), https://www.economist.com/international/2020/06/27/the-pandemic-has-accelerated-the-growth-of-e-sports.

96. Tobias Seck, *How COVID-19 Changed the Esports Industry in 2020*, The Esports Observer (Dec. 23, 2020), https://esportsobserver.com/covid-19-finance-2020/#jeg_loginform.

97. *Id.*

98. Colby Stivers, *The First Competitive Video Gaming Anti-Doping Policy and Its Deficiencies Under European Union Law*, 18 San Diego Int'l L.J., 263, 269–70 (2017).

2020, the Food and Drug Administration announced its approval of the first-ever video game, called EndeavorRX, to help alleviate the ADHD symptoms of children.[99] Although the game is not designed to supplant prescription medication, it does aim to help children increase focus.[100] With the advent of this new game designed to help children with ADHD, parents may become more comfortable letting children as young as eight begin playing video games.[101] In turn, this could potentially spark interest in future professional gaming careers from elementary and middle school-aged children with ADHD diagnoses. If these children seek out professional gaming careers in their teenage years, esports leagues must be ready with policies in place to help them succeed at a competitive level.

---

99. Sy Mukherjee, *How the first-ever digital ADHD treatment—a video game—got the FDA's blessing*, Fortune (Jun. 17, 2020, 12:30 PM), https://fortune.com/2020/06/17/digital-adhd-treatment-fda-akili/.

100. *Id.*

101. *See* Sean Hollister, *The FDA just approved the first prescription video game—it's for kids with ADHD*, The Verge (Jun. 15, 2020, 8:22 PM), https://www.theverge.com/2020/6/15/21292267/fda-adhd-video-game-prescription-endeavor-rx-akl-t01-project-evo.

CHAPTER 12

IMMIGRATION LAW

The Globalization of Esports

In 2016, there were 121 million frequent viewers of esports across the globe.[1] By 2022, Newzoo, a market research company, predicts that the esports audience will reach 300 million frequent viewers worldwide.[2] Esports' increase in global popularity has stemmed in part from streaming platforms like Twitch, which reached a record high of 3.1 billion hours watched in the first quarter of 2020.[3] As Twitch presents fans with a unique opportunity to engage with their favorite gamers,[4] it comes as no surprise that players from across the globe seek to pursue a career in esports.[5]

International interest in esports will likely increase because, for example, more than 50 percent of *Overwatch* League (OWL) players hail

---

1. Brad Adgate, *Esports Is Filling the Programming Void*, FORBES (Apr. 21, 2020), https://www.forbes.com/sites/bradadgate/2020/04/21/esports-is-filling-the-programming-void/#744f6be2533b.

2. *Id.*

3. *See id.*

4. Smith, *supra* note 42; Brett Molina, *Why watch other people play video games? What you need to know about esports*, USA TODAY(Jan. 12, 2018, 10:02 AM), https://www.usatoday.com/story/tech/news/2018/01/12/more-people-watch-esports-than-x-dont-get-here-basics/1017054001/. [Not sure which note to point this supra to because note 366 in the version of the manuscript that had consecutive numbers for the footnotes (i.e., 1–1,043) did not contain any info relating to a publication by Smith.]

5. *See* Noah Parson, *Immigration and ESports: The Issue of Legitimacy and Its Impact on the United States Visa Process*, 43 FORDHAM INT'L L.J. 1187, 1198–99 (2020).

from South Korea, and the *League of Legends* Championship Series (LCS) features players from countries ranging from Turkey to Thailand.[6] Considering that the LCS and OWL are two of the most popular esports leagues[7] and the LCS and OWL each play most of their games and matches in California,[8] questions loom surrounding how players from other countries can play for U.S.-based teams and leagues. While obtaining a visa seems like the logical answer, if an international esports athlete were to enter the United States after acquiring the incorrect type of visa, the athlete could create liability issues for themselves and for a league.[9] Moreover, in esports, the game developer owns the intellectual property that grants permission for the game to be used in tournaments.[10] Because the game developer ensures the viability of a league and game developers are sometimes the parties compensating the players,[11] garnering the wrong visa could also render game makers liable to suit.[12]

Overview and History of Visa Issues in Esports

To date, two well-known professional esports players have successfully obtained visas. The first was Canadian Danny "Shiphtur" Lee in 2013,[13]

6. *Id.* at 1200; *Worlds 2019: Player Nationalities*, DEVTRACKERS.GG, https://devtrackers.gg/leagueoflegends/p/f4f91134-%20worlds-2019-player-nationalities (last visited Sep. 29, 2020).

7. Rebecca R. Rosenthal, *A Tough Pill to Swallow: Making the Case for Why eSports Leagues Must Adopt Strict Banned Substance Policies to Prevent Disability Discrimination*, 2021 Va. Sports & Ent. L. J. (forthcoming Spring 2021).

8. *See* Andrew Webster, *Blizzard explains how home and away games will work in the Overwatch League*, The Verge (Jul. 16, 2019, 8:00 AM), https://www.theverge.com/2019/7/16/20694642/blizzard-overwatch-league-home-away-games-esports-2020; *LoL Championship Series*, Liquipedia, https://liquipedia.net/leagueoflegends/LCS (last visited Sep. 29, 2020).

9. Maryanne Kline, *The Thrill of a Visa, the Agony of Denial: Visa Challenges for the Esports Athlete*, The National Law Review (Feb. 22, 2019), https://www.natlawreview.com/article/thrill-visa-agony-denial-visa-challenges-esports-athlete.

10. Parson, *supra* note 5, at 1196–97.

11. *Id.*

12. Employers have the responsibility to verify the identity and employment authorization of all employees including the possession of proper eligibility for the work they are being hired to perform. Failure to adhere to government verifications could subject the employer to civil and criminal penalties. *See I-9 Penalties*, United States Citizenship & Immigration Services, (updated Jul. 10, 2020), https://www.uscis.gov/i-9-central/legal-requirements-and-enforcement/penalties.

13. Jonathan Brannon, *Are You Not Entertained? Considering the P-3 Visa as an Alternative Option for International Esports Professional Gamers*, 60 Ariz. L. Rev. 753, 754 (2018).

and the second was South Korean Kim Dong-hwan that same year.[14] Both players obtained a P-1A visa from the United States Citizenship and Immigration Service (USCIS).[15] P-1A visas grant "athletes" permission to enter the country due to their "internationally recognized level of performance,"[16] and are valid for a period of up to five years.[17]

Despite the victories Lee and Dong-hwan achieved obtaining P-1A visas, player success obtaining P-1A visas has been "sporadic and unpredictable."[18] For example, in 2015, world-ranked William "Leffen" Hjelte was deported while on his way to a *Super Smash Bros.* tournament.[19] Because the USCIS believed that Leffen lacked status as an "athlete," they denied his P-1A visa application.[20] Although Leffen acquired a P-1A visa the following year, his deportation caused him to miss out on significant cash prizes.[21] As esports players have shorter average career lengths in comparison to traditional professional sports athletes and success in competition means the highest possible paycheck,[22] Leffen's deportation was likely detrimental to his career.

While the P-1A visa is arguably the best option for professional esports players, the USCIS only approves P-1A visas on a "case-by-case basis."[23] In the case of Leffen, the USCIS determined that the *Super Smash Bros.* tournament he was scheduled to play in was not a "legitimate sport."[24] As a result, it seems that the "obstacle between esports players and P-1A visas is not their inability to provide evidence of high performance, but rather . . . [societal] resistance to . . . recognize esports as a sport and gamers as athletes."[25] Despite the fact that USCIS precedent calls the legitimacy of esports as a professional sport into question, deferring to definitions

14. Alan Yu, *U.S. Recognizes A South Korean StarCraft Player As An Athlete*, NPR (Dec. 15, 2013, 3:05 PM), https://www.npr.org/sections/alltechconsidered/2013/12/15/250793493/u-s-recognizes-a-south-korean-starcraft-player-as-an-athlete.

15. Kline, *supra* note 9.

16. Bridget A.J. Whan Tong, *A New Player Has Entered the Game: Immigration Reform for Esports Players*, 24 Jeffrey S. Moorad Sports L.J. 351, 369 (2017).

17. *eSports Visa Requirements in 2020*, Johnson & Matsumi (Aug. 3, 2020), https://www.johnsonmasumi.com/esports-visa-requirements-in-2020/. P-1A visas are limited to five years but are eligible for renewals up to a maximum of ten years in aggregate. Immigration & Nationality Act §214–PL 116-133 (2020).

18. Parson, *supra* note 5, at 1188–89, 1210.

19. *Id.* at 1209.

20. *Id.*

21. Kline, *supra* note 9.

22. *See* Rosenthal, *supra* note 7.

23. Parson, *supra* note 5, at 1211.

24. *Id.* at 1210.

25. Tong, *supra* note 16, at 383.

promulgated by the International Olympic Committee (IOC) and National Collegiate Athletic Association (NCAA), as well as looking to case law concerning the definition of "sport," proves that like athletes in traditional professional sports, esports athletes likely also qualify for P-1A visas.[26]

In 2017, the IOC explained that because esports players "prepare and train with an intensity . . . comparable to athletes in traditional sports," competitive esports constitute a sport.[27] Although the NCAA has yet to determine whether it will host esports competitions, it defines sport as an "activity involving physical exertion with the purpose of competition versus other teams or individuals."[28] Additionally, the Second Circuit Court of Appeals has suggested that for an activity to constitute a "sport," it must involve some form of a recruiting process, have a formal set of governing rules, and include teams that compete against one another in the same activity.[29] As a whole, the IOC and NCAA definitions and case law illustrate that for an activity to constitute a "sport," it must involve (1) a formal set of rules or regulations; (2) a competition against other competitors or teams who participate in the same activity;[30] and, (3) the activity must require physical exertion.[31]

Looking at the definitions proffered by the IOC, the NCAA, and case law suggests that esports are likely a sport and that esports players are athletes. Specifically, physical exertion is present in esports competitions because players make up to 400 movements on a mouse or keyboard each minute.[32] Additionally, the players' heartbeats fall somewhere between 160–180 beats per minute (akin to running a marathon).[33] Moreover, top esports leagues like the *Overwatch* League (OWL), *League of Legends* Championship Series (LCS), and *Call of Duty* League (CDL) all have a set of governing rules, and each host tournaments where teams compete

---

26. *See* Rosenthal, *supra* note 7.

27. Jacqueline Martinelli, *The Challenges of Implementing A Governing Body for Regulating eSports*, 26 U. Miami Int'l & Comp. L. Rev. 499, 506 (2019) (citing The Local, *Olympic commit recognizes video games as sports*, The Local, (Nov. 18, 2018), https://www.thelocal.ch/20171030/olympic-committee-recognizes-video-games-as-sports).

28. Rosenthal, *supra* note 7 (quoting Daniel Kane & Brandon D. Spradley, *Recognizing ESports as a Sport*, The Sport J., https://thesportjournal.org/article/recognizing-esports-as-a-sport/).

29. Biediger v. Quinnipiac *U.*, 691 F.3d 85, 103–05 (2d Cir. 2012) (holding that Quinnipiac University's cheerleading team did not qualify as a sport).

30. *See* Rosenthal, *supra* note 7.

31. *Id.*

32. Martin Schtz, *Science shows that eSports professionals are real athletes*, DW (Dec. 3, 2016), https://www.dw.com/en/science-shows-that-esports-professionals-are-real-athletes/a-19084993.

33. *Id.*

against one another in the same game.[34] As such, esports are indeed a sport, and professional esports players are athletes.

From B to P: The Alphabet Soup of Visa Options

Although esports are likely a legitimate sport, and thereby, professional esports players are athletes, the inconsistent USCIS precedent surrounding P-1A visas is unsettling. Consequently, applying for visas other than the P-1A could be beneficial for professional esports players. On top of the P-1A visa, there are two additional visa options for professional esports players —an O-1A visa or a P-3 visa.[35]

Despite some contention that B-1 and B-2 visas may be appropriate for esports players,[36] this appears unlikely for a professional esports player on a team within a league like the LCS or OWL. Under a B-1 visa,[37] an individual may not have a "contract or other prearranged employment,"[38] and the USCIS only grants B-2 visas for "pleasure."[39] "Pleasure" includes "activities of a recreational character, including tourism, amusement, visits with friends or relatives, rest, medical treatment, and activities of a fraternal, social, or service nature."[40] Professional esports players who play for leagues like the LCS, OWL, or CDL receive minimum contract guarantees and signing bonuses,[41] and would not qualify for a B-1 visa due to

34. *See* Overwatch League Summary of Official Rules 2019 Season, Overwatch League, https://bnetcmsus-a.akamaihd.net/cms/content_entry_media/bb/BB6C3OEC530B1549590044543.pdf (last visited Sep. 29, 2020); Call of Duty World League 2019 Official Handbook, Call of Duty, https://www.callofduty.com/content/dam/atvi/callofduty/esports-new/2019-rules/2019_CWL_Handbook.pdf (last visited Sep. 29, 2020); 2020 Official Rules, League of Legends, https://nexus.leagueoflegends.com/wp-content/uploads/2020/01/2020-LCS-Rule-Set-v20.1_6bkbwz26cgp7fngeat6a.pdf (last visited Sep. 29, 2020).

35. *See generally* Brannon, *supra* note 13.

36. *See* Tong, *supra* note 16, at 369.

37. B-1, or temporary business visitor visas are issued for limited purposes like attending conferences, settling an estate, or participating in short-term training. *See* B-1 Temporary Business Visitor, United States Citizenship & Immigration Services (updated Apr. 22, 2020), https://www.uscis.gov/working-in-the-united-states/temporary-visitors-for-business/b-1-temporary-business-visitor.

38. 22 C.F.R. §41.31(b)(1) (2020).

39. 22 C.F.R. §41.31(b)(2) (2020).

40. *Id.*

41. *Blizzard reveals Overwatch League player salaries and contract status*, Millennium (Oct. 8, 2019), https://www.millenium.us.org/news/6789.html; Darren Heitner, *Watching Video Games Is Now Bigger Than Traditional Spectator Sporting Events*, Inc. (Apr. 2, 2018), https://www.inc.com/darren-

their "contract[s] or other prearranged employment."[42] Likewise, LCS, OWL, and CDL players rely on these leagues for retirement and healthcare benefits,[43] and these leagues either provide players with housing or dedicated training facilities.[44] On account of this, professional esports athletes do not play for leagues for recreation or tourism purposes—these leagues are their primary source of work and income. Therefore, these players would also not qualify for B-2 visas.

Further, some posit that professional esports players could seek H-1B visas to compete in the United States. The H-1B visa requires that an individual engages in a "specialty occupation."[45] Prerequisites for engaging in a "specialty occupation" include a bachelor's degree or equivalent experience in the specialty area in which the individual seeks to work.[46] As three years of experience equates to one year of a bachelor's degree, players seeking H-1B visas need either (1) a college or university degree focused on esports or relevant skills, or (2) twelve years of experience in professional esports.[47]

Even though universities in China and Singapore offer esports programs,[48] it is likely that if an individual completed one of these college programs, this individual would not have dedicated the amount of time to a particular game needed to garner a coveted spot in a top esports league.[49] Additionally, most top esports players choose to forgo a college degree to

---

heitner/watching-video-games-is-now-bigger-traditional-spectator-sporting-events.html; Kevin Webb, *I attended the launch event of the $300 million Call of Duty League and it was a wild three-day whirlwind showcasing the potential of the esports industry*, Bus. Insider (Feb. 1, 2020, 7:00 AM), https://www.businessinsider.com/call-of-duty-league-esports-launch-kickoff-minneapolis-minnesota-rokkr-2020-1.

42. *See* Brannon, *supra* note 13, at 767.

43. About the League, Overwatch League, https://overwatchleague.com/en-us/about (last visited Jan. 23, 2020); Webb, *I attended the launch event of the $300 million Call of Duty League*, *supra* note 41.

44. *Overwatch League*, Wikipedia, *supra* note 62; Noah Higgins-Dunn, *supra* note 62; Harrison Jacobs, *Here's the insane training schedule of a 20-something professional gamer*, Bus. Insider (May 11, 2015, 12:05 PM), https://www.businessinsider.com/pro-gamers-explain-the-insane-training-regimen-they-use-to-stay-on-top-2015-5; Noah Smith, *Esports training facility brings gaming another step closer to traditional pro sports*, Wash. Post (May 10, 2018, 10:30 AM), https://www.washingtonpost.com/sports/esports-training-facility-brings-gaming-another-step-closer-to-traditional-pro-sports/2018/05/10/c102e684-4e2f-11e8-84a0-458a1aa9ac0a_story.html.

45. 8 U.S.C. §1101(a)(15)(H)(i)(b) (2020).

46. Parson, *supra* note 5, at 1203.

47. *See id.*

48. *Colleges are starting degrees in esports, with $36,000 programs*, CBS News (Oct. 1, 2019, 3:32 PM), https://www.cbsnews.com/news/college-esports-universities-launch-degrees-in-esports/.

49. *See* Parson, *supra* note 5, at 1204.

pursue a career in esports.[50] Thus, for players without a bachelor's degree to obtain an H-1B visa, they would need twelve years of relevant experience.[51] Because the average age of a professional esports player is twenty-two,[52] it seems improbable that an individual could seek an H-1B visa for professional esports without taking the college degree route. Overall, since professional esports players likely do not qualify for B-1, B-2 visas, or H-1B visas, it is most appropriate to consider O1-A and P-3 visas as alternatives to the P-1A visa option.

O-1A Visas

O-1A visas are for individuals who exhibit "extraordinary ability" in athletics, "which has been demonstrated by sustained national or international acclaim."[53] "Extraordinary ability" means "a level of expertise indicating that the individual is one of that small percentage who ha[s] risen to the very top of the field of endeavor."[54] O-1A visas are also valid for up to three years.[55] This is beneficial because players frequently travel internationally to attend competitions, and some players even change teams (which can require relocating to a new geographic region) after each season.[56]

Because O-1A visas allow individuals to "enter the United States to continue to work in the area of extraordinary ability,"[57] they are distinguishable from B-1 and B-2 visas and remain a viable option for professional esports players. That being said, O-1A visas proffer a "high evidentiary standard" for proving "extraordinary ability."[58] While a player could perhaps demonstrate "national or international acclaim" through past competition performance or even his or her number of Twitch subscribers, a player likely needs a major championship win to meet the high

---

50. *Id.*

51. *Id.* at 1203.

52. Nick Summers, *The esports elders defying their age*, Engadget (Mar. 9, 2020), https://www.engadget.com/2020-03-09-the-esports-elders-defying-their-age.html.

53. 8 C.F.R. §214.2(o)(1)(ii)(A)(1) (2020).

54. 8 C.F.R. §204.5(h)(2) (2020).

55. Khuong B. Nguyen, Amy L. Peck, & Gregg E. Clifton, *Visas For eSports Gamers On The Rise*, Lexology (Mar. 25, 2019), https://www.lexology.com/library/detail.aspx?g=8627c380-f3ae-4945-af7f-5162ba4eff1e.

56. Parson, *supra* note 5, at 1200.

57. Tong, *supra* note 16, at 379.

58. *Id.*

success threshold required for an O-1A visa.[59] The O-1A visa may provide an advantage over the P-1A visa because the O-1A visa is not tied to a specific event like the P-1A.[60] Indeed, a number of prominent Brazilian mixed martial arts competitors were denied entry to the United States after UFC 250, a competitive mixed martial arts event hosted by the Ultimate Fighting Championship, was postponed as their P-1A visas were tied specifically to that event.[61] Additionally, if esports players only sought O-1A visas, this would "essentially restrict US Esports competitions to players who have already won major championships."[62] Consequently, it could "prevent up-and-coming players from succeeding."[63]

The Prospect of the P-3 Visa

The P-3 visa classification applies to those who are coming to the United States "temporarily to perform . . . as artists or entertainers, individually or as part of a group, under a program that is culturally unique."[64] "Culturally unique" encompasses "a style of . . . methodology, or medium which is unique to a particular . . . group of persons."[65] To petition for a P-3 visa, an individual must provide expert testimony via affidavits or letters, which prove that the expert has first-hand knowledge of the visa-seeking individual's skill.[66]

Professional esports players seeking entry into the United States might qualify for a P-3 visa if three main elements are met. First, the individual would have to prove that they seek temporary entry to the United States to act as an entertainer (professional gamer), either alone or as part of a team.[67] Second, the individual would need to establish that their performance as a professional gamer involves implementing a method unique to a particular group—in this case, high-skilled video-game playing that is unique to the world of professional esports.[68] Third,

59. Parson, *supra* note 5, at 1205.

60. Sherrod Seward, *Brazilian MMA Fighters With P-1 Visas Denied Entry For UFC 250*, Sherrod Sports Visas, https://www.sherrodsportsvisas.com/ufc250 (last visited Oct. 8, 2020).

61. *Id.*

62. Parson, *supra* note 5, at 1205.

63. *Id.*

64. 8 U.S.C. §1101 (a)(15)(P)(iii)(II) (2020).

65. Brannon, *supra* note 13, at 774.

66. *Id.*

67. *See id.* at 772–74.

68. *See id.* at 776–79.

the individual would need to authenticate his or her skills via an "expert" opinion.[69]

To date, there is no evidence that the USCIS has granted a P-3 visa to an esports player.[70] While the eligibility of esports professionals for a P-3 visa is speculative, the visa has two key advantages. First, the P-3 visa does not require the high level of performance associated with P-1A or O-1A visas, and second, the P-3 visa is good for a period of up to one year,[71] which would cover the twenty to thirty weeks of a professional esports season.[72]

What's at Stake?

American esports were predicted to surpass $252.8 million in total revenue by the end of 2020.[73] Even though many prestigious esports competitions are held in the United States each year, most of the world's best esports players are citizens of other countries.[74] If the United States is to maintain its position as a destination for esports competitions and command a sizeable market share, visa reform is needed in the esports space, and the reform may be as simple as an opinion letter from the USCIS declaring that esports competitors qualify for P-1A and O-1A visas.[75]

One might argue that with the popularity of streaming platforms like Twitch, which allow amateur players to become international sensations, nearly anyone with a significant enough fanbase can meet the "internationally recognized level of performance" standard required for a

69. *See id.* at 774.

70. Brannon, *supra* note 13, at 772.

71. *P-3 Artist or Entertainer Coming to Be Part of a Culturally Unique Program*, U.S. Citizenship and Immigr. Servs., https://www.uscis.gov/working-in-the-united-states/temporary-workers/p-3-artist-or-entertainer-coming-to-be-part-of-a-culturally-unique-program (last visited Oct. 1, 2020).

72. *See* John T. Holden & Thomas A. Baker III, *The Econtractor? Defining the Esports Employment Relationship*, 56 Am. Bus. L.J. 391, 409 (2019); Hunter A. Bayliss, *Not Just a Game: The Employment Status and Collective Bargaining Rights of Professional ESports Players*, 22 Wash. & Lee J. Civ. Rts. & Soc. Just. 359, 378 (2016) (discussing *Riot Games Terms of Service*, Riot Games, https://www.riotgames.com/en/terms-of-service (last modified Jan. 15, 2020)).

73. Dean Takahashi, *Newzoo: Global esports will top $1 billion in 2020, with China as the top market*, VentureBeat (Feb. 25, 2020, 7:00 AM), https://venturebeat.com/2020/02/25/newzoo-global-esports-will-top-1-billion-in-2020-with-china-as-the-top-market/.

74. Brannon, *supra* note 13, at 759.

75. *See* Brannon, *supra* note 13, at 760. The issuance of P-1 visas reached near capacity of 25,000 every year between 2015–2019. *See Nonimmigrant Visa Issued by Classification (Including Border Crossing Cards) Fiscal Years 2015-2019*, Dep't of State (last visited Oct. 9, 2020), located at https://travel.state.gov/content/dam/visas/Statistics/AnnualReports/FY2019AnnualReport/FY19AnnualReport-TableXVI-B.pdf.

P-1A visa. With the advent of platforms like Twitch, more esports players could qualify for a P-1A visa; however, the USCIS grants a maximum of 25,000 P-visas each year.[76] Therefore, esports competitors could be victims of a visa shortfall. Overall, clarification surrounding immigration law issues is needed in the esports space. By continuing to issue inconsistent decisions on visa applications and not setting clear guidelines for professional esports players, the USCIS is harming the burgeoning billion-dollar industry that esports presents.

76. *P visa*, Wikipedia, https://en.wikipedia.org/wiki/P_visa (last visited Oct. 2, 2020).

Conclusion

When more than 127 million fans across the globe joined together to watch the Midseason Invitational of *League of Legends* online in May of 2018, that was our sign—as attorneys and law professors—that market demand for esports had grown large enough to merit writing a full-length book about the industry. And yet, even as the esports industry has continued to grow in the years since, a large segment of the U.S. population remains in disbelief that esports is a *bonafide* source of employment for gamers, or that lawyers and businesspeople should dedicate their time to the cause.

Not long ago, one of the authors of this book recalled a story that his father had shared with him about one of his colleague's nephews—long considered his family's black sheep—who had dropped out of college and was seen by his family as floundering in life. And then, one day, entirely unexpectedly, he closed on a multimillion-dollar home in the suburbs. The secret to this young man's wealth? He had become one of the most successful gamers in the world.

Of course, none of this is to say that everybody who enjoys playing video games will become a multi-millionaire, much the same as every young person who spends hours shooting hoops in the playground is not going to become the next Michael Jordan or Sue Bird. But, at the same time, the parallels between the perceptions of esports today and traditional sports nearly one hundred years ago are astounding. Indeed, it was roughly one hundred years ago when the mentors of Harold "Red" Grange, upon his anticipated graduation from the University of Illinois, sat him down and tried to encourage him to become a journalist because they believed there would be no money in playing football professionally in the startup National Football League. Grange did not listen. He went on to become one of the most famous running backs in Chicago Bears history and thereafter a renowned coach for the team.

Since beginning the writing of this book, several changes in the world have only helped to reinforce the promise of esports emerging as America's next national pastime. Perhaps, the most significant change was the early and unexpected arrival of a dangerous virus, COVID-19, in March of 2020. As the world was forced indoors and into quarantine during the spring and summer of 2020, all forms of group sporting activity hit the pause button. However, based on the miracle of the internet, competitive videogaming was able to sustain itself, at least in some form, during this health crisis.

During the COVID-19 pandemic, when courses for college students moved online and business meetings were held remotely, the notion of esports being something "real" became far less of a stretch. If political conventions and weddings could be shifted to the internet, why should a competition tied to an online video game still be seen as anything less real than a competition linked to a real-world physical event? By early 2021, even the historical children's hobby of collecting physical and tangible baseball cards was supplemented by the new digital craze of collecting non-fungible tokens (NFTs). To quote the legendary singer and songwriter Bob Dylan, "the times they are a-changin'."

And yet, even as commercial esports continues to fortify itself as a sustainable segment of both the U.S. and global entertainment industry, it is reasonable to suspect that the esports industry too will undergo changes —both as the world emerges from the COVID-19 pandemic, and as the business and legal structures of esports continue to level up to match the growing revenue streams associated with the industry. Among other things, it is likely that many of the large law firms that currently represent the professional sports industry will make inroads into representing esports stakeholders.

In addition, as the esports industry continues to mature, not only will novel issues emerge within this rapidly growing industry, but many of the issues discussed in this book are likely to increase in prominence—with some perhaps even playing out in the form of public policy debates before the national media. It seems inevitable that issues pertaining to intellectual property rights within esports will take center stage as publishers attempt to protect their copyright in underlying video games and esports participants seek to monetize their names, images, and likenesses. One matter of particular concern in the esports world will seem to relate to the interplay of copyright law and antitrust law as video game publishers may reasonably attempt to monopolize competitions based on the games they produce by making these games unavailable to potential competitor entities. In many cases, antitrust law does not require the holder of intellectual property to license rights to use that intellectual property to others, even if the absence of such licensing were to yield highly concentrated markets. Employment issues meanwhile represent another source of inevitable legal questions as the esports industry matures. Not only will there likely be a battle as to whether esports participants are properly classified as employees or independent contractors, but, in all likelihood, we will see efforts by certain esports participants to form unions to bargain collectively over their terms and conditions of employment.

From a social policy perspective, the coming years will also likely experience the emergence of questions that will require federal and state legislators to think deeply about how to regulate the esports industry. For example, the emerging world of fans betting on esports events yields not only all of the same novel questions that arise from the emerging markets in the U.S. for sports betting, but also raises new and important questions about whether under existing laws, esports constitute "sports." Other policy concerns that will likely garner increased attention are the issues of substance abuse (primarily in the form of both legal and illegal amphetamines) and the systematic harassment of female gamers. Further, with regard to social policy, questions will arise surrounding free speech, especially as the Chinese company Tencent Holdings Ltd.—the company that shut down Chinese broadcasts of National Basketball Association games in China after a former Houston Rockets general manager retweeted a message supporting Hong Kong protesters—also has strong inroads in esports. Moreover, unlike most physical sports, esports leagues are genuinely global in scope. As an early entrant into the commercial esports marketplace, China's government and its business interests exercise a strong voice over the global esports industry as a whole.

Lastly, the oversight of esports at the college level will likely receive ample attention in the years ahead, if nothing more than based on the contrast of the financial rights and freedoms between young esports contestants and young athletes in physical sports. Although NCAA leaders publicly voiced a wide range of concerns about the esports industry, in earnest, one reason why the organization may have stayed out is that it is far harder to take away monetary rights from those who already enjoy these rights. And, at the same time, it would be hard for the NCAA to juxtapose a policy that allowed college gamers to earn prize money while continuing to deny athletes in traditional sports of these same opportunities. Nevertheless, with the U.S. Supreme Court's June 2021 decision in *NCAA v. Alston* that overturned NCAA limits on in-kind educational benefits provided to student-athletes and the NCAA's subsequent lifting of its rules preventing college athletes from commercial licensing the use of their names, images, and likenesses, the economic dichotomy between college athletes and esports competitors seems to be lessening.

While it is always possible that, like the X-Games, esports will level off in terms of consumer interest, in seems unlikely that after all of the great sums of money that game developers, investors, and even professional sports ownership groups have invested into building the infrastructure of the industry that professional esports will disappear anytime soon. The global nature of esports, coupled with its ability to operate primarily in an online universe, is attractive to an entirely new generation, with the world's top gamers beginning to enjoy similar celebrity status to actors, singers, and even real-world athletes.

In the years ahead, creating stable organizational structures for the esports industry will present challenges for the next generation of attorneys in this space. And, much like with the traditional sports leagues from one hundred years ago, the ability to harness these legal issues will indubitably help to set the course for the industry's growth over the next century.

Glossary Terms for Esports and the Law

battle royale
A genre of online multiplayer video games in which players must eliminate other players as part of a survival contest with the goal of being the last person standing. The name for this genre is believed to stem from the Japanese film *Battle Royale* (2000), which is based on the 1999 novel by Koushun Takami. Popular battle royale games include *PlayerUnknown's Battlegrounds* (*PUBG*), *Fortnite Battle Royale* (*Fortnite*), *Firestorm*, *Apex Legends*, *Fall Guys Ultimate Knockout*, and *Call of Duty: Warzone*.

broadcaster
This term refers to a person or organization that transmits (or broadcasts) a radio or television program. The term more often applies to the specific individual(s) who present radio and television programs.

esports
Is an umbrella term that applies to all types of electronic video game competitions. Similar to traditional sports, esports includes amateur, collegiate, and professional esports competitions.

esports league
Following models for competition established within traditional sports, esports leagues also take a tournament or season format in which individuals or teams compete against each other with the purpose of winning a league championship or title. The *Overwatch* League is the first esports league to adopt a franchise approach to league development, based on the North American model for sports leagues. Esports leagues may be amateur, collegiate, or professional, and some professional leagues (e.g., League of Legends *League Championship Series*) provide salaries for their players.

esports tournaments
A series of esports contests between a set number of participants who compete, often in a format in which losers of matches are eliminated along the way until only one team or competitor is declared champion.

fighting game
Is a video game genre in which one opponent engages another in combat until one defeats the other or until the expiration of a set period of time. To be successful, players must master various defensive and attacking techniques. Often, players are restricted in fighting games to a specific space during combat and if they leave that space they forfeit the match. Some popular fighting games include the *Street Fighter*, *Mortal Kombat*, *Tekken*, and *Soulcalibur* series of video games.

first-person shooter (FPS)
This is a shooting-style genre of video games that is centered from a first-person perspective. While the context and combatants may vary from one game to the other, FPS games all involve gameplay in which players guide the protagonist and see from that person's perspective while shooting various antagonists (typically zombies or other types of monsters). Popular FPS games include *Doom*, *GoldenEye 007*, *Halo*, *Wolfenstein 3D*, *Call of Duty*, *Far Cry*, and *Resident Evil*.

gamer
Refers to persons who play interactive games, whether those games are electronic video games or tabletop role-playing games (RPGs).

headset
This is hardware that connects, whether through wires or by Blu-ray, to another electronic device such as a telephone or computer, so as to allow the user to go hands-free while communicating with others.

live streaming (or streaming)
A live stream is the transmission of live video and audio content over the internet. Live streaming is the act of streaming live content across the internet.

multiplayer online battle arena (MOBA)
This is a subgenre of real-time strategy games in which two teams compete against each other on a battlefield. Each player controls one character within the game and each character has specific abilities that must be best utilized by teams in order to be successful. Typically, MOBA games involve groups of characters who serve specific functions on teams that operate with the purpose of destroying the opposite team's base.

multiplayer video game
Any video game in which multiple people may play at the same time, either with or against each other.

online platform
An online platform is a digital service provider that offers a medium for facilitating interactions between individuals or groups of individuals in an online space. For example, Facebook, Twitter, YouTube, and Twitch are all examples of online platforms.

player
A player is someone who is actively engaged in video gameplay.

real-time strategy (RTS) game
Games of strategy that do not progress from stage to stage incrementally but instead take place simultaneously, or in real time.

role (or role-playing) games (RPG)
These are games in which players assume roles based on the characters they select, characters that may only take action based on established rules or guidelines. There are various types of RPGs, including role-playing video games, tabletop or board games, live action role-playing (LARP), or card games.

skins
A skin is a commodity in electronic video games that permits players to change the appearances of characters in video games. Skins do not have any practical functionality for players: they serve an aesthetic purpose. For many video game producers, skins are a primary or significant source for revenue as consumers spend money to personalize their in-game characters.

sport video games (SVGs)
Sport video games are those that attempt to virtually simulate traditional sport contests as electronic games. For example, a video game built around baseball, football, or soccer would function as a SVG.

stream
The process of transmitting content over the internet in a consistent flow.

streamcasting
The process of streaming content over the internet that is also broadcast on television or radio.

streamer
A person who transmits content over the internet (streaming) in a consistent flow.

traditional sports
This term is often used within electronic gaming (esports) to refer to traditional or nonelectronic sports such as hockey, distance running, baseball, soccer, etc.

Twitch
Is a live-streaming platform used by gamers and esport tournament producers to transmit gameplay on the internet. Like with YouTube, Twitch provides a platform for anyone to become a content creator through streaming. While Twitch is often used for streaming content unrelated to electronic gaming, the platform grew in popularity mostly from esports or gaming-related content.

video game (or computer game)
A game played electronically (often on a computer, console, phone, or other handheld gaming device).

video game console
An electronic gaming device that outputs a video signal in the form of a video game. Sometimes these are referred to as home video game consoles because their advent allowed gamers at-home enjoyment of the games they would otherwise have had to play in arcades. The Nintendo Switch, Playstation 5, and Xbox One are examples of video game consoles.

video game designer
Someone who develops video games. These persons specialize in various aspects of game development ranging from building code to creating story content/plots, character design, and music, for example. Sometimes these persons are referred to as video game developers or video game makers.

video game genre
A genre is a category of artistic composition that is similar in style. For the purpose of video games, the term genre means the types of games categorized based on style of play. For example, first-person shooter games are a genre distinct from fighting games.

video game industry
This term refers to the economy (industry) that produces video games, and it includes the development, marketing, and distribution of electronic games.

video game producer
This term applies to the head of video game production for a specific game title. This person oversees all aspects of game development.

video game publisher
The company that publishes a video game, which may have been developed in-house by the publisher, or by an external game developer who sold the product to the publisher.

virtual reality (VR)
Computer technology designed to create simulated real-life environments for users. VR games are those that permit players to interact with artificial three-dimensional environments by using devices such as electronic headsets, goggles, or special gloves that are fitted with sensors.

YouTube
A video-sharing platform that provides users with the opportunity to create video content, or to watch video content on their electronic devices. YouTube may be used to distribute produced video content or live-streaming content.

INDEX

About the Authors

Marc Edelman is a tenured Professor of Law at the Zicklin School of Business, Baruch College, City University of New York, where he teaches in the areas of sports law, antitrust law, intellectual property law, and gaming/fantasy sports law. He has published upwards of 60 law review articles in leading journals and is regularly cited by the media on topics including how the Sherman Act applies to professional sports leagues, how gaming laws apply to fantasy sports contests, and how both labor laws and antitrust laws apply within the college sports industry.

In addition to his full-time role as a law professor, Professor Edelman is the founder of Edelman Law, where he provides legal consulting and expert witness services to businesses in the commercial sports, entertainment and online gaming industries. Some of Professor Edelman's recent clients include a Major League Baseball team, an international sportsbook, the Arena Football League Players Union, and several online fantasy sports providers.

A magna cum laude graduate of the University of Pennsylvania's Wharton School and a cum laude graduate of Michigan Law School, Professor Edelman began his professional career by practicing antitrust and sports law with the law firm Skadden, Arps, Slate, Meagher and Flom LLP. Thereafter, Professor Edelman practiced both litigation and transactional law in the sports and intellectual property practice groups of Dewey Ballantine LLP.

He resides in Manhattan, New York with his wife Rachel.

Dr. Thomas A. Baker III is a tenured Professor of Sport Law at the International Center for Sport Management (ICSM), University of Georgia. He is also the Editor-in-chief for the *Journal of Legal Aspects of Sport (JLAS)*, the only peer-reviewed sport law journal in the United States and a contributor to Forbes on subjects related to sports law. Dr. Baker's research primarily focuses on the application of law to sport and within that focus he specializes in how commercial laws influence sport, such as legal issues concerning brand image/management and the regulation of marketing through advertisements and social media. He also conducts injury prevention research that focuses on the risk of sexual violence in sports, with a particular focus on methods for preventing violence against children.

Dr. Baker has more than 60 scholarly publications and has written extensively on the influence of law on student-athlete regulations. Dr. Baker's research was admitted into evidence in *Alston v. NCAA* and has been cited by the Kentucky Supreme Court in *Jamgotchian v. Kentucky Horse Racing Commission*. He also co-authored an amicus curiae brief that was submitted to the Ninth Circuit in *O'Bannon v. NCAA* on behalf of sport management professors. Dr. Baker received his Ph.D. from the University of Florida where he was a Dr. Charles W. LaPradd Fellow. He earned his J.D. from Loyola University of New Orleans School of Law where he graduated in the top 10% of his class and earned the distinction of William L. Crowe Scholar.

He lives outside of Atlanta, Georgia with his wife Susana.

John T. Holden is an Assistant Professor in the Department of Management in the Spears School of Business at Oklahoma State University. Prior to his arrival at Oklahoma State, John worked for two years as a Visiting Scholar at Florida State University in the Department of Sport Management. John's academic scholarship is focused on legal and regulatory issues in the esports and sports gambling industries. He is the author of more than 50 academic articles on these and related subjects.

John has also testified and submitted written recommendations regarding the legalization of sports betting and daily fantasy sports on the state and national level. John filed two amicus curiae briefs at the Supreme Court during the litigation that paved the way for legalized sports betting. He has also been quoted in a variety of news outlets including: *USA Today, The Wall Street Journal, The New York Times, and NPR.*

John is a licensed attorney in the state of Florida. He earned his Ph.D. from Florida State University, his LL.B. from the University of Ottawa, and his J.D. from Michigan State University.

He lives in Stillwater, Oklahoma with his wife Cassandra and his two children Cameron and Jack.

Rebecca Rosenthal is an Associate at a law firm in New York City, where she focuses her practice on employment and business litigation. She earned her J.D. from the University of Wisconsin Law School, where she served as the Senior Articles Editor of the *Wisconsin Law Review*, coached

Wisconsin's Labor and Employment Moot Court team, and worked as a Summer Law Clerk for the NFL. Prior to law school, Rebecca received her B.A. from the University of Michigan. Rebecca is the author of a law review article on the employment law challenges presented by the lack of banned substance policies in professional esports.